PENGUIN BOOKS

French Toast

Peta Mathias is a respected chef, author and tele-vision presenter. Her culinary love affair began in Paris with her restaurant Rose Blues and she returned to New Zealand 10 years later to cook and write. Peta has written eight books about food and travel including *A Cook's Tour of New Zealand* (2005).

After presenting the popular television food and travel show 'Taste New Zealand' for 10 years, Peta has recently completed an international version called 'Taste Takes Off'. Peta's latest venture is a cooking school in the south of France.

www.petamathias.com

French Toast

Eating and Laughing Your Way Around France

PETA MATHIAS

PENGUIN BOOKS

PENGUIN BOOKS

Published by the Penguin Group

Penguin Group (NZ), 67 Apollo Drive, Mairangi Bay,
Auckland 0632, New Zealand (a division of Pearson New Zealand Ltd)
Penguin Group (USA) Inc., 375 Hudson Street,
New York, New York 10014, USA
Penguin Group (Canada), 90 Eglinton Avenue East, Suite 700, Toronto,
Ontario, M4P 2Y3, Canada (a division of Pearson Penguin Canada Inc.)
Penguin Books Ltd, 80 Strand, London, WC2R 0RL, England
Penguin Ireland, 25 St Stephen's Green,
Dublin 2, Ireland (a division of Penguin Books Ltd)
Penguin Group (Australia), 250 Camberwell Road, Camberwell,
Victoria 3124, Australia (a division of Pearson Australia Group Pty Ltd)
Penguin Books India Pvt Ltd, 11, Community Centre,
Panchsheel Park, New Delhi – 110 017, India
Penguin Books (South Africa) (Pty) Ltd, 24 Sturdee Avenue,
Rosebank, Johannesburg 2196, South Africa

Penguin Books Ltd, Registered Offices: 80 Strand, London, WC2R 0RL, England

Previously published as *Salut!* by Random House New Zealand, 1998
This edition published by Penguin Group (NZ), 2006

3 5 7 9 10 8 6 4 2

Copyright © Peta Mathias, 2006

Designed by Mary Egan
Typeset by Pindar NZ
Printed in Australia by McPherson's Printing Group

ISBN 978 0 14 302101 8
A catalogue record for this book is available
from the National Library of New Zealand.

www.penguin.co.nz

Deep affection and thanks to my French friends and colleagues who all said they would sue me if I said one word about them.

Contents

Introduction

JUST AS THE AMERICANS say you end up with the face you deserve, the French maintain a country has the cuisine it deserves. If a place has lousy food it is only because the population are not appreciative enough to demand better.

They say the way to a man's heart is through his stomach (if only it were that easy). Well I wanted to tune into France's heart through its cuisine, having studiously explored other avenues.

I lived in Paris for 10 years in the 1980s, owned a restaurant in the 5th arrondissement called Rose Blues and dedicated myself to gastronomy in a most selfless way. Here I was again years later, having forsaken the life of a chef for television and writing, looking around France for adventure and culinary nirvana. Surely French cuisine wouldn't change in a handful of years, you might say. Well, if the New World has moved on from parsley sauce and boiled carrots, there's no reason to believe the French have been cooking nothing but *coq au vin* over the past few years. Many, however, believe that's just what they should be doing.

It had long been rumoured that French cuisine was in trouble – reputable restaurants closed, famous palaces of gastronomy went bankrupt, brilliant three-star chefs committed suicide from the strain of having to live up to the murderous standards of the culinary guides and war had broken out between the top chefs as to what constituted true French cuisine. Chefs became '*refusés*', requesting exclusion from the Michelin Red Guide but the famous Tour d'Argent in Paris was not amused when in 2006 they were demoted to one star.

In the late 1990s Joël Robuchon puréed his last potato in his illustrious restaurant on Raymond-Poincaré in favour of retirement, saying, 'I have done everything I wanted to do. I have nothing more to prove. Now I will consecrate myself to teaching.' He also said he was appalled at the tendency to mix everything with anything on a plate to give the impression of innovation at any price. He drew up a 'manifesto' and stated his case for purity, tradition and back-to-basics, deriding experimental chefs for suffocating the national cuisine with a battery of alien flavours. 'Nobody knows what they are eating any more.' This so incensed him, he turned around and opened a new restaurant called La Table, an ode to simple food, which Michelin have just awarded a second star.

Enter the rival group of well known experimenters, led in their charge by my hero Alain Senderens of the Lucas Carton in Paris. He accused Robuchon and his followers of downright treachery, not to put too fine a point on it. 'It is not right for chefs to turn against one another. We are artists and we should respect rather than attack each other's differences.' Quite right too. They called the purists culinary nationalists, unable to assimilate from other cultures and open up to new ideas, adding that the glory of French cuisine has always rested on their tradition of giving the right of asylum to flavours from around the world. Senderens had his finger right on the pulse as far as I am concerned and I suspected it would be he and his ilk who would save French cuisine. He is most famous for using vanilla and cinnamon in pigeon and lobster dishes, an innovation that was considered breathtaking in the 1990s. He became a refusé, closed his three-star Lucas Carton restaurant and opened another named after himself, saying he wanted a different style of restaurant that was less expensive and more comfortable. Ironically enough, Michelin awarded him two stars within a matter of months! This is the fastest promotion in the guide's 105-year history.

I like these fights because it clears the air and inevitably results in even better dishes for us ordinary civilians to eat. Even on the fast-food level, the French started to say *non*. My old *quartier*, Montparnasse, traditionally frequented by people suspected to possess a third of the world's known supply of intelligence, said 'over my dead body' to McDonald's. A determined band of revolutionaries called the Joyous Anti-Fast-Food Network forced the hamburger chain to abandon plans to set up shop where Matisse and Picasso (and my mother) once bought their paints. They sawed off 'Ronald' statues and daubed anti-McDonald's slogans on the fast food outlets, condemning them as an invasion by a pseudo-American subculture! I admire this about the French. They say what has to be said and won't put up with something they feel is not right – and this goes for all walks of life. I always know where I stand with them because they're very easy to read emotionally – they say what they think and they show what they feel.

Of course their inability to put up with things they don't like can be a bore when you're on the receiving end. One winter in the 1980s when I was living in Paris the métro, the buses, the post and the electricity all went on strike at the same time as certain nationalities delivered bombs to department stores and restaurants. Personally I didn't think it was the correct time to strike when half the customers of the Jewish deli around the corner from me had been blown up. I had to walk in the snow to my restaurant in the 5th from my apartment in the 3rd four times a day, not knowing if I would be missing an arm or a face when I got home; old people died in their freezing apartments and there were no letters from home. It was like living in a war zone. And of course, as always in times of tragedy and hardship, what did the people do? Of course ... and Paris was graced with lots of babies in the autumn.

People were also saying that the best cooking and fashion were now coming from outside Europe. In the past the French treated cookery almost as an extension of foreign policy and used it to establish global culinary supremacy. Escoffier claimed that French cooking was a branch of diplomacy and that he had personally placed 2000 French chefs around the world. In fact if you read Escoffier today you will see there is nothing new – and he died in 1935. Although he fought hard to improve the general lot of the chef, Escoffier was actually a naughty boy. Few people remember that he diddled the Savoy out of an enormous amount of money and was sacked in 1989, along with his mate Ritz. He brought more dishonour on the vocation than any other chef in history and yet we remember him as a hero.

Say *nouvelle cuisine* to the French people and they go cross-eyed, so traumatised were they by this cult. The great chef Raymond Blanc says the French are arrogant and some of them cannot look beyond the hexagon of France, which means French food is not reinventing itself fast enough. He insists that a thoughtful chef will take authentically from another culture to enrich his own.

The English chef Marco Pierre White reckons the French are still the greatest cooks in the world and anyone who says otherwise can't be taken seriously. Michel Roux said it's complete bollocks that French cooking is in decline and anyone who says the contrary is talking out of their backsides. However, highly respected gastronomic critics who love the French dared to suggest that there were American, English,

New Zealand and Australian chefs who were producing cooking that was genuinely new and better than French cuisine. As it stands the three-star Fat Duck in Bray, England, is considered by some to be the best restaurant in the world. These chefs took like magpies from other cultures, mixed things up and created entirely new styles, thus liberating food from the rigid embrace of tradition. Then in the 1990s Paul Bocuse entered the halls of feathered nudity, mile-high head-dresses and sparkly tassels. He took over supervision of the kitchen at the famous Lido on the Champs-Elysées, serving up such titivations as smoked Scottish salmon tartare, artichoke and *foie gras* aspic, monkfish cheeks with shrimps, turbot roasted with meat *jus* and fried onions and strawberry *mille-feuille.*

And what about women cooks in France? The rumble is that they don't want to cook at home but they do want to excel in restaurants as chefs. Recent surveys have shown that French women are still sexy as all hell but they don't know the difference between a *blanquette* and a *brandade* when it comes to the kitchen. Everybody's weeping into their *bouillon* about this and it has happened for purely socio-economic reasons – (a) the daughters of women who embraced feminism in the 60s and 70s were not taught to cook at their mother's elbows and (b) women now work outside the home and don't have time to cook the nourishing and delicious *bourgeois* meals of the past. What's more, they're not even interested in cooking – one recent questionnaire revealed that a third of French women considered cooking as dreary as housework. They didn't know how to make such simple things as a *gratin dauphinoise*, a *soufflé* or a chocolate mousse. Sociologist Jean-Pierre Poulain reported that dinner is now almost extinct, there's not even a starter, there's no garnish, they eat pizzas. *Zut alors!* Lunch used to be a two-hour break to go home and eat; it is now a snatched snack at the desk.

But fear not. All is not lost. Critics and food writers are increasingly noticing the work of female chefs. Traditionally women have always been on the margins of restaurant cooking but recently the girls have been taking over famous family restaurants, once manned only by their fathers, uncles and brothers. There are no Michelin three-star women chefs in France but there are two two-stars – Helene Darroze of Restaurant Helen Darroze in the Latin Quarter in Paris and Anne-Sophie Pic of La Maison Pic in Valence. Thirteen other women have one star. This in contrast to 26 male chefs with three stars, 68 with two and 389 with one. There has only been one woman chef in the history of French cooking who was acclaimed like a male – Eugenie Brazier 'la Mère Brazier' of Lyons and that was 60 years ago. Iconoclastic food writer Gilles Pudlowski has written a book called *Elles Sont Chefs*, highlighting the work of 35 top women chefs, praising them for their generosity and sensitivity. Pudlowski is memorable in my life for reviewing a restaurant I worked in in Paris in the 1980s called L'Assiette, describing me in his review as 'having the chauvinism distinct to my quartier'. I remember him ordering many things, sitting hunched over and taking precisely one bite from each dish. Lulu, my friend and chef of L'Assiette, ran in and out of the kitchen, fetching morsels for him, chattering non-stop in her strong Po accent. He has always respected women chefs, unlike a lot of French critics.

In 1998 Anne-Sophie Pic took over the well-known restaurant in Valence, previously run by her grandfather, father and brother, and has succeeded in shining it up. She cooks things like iced truffle-flavoured dumplings and pomegranate and passionfruit sparkles. She says that women have a greater finesse and more sensitivity in the kitchen, bringing serenity, respect and gentleness. There is less of the famous male chef verbal (and physical) violence, therefore their workplaces are less stressful. Her colleague Helene Darroze has written an unusually intimate cookbook that combines those two great past-times – food and sex. In one chapter she talks about the wild night of passion that led her to invent her star dish of *crème brûlée au fois gras*. Jacques Chirac hand-wrote her a letter of appreciation for the book. She feels that although men are technically brilliant in *haute cuisine*, women contribute instinct, feeling and a fresh approach. Both women have had problems with male staff, leading them to found The New Mother Cooks club, set up to defeat centuries of sexism in French kitchens. In the old days the women chefs were called 'les Mères' because that's what they also were, hence the slightly tongue-in-cheek name.

So, the state of French cuisine is a subject of hot debate – and it's so typical of the French to turn food into an intellectual pursuit. Though it is much more than that – it's the jam in the sandwich of relationships in France, and brought me together with such a rich assortment of people – all of whom are real. Any resemblance to fictional characters is purely coincidental. The stories I really can't tell due to fidelity, respect and French libel laws will no doubt find their way into future fiction. Some people, when they learn you are a writer, immediately urge you to sign a piece of paper saying you will never talk about them; and others, when they see the notebook come out, blossom into Laurence Oliviers, Paul Bocuses and Vivienne Westwoods. Some turn the tables on you and answer each question with a question – always much more probing than yours. Sometimes I asked for a mushroom and got a whole feast, and almost always there was humour, interest in my project and hospitality way above and beyond the call of duty. I got involved in family dramas, psychological lift-offs from reality and falling in love with children, something I normally reserve for my immediate family.

Unlike the Italians, the French are not natural people-lovers with inbred gregariousness but I really like their sharp edge, I like that they make you work, I like that they are a nation of angry gourmets, endlessly analysing food and wine.

It's like constantly striving to please an uncompromising parent or teacher (and God knows I've had a lot of experience in that domain) because although you would just like them to get over themselves, you always learn something, you always come away richer. Their ability to detect minor imperfections in cooking and presentation is truly mind-boggling.

As often as I cursed my methods of transport, in the end I was glad I seldom had access to a car because as any trainwatcher will tell you, train travel provides a unique opportunity to eat revolting food, meet harmless lunatics you wouldn't talk to in a month of Saturday nights, and sit doing nothing – which, as everyone knows, is why a person becomes a writer. I have learned not to allow people to talk to me on trains or planes, not because I am Anglo-Saxon and retentive but because I have NEVER had an interesting conversation with anyone on public transport. The stories are always the same. ALWAYS. It's usually a man, he has usually been undone by some slattern he was married to for 20 years and he never notices when you fall asleep on him in mid-sentence.

Bars, clubs, private homes and markets are a different story. There you meet people who tell you their dreams, their theories on capitalism or the decline thereof, the history of cigar-making and I even met one person in a market bar in the South of France who told me the French bombed the *Rainbow Warrior* for the sole purpose of getting hold of succulent New Zealand lamb. I would have preferred to travel by candle-lit, horse-drawn carriage (décor Louis XIV) with four young slaves to look after my womanly needs and another four to fold and iron my clothes by lying on them. I would have preferred to be long and alabaster of leg with stars in my raven locks, have a nature so sweet and dulcet that the sun came out merely at the mention of my name and wear nothing but black satin gowns cut on the cross to reveal my curvaceous but firm body. But you see, there I was

– five foot four, carrying a ridiculous amount of luggage *sans* assistance, covered in *taches de rousseur* (freckles) and with hair so red, an Irish pilot suggested I be used as a landing light for planes.

The French are very poetic and pepper their conversations with little dollops of incidental tenderness when you are least expecting it. At a picnic a man said the flowers should hide in shame, so lovely were the women there. Often a part of a poem enters the conversation in a radio interview. Men kiss each other on both cheeks and ask you to dance in the rain, then kiss you. I bought a ribbon from a woman who described the colour as crushed raspberries – late season. I bought fabric from another woman who explained to her assistant how to cut plain material straight – 'you can sense the warp. It's like crossing the mountains from Spain . . . you just follow your feelings'. Gabriella on the métro carrying around her family silver. The taps in the toilets at Café Marly at the Louvre run as soon as you put your hands near them. Someone you've met for 15 minutes writes you a love letter. These things I found very poetic.

For a sociable loner I didn't do too badly – only a few tears, lots of bursting into laughter, many days of hibernation, a small handful of temper tantrums and unlimited nosiness. This is the character of the traveller. I'm always amazed at travel writers who are nasty and lacking in graciousness. How do they get people to talk to them? How do they get into people's homes? Who would feed the person who is a hand-biter? And how come they sell millions of books? And then of course there's the periodic loneliness or disappointment in a place that one isn't expecting. There's no such thing as a wonderful, beautiful or moving place. There is only your reaction and relationship to it that makes it worthwhile or not. When I first saw Provence again I thought, what is this barren, dry, colourless place? But then it grows on you like beautiful hair or a reluctant smile. I cooked in kitchens that were unmitigated tips, on castle moats, on barges, in restaurants, in farmhouses with chickens and mud underfoot and in kitchens so spotless and well equipped I wondered if the owners might have sexual problems. The people I dined with were not of the bourgeois, copper-pot, designer-kitchen school of cooking. They were of the 'let's talk about the meaning of life, get the wine open, all you need is fresh ingredients' school of cooking. They were of the 'food is love' school.

This book was written over a period of years and is a personal journey where I was blown by the winds of work, festivals, weather, love and circumstance. Lots of places were left out, which will only make them sweeter when I do get to them. The provinces of France are so different in geography, history, food and sometimes even dialect, that it's like being in different countries. In my opinion the best way to arrive upon French soil is to come from London by Eurostar (the underground train between England and France), bursting silently into the centre of Paris without the experiential dilution of finding your way around the airport and driving in through the suburbs, neither of which experience is of any use to anyone. The second-best way is to enter from Italy or Spain, hit the emotional warmth of the southern French and gradually enter cooler and more sophisticated climes as you ascend.

French eating was in the past entirely centred on agriculture and seasonal availability, and local produce determined the development of recipes. Now, of course, you can get anything anytime, but over and over again I noticed my friends eating seasonally and looking forward to certain foods that might have been available for only two weeks of the year, but they knew those two weeks and waited for them all year. In the country there are always festivals celebrating the arrival of cherries or walnuts or garlic or wine. I went to a village dinner to which everyone from miles around was invited to celebrate the eating of a certain dish called *aligot*. If there's a food and wine celebration going on in France, you can be sure music and a knees-up are not far behind, characterised by lots of country sweat, unbelievable consumption of wine that seems to have no effect, and extremely dubious fashion statements.

Also, in many towns there are grapevines right on the outskirts (there is even a vineyard in the north of Paris) so people are close to their local wine and everyone knows the winemakers. Without question, it is always best to eat regional food in its region, fish in a fish restaurant, seafood and oysters in the months that end with '*bre*' (*octobre*, *novembre* and *décembre*) and flirt with boys in the springtime. Although there are serious pretenders to the throne, the French still produce the best cuisine and the most superb wines in the world, and I suppose their greatest gift to civilisation has been their quality of restraint – the grand pursuit of moderation, the avoidance of exaggeration and grandiosity, the maintenance of balance and measure. They have a horror of strong flavours that are showy or lacking in subtlety.

French family life has broken down to a certain extent, as it has in most western countries, but families are still very close-knit, if spread out. City people maintain close ties with their country cousins who bring food from the farm up to the city, and every family get-together is a reason for feasting. Of course there are contradictions everywhere in French style, fashion and cuisine. If they're so tasteful how come the hotel wallpaper sucks, how do you explain the fact that they've worn jeans and black leather jackets for the last 50 years to the exclusion of all else and why do they eat so much McDonald's?

If I didn't do what I do, I'd have a potato stall in a market in the South of France, where I would stay abreast of political developments, be courted, give and receive recipes, philosophise, meet friends, give to the poor, sing with the happy peasants and eat potatoes to my heart's content. When I was 20 my father said that all he really wanted to do was live on a hill and grow potatoes, and he had no idea how he ended up with six children, a horrendous mortgage, two cars, two houses and a job as an accountant. My mother said, 'Don't be silly, dear, you know perfectly well you couldn't bear to live on a hill.'

I expect the same goes for me. Barking absurdity to think I'd be happy with a potato, really.

Paris

WHEN I FIRST SET FOOT on French soil in Christmas 1979, I was incandescent with openness, positively radiating innocence, and had few preconceptions of what it would be like apart from the vague expectation that Latin lovers would fall at my feet which would always be dancing the java. My inability to see the downside actually protected and served me, and I have never lost it. Only when I am in France do I get the feeling I got in those first three days all those years ago, the feeling of total comfortableness and rightness and 'Oh, is this how it is to be happy?'

'Do you know what the time is?'
    'Yes. It's 7.45 p.m.'
    'You told me your plane was getting in at 4.45.'
    'No. 6.45.'
    'That's not what you told me.'
    'Yes it is.'
    'I waited at the airport until 6 o'clock and then I went home.'
    'Oh God, oh God.'
    This was not what I had in mind for the first night of my follow-up visit to France – an expensive taxi ride into Paris, no welcome, a furious friend and Saturday night alone.
    I was shocked at the turn of events. There I was with presents for the children, a rug for my friend Renate and

four heavy bags to carry. Right, I thought, first I'll drink the
duty-free whisky in the taxi then I'll consider my options.
The thing about being miserable in Paris is that it just doesn't
work. What can I tell you? Paris just takes you in her arms
and looks after you. Everybody hates the French except me
and when I say that Parisians are nice to me, this information
is always met with derision and narrowing of the arteries. I
had reserved a room at Hotel Le Chopin, and a fax confirming
my reservation said: *Chère Madame, J'espère qui'il fera du
soleil lorsque vous viendrez chez nous le 24 Mai. C'est bien parti!*
(I hope it will be sunny when you come to stay with us. It's
looking good!) Overflowing with charm, this two-star place,
surely one of a kind, has tiny rooms with good bathrooms,
lovely staff and something unheard of in Paris – quiet, due
to the fact that it is surrounded by other buildings. The taxi
driver was congenial and kind, the clerk at the Chopin was
gentle and helpful and the waiters at the brasserie were
falling over themselves to spoil me – a woman in a black
dress, dining alone on a Saturday night with nothing better
to do than scribble in a notebook. I tried to look as if I was
waiting for Gérard Depardieu.

It was a cheap, touristy brasserie on the Boulevard
Montmartre, which was exactly what I wanted – the only
place I could trust to slap up something completely unimaginative and banal. One doesn't want always to be stimulated,
impressed or moved to tears by a meal. Sometimes (when one
is near tears anyway) one requires the unsurprising, the staid,
the reliable. That must be why some people have husbands.
Sometimes being a merry widow is not all it's cracked up to
be. I ordered a *kir* (*cassis* and white wine) and was presented
with a little plate of potato chips to accompany it. My invol-
untary eye movement was immediately understood by
the *maître d'*. He signalled the waiter. '*Madame ne veut pas
de chips. Tu ne vois pas que Madame fait attention à sa ligne?*
(Madame doesn't want chips. Can't you see she's looking after

her figure?)' Chips snapped into thin air out of offending distance. *'Madame préfère peut-être des olives ou des petites crevettes?* (Would Madame prefer olives or perhaps little shrimps?)' Hands behind back, bowing slightly. *'Vous n'avez qu'à demander, Madame.* (You only have to ask.)' I inclined my head a third of a centimetre towards the shrimps. There are not half enough people in my life who bow when they address me.

It was a warm, early summer evening and at 9.45, the light was only just beginning to give in to the inevitable seduction of darkness. A raggedy *confit de canard* (preserved duck) that looked like it had walked all the way from Périgord on its own and basement-temperature pasta arrived – and back it went with a pleading smile for something more edible. Profuse apologies and a glass of red wine to see me through. Dinner came back transformed and I made a mental note to always complain in future, no matter what. This time the confit returned in one large, plump thigh with the pasta served warm on a separate dish with a side dish of cheap, grated cheese. I thanked the maître d' for the new improved meal. *'Vous le méritez, Madame.* (You deserve it.)' I think when someone has made an effort one must recognise and acknowledge it. He could EASILY have brought back something equally as unpalatable as the first meal to make sure I understood who was boss, but he didn't. It was a small gesture in the scheme of things and probably wouldn't contribute to world peace, but in my pathetic mood I found it touching.

Suddenly the second glass of wine unplugged the true horror of my situation – eating alone in Paris on Saturday night. I could have stayed alone in the hotel room but then I would have starved to death. The pasta, salted by my tears, was delectable. The maître d' slid over, took in the scene and screamed to the bowels of the restaurant, *'Un café soigné. Tout de suite! C'est pour une amie.* (A well made coffee. Now! It's for a friend.)' Why does everybody hate the French?

I trooped back to my tiny room and flung open the lace-curtained windows to reveal the rooftops of Montmartre. Even though there was no traffic noise, the walls were like crêpes. 'Do you love me?' yelled my neighbour. 'Well, do you?' Oh God, there's no true answer to that question, I thought, I hope his girlfriend gets it right. My neighbour on the other side snored enthusiastically. I turned the TV on loud to keep up with the noise level and at 2 a.m. watched what was actually much more interesting than evening TV. Just like every other country – if it's interesting, put it on when nine tenths of the population are either unconscious or begging for love or otherwise occupied. First there was a documentary on famous French writers all being very intense and vulnerable looking, then the marvellous, erudite *Apostrophes*. *Apostrophes* was a very civilised, highbrow show around literature and authors, presented and choreographed by a razor-sharp intellectual, one Bernard Pivot. The guests all sat around being skilfully witty and brilliantly cultivated. Considering that there are supposedly only a few people left in France who still read, *Apostrophes* was a gift from heaven.

I was in Paris to publicise the translation of *Fête Accomplie* my book about living in France, particularly Paris, through my stomach. The editor took me out to lunch in a local bistro. In between the *jarret de porc aux patates à la dijonnaise* and the *clafoutis* I asked the obvious question: 'Why would the French read a book about themselves?' And got the reply: 'because we're as fascinated by us as you are.' Phyllis Diller always said there was absolutely nothing more wonderful than curling up in bed with a good book, or someone who had read one, so maybe the French were the same.

The minute my fellow diners had finished eating, they lit up. I was briefly shocked but then decided to get a life. What did I care anyway? Finally I was back in Paris, and smoke getting in my eyes was part of the deal. The journalists who interviewed me all had different attitudes, ranging from arrogant lack of interest and smoking in my face, to genuine fascination that I had turned the French into likeable and admirable people. I ate a rack of lamb in a Basque restaurant down the road from my publisher with the publicist Catherine and a nice Burgundian journalist whom Catherine considered to be chic that day as he usually didn't bother to get dressed up. The menu carried such Basque specialities as *ttoro à la kaskarot* (Basque-style bouillabaisse), *piment al piquillo à la morue* (salted cod with hot pepper) and *chipirons à la basquaise* (whitebait).

Laurent the journalist considered that I was suffering from some sort of altered state. '*Mais les Parisiens sont stressés, moches, aggressifs. Ils n'aiment personne, surtout pas le Parisiens.* (Parisians are stressed out, ugly and aggressive. They don't like anyone, they don't even like each other.)'

'No, no,' I said, stuffing a juicy morsel of lamb into my mouth, 'you French are so negative. You all have good educations, you live in a country so beautiful that you have the most tourists in the world in spite of your efforts to humiliate and alienate them, and you have arguably the best cuisine and wine. But still you complain. Still you can't allow yourselves to be happy.'

'It's true,' he replied, 'we're very insular and it's revealing to hear how foreigners see us and how kind you are to us. We don't deserve it.'

'Also you Froggies have this national passion for gastronomy that you use to make yourselves feel slightly less miserable.'

'Ah, *non*. Young people only eat steak and chips and McDonald's now and they're addicted to Heinz ketchup – they know nothing about food.'

'So I hear. Do you know, Laurent, that a third of French people don't even know how to make mayonnaise?'

'Only a third? I am surprised that anyone knows how to make it.'

Catherine with her round open face, blue/grey eyes and dark red hair, was always good company and, like most people, smoked. Parisians still smoke in the office, light up in restaurants the second they've finished eating (no question that they would wait until you've finished), inhale deeply when they're pregnant, on the street and in bed. In spite of the Minister of Culture's efforts, they still use a lot of English words in their sentences. For example, they order *un café strong* and go to the country on *le weekend* and they *faire du shopping*. We got into a big discussion about whether we were happy or not. Laurent asked me what my dream was and I replied without hesitation that I was living it, my biggest fear being that it would all come crashing down on my head and the dream would be taken away. 'You're being French,' he laughed. 'Don't be negative.'

The French have always been a nation of paranoiacs and hypochondriacs, bless their silk socks, but a study called *Francoscopie* by researcher Gérard Mermet has found them to be the most anxious people in Europe. No wonder they're thin. The average Froggie has three times the 'prescription drug intake of other European countries – sleeping pills, anti-depressants, painkillers, sedatives and of course, the ever present liver problems. No one else in the world has *crises de foie* like the French. No one else in the world is even aware of their livers. One in five adults take mood altering medication which has unfortunately not improved the nation's sense of well-being. They have a rich history, are good-looking and reasonably wealthy, but are convinced fate is against them and everything is going wrong, inventing social, economic, political and medical ills. The fact is that everyone envies the French their lifestyle and wants to live in France – except the French.

They think they have become poorer and less healthy and that their culture is being destroyed by America, but the truth is their wealth has grown, they live longer and their food and wine are still sought after worldwide. No one would prefer American culture over French culture in a zillion years. This year France had the most tourism in the world, the three most popular reasons being the food, the countryside and the women (or men depending on your preference), but still the Froggies, against all logic or reason, are unhappy. When several nationalities were asked, 'Are you satisfied with your life?' the French were the only ones who perceived a huge discrepancy between their country's objective and subjective standing. Despite having beautiful architecture, great clothes and the sexiest-sounding language on earth, France's suicide rate is the third-highest in Europe.

The area my small publishing house has chosen to do business in is in a very dangerous part of Paris, the 2nd arrondissement – full of Jean-Paul Gaultier, Kenzo, Stéphane Kélian and Robert Clergerie shops; small old-fashioned bistrots, exclusive kitchen shops and mysterious passages. The five-minute walk from the métro to my publisher right smack in the middle of rue Croix des Petits Champs took me at least half an hour each time we had a meeting. I would take the tiny lift up to the fourth floor, turn left and enter a world of sunlight and books. Entirely white with coir-covered floors and large portraits of their authors, the offices all opened into each other. I spent most of my time in Catherine's room getting instructions about publicity and interviews. All the women who worked there were softly spoken, pretty, smart and very feminine, and the young man at reception was good-looking. I wondered if the publisher had deliberately arranged things this way – I supposed that she had.

At another lunch the journalist didn't ask me any questions, didn't take any notes and appeared to be there as a friend to pass the time of day. With relief I understood that I didn't have to tell my story one more time and we settled into gossiping about famous French film stars. I found out everything about Isabelle Adjani, Gérard Depardieu, Sophie Marceau, Stephanie and Caroline of Monaco and Juliette Binoche. We even covered Mitterand and Chirac. When I asked later why I had even been present at the lunch, Catherine explained that sometimes even though journalists have all the information on the author, they still want to get a look at them and see what they're like.

After leaving my hotel I stayed at my friend Michèle's apartment in the 15th arrondissement, a 20-minute walk from Montparnasse. She is a top-level translator and everything was exactly the same *chez elle* as when I was there 15 years ago except that now there was a huge, early 19th-century Algerian curtain hanging over the entrance to the main room. This magnificent work of art was made of faded green, red and brown silk and embroidered with gold thread. Michèle had found it in the basement of her aunt's estate where it had lain for many years, forgotten and protected from the light, waiting for someone who would love it again. It really belonged in an Arabian *souk* – and there it was in a small apartment in Paris.

Persian rugs covered the floors and bookshelves covered the walls from floor to ceiling, housing collections of Proust, Molière, Balzac, Victor Hugo, Gusave Flaubert. There were gigantic dictionaries, fabulous books on art, important authors she had translated and lots of modern American writers. Every other space on the walls was taken up with gilt-framed paintings; all the cutlery, glasses and dinnerware were antique or at least collectable from her days as a dealer at the *marchés aux puces* (fleamarkets); always a good collection of whiskies on the shelf in the main room; cigarette ashes everywhere. The beds were made up with real linen sheets, and heavy velvet curtains lined with flowered damask hung on the bedroom windows. There was one nutty thing about the apartment, and that was the kitchen on a tiny mezzanine floor, overlooking the proceedings in the main room. In this ridiculous space which contained a fridge, a stove, a sink, three square centimetres of bench space, shelves and cupboards, Michèle had produced dinners for a dozen or more people without any problem. Parisians are experts at making small spaces work.

Michèle rose in the morning, immediately made a coffee that would give a normal person cardiac arrest, lit a cigarette, put on some Bach and started working. She washed and got dressed at some other time of the day, depending on whether she had to go out or not. She sat at her desk by the window all day reading and taking notes, pausing occasionally to eat a sandwich of grainy *ficelle* (skinny little baguette), butter and *jambon de Bayonne* (cured raw ham), occasionally throwing crumbs out the windows to the birds. I was very inspired by her ability to apply herself and not move for hours, something I had yet to learn. However when she went away to Marseille leaving me alone, I found that if I sat at her desk and drank her whisky, I assumed her habits and wrote for very long periods.

Tiny and slim with feet the size of a doll, hair the size of a Rastafarian's without the dreadlocks and an aristocratic face, Michèle is typical of a certain type of Frenchwoman – chic and tasteful in her dress, lucidly intelligent, viciously funny, nervously intense and a master of verbal stiletto. We had long, whisky-fuelled conversations about writing and translating. On *Apostrophes* I listened to a charming, unconventional man, the philosopher and writer Jean Steiner, talking about the thankless job of the translator. He said Nabokov in particular terrorised translators who didn't know the words he used, considering them the lowest form of life. Unloved, badly paid and mistreated by both publishers and writers, translators do it for the love of literature and often rewrite the books they translate to great advantage. If they're not desperately poor, it's because they have some other form of support, e.g. a husband, or family money. Or maybe they lead a double life as prostitutes – I don't know. For French intellectuals, the best writing is now coming from the new world, especially America.

During the day, when I didn't have interviews or photographers, I wrote at Michèle's late 18th-century dining table, sharing it with a bowl of fresh walnuts and crunchy apples. I spent one afternoon in the company of a very attractive American photographer called Adine, with a honey-like voice and gentle manner, who carried around two bags of equipment and a six-month pregnancy. She took 36,000 photographs in a pretty restaurant on the rue de Poitou in the Marais then took another 6,000 in a little park around the corner. We liked each other and, as is common with women from America, immediately fell into quite intimate conversation, something that takes a long time to happen with French women. We watched people in the park – children, lovers, elderly strollers. Parisian women annoy and restrict their children a lot, especially the girls. I suppose that's why they are so softly spoken and agreeable when they grow up. The children tried really hard to have a good time in the park but the mothers and nannies were constantly admonishing them and preventing them from fully experiencing their little lives. Why should they care if their smocked dresses got dirty? Why shouldn't the kid explore one end of the little park to the other? No wonder they become addicted to ketchup.

I used to live in the Marais in an apartment up nine flights of stairs without a lift, so while I was in the area I went for a sentimental sidle. I came across a tea shop on rue du Bourg-Tibourg where I often shopped in the old days, called Mariage Frères. When you walk into this wonderful, old-fashioned place you are immediately hit by the smell of sweetness and aromatic smokiness. The tea shop is downstairs with its huge selection of teas (almost a thousand) from China, Taiwan, India, Ceylon, Japan, Russia, Iran, Turkey, Latin

America, Africa and even Australia. There are beautiful teapots, cups and saucers, kettles, books on tea and other paraphernalia for sale at the counter from the white linen suit-clad assistants. One glides across the polished floor, runs one's hand along the mahogany fittings, takes in the palms and wooden ceiling fans and slides into the little tea room to have tea and cakes with classical music. Upstairs there is a tea museum where you find out that Nicolas Mariage started the business importing tea in 1660. It is a lovely, restful room full of antique tea boxes, weighing machines, labels, order books, tea chests, picnic baskets and teacups.

There are six categories of tea in the world – white, green (non-fermented), semi-fermented, black, perfumed and compressed. They sell a Chinese white tea from the Fujian province called Yin Zhen that costs 70€ per 100g and a Japanese green tea called Gyokuro for 75€, but the most extravagant is a Hunan tea called Five Dynasty Yellow tea that sells for a whopping 40€ per 20g. Most of the prices are a lot more affordable than that and you can get a cup of the brew that cheers but does not inebriate for an average of 6€ per 100g. Tea from Asia is the crème de la crème, the oldest plantation in the world, the 'king of tea plantations' being situated in the Nanhuo valley in Yunan. This tea, which has been grown for eight centuries, is from the camellia family – *Camellia sinensis*. Like wine, each growth reflects the characteristics of the area – the type of soil, climate, sun, rain and the moment of harvest. Green tea is an antioxidant. I thought that would get your attention. I've always loved ordering green tea in Chinese restaurants, but because I liked the mellow clear taste, NOT because it helps you lose weight, is a diuretic, lowers blood pressure, prevents tooth decay and helps digestion. I don't care about any of those things – I'm sold on the lovely, refreshing aroma.

I walked down rue des Rosiers and past the best kosher restaurant in Paris – Jo Goldenbergs, where all those people were mowed down by Arab terrorists the day after I had eaten there. Their window was full of gefilte fish, matzo balls, chopped liver with onions and grated eggs, marinated herrings, pastrami, borscht, smoked kippers and pickled beef – heaven. The street was lined with fabulous Jewish pastry shops bursting with poppyseed strudel and prune shortbread, kosher supermarkets, fish shops, religious supply shops where I used to buy my candles, charcuteries specialising in Eastern European food, and Jewish bookshops. At the far end of the street towards rue Pavée were avant-garde fashion shops, my preferred of which L'Eclaireur. What more could you ask for in one little street? Food, fashion and spiritual sustenance.

I enjoyed a mad bus ride home, lurching through the seven o'clock rush hour, arriving at Michèle's to be met by the unmistakable smell of mushrooms cooking. Table set, wine open, Schubert playing, lights low, dinner on and whisky placed in the hand. God! I thought, this must be what it's like in heaven. To come home to a meal cooked when you're not expecting it. Just like having a husband. Michèle has a horror of anything light or not thoroughly cooked or that smacks of 'healthy'. The idea of sushi or raw marinated fish sends her into spasms of horror. Her one concession to health is that she now buys low-fat cream. This was the menu: thin pork chop beaten to within an inch of its life and fried until it no longer resembled meat in any way, served with a cream, mushroom, white wine and thyme sauce; polenta, tinned gourmet peas and crunchy ficelle. The wine was a somewhat disappointing Bordeaux.

Arraying myself in a snappy blue and white sailor T-shirt and a daring swish of the perfume worn by my mother and grandmother, Chanel No 5 *n'est pas*, I went on a sentimental tour of Montparnasse. My first stop was for a snack at Le Select where my friends and I had spent many, many hours resolving the fashion problems of the passers-by.

Didier, who always served us, met me at the door with a huge smile and kisses. Presently the manager, Francois, came over to shake my hand, refusing to believe we hadn't seen each other for five and a half years. I settled in and waited, fully expecting my old friends to walk in. Didier gave me a look that said, '*Comme d'habitude?*' And 10 minutes later it arrived in the form of three huge slices of *jambon du pays*, little pickles, slices of baguette, packets of butter and the necessary lettuce leaf. The rest of the world gave up the tired lettuce garnish at about the same time they got rid of the horse and cart, but cafés in Paris are still very attached to it. A few glasses of Bordeaux later and it was as if I'd been away only a few months.'

I looked up my Brazilian actress friend Gabriella – which is the same thing as looking up a social secretary. Small, pretty, laughing and full of energy, she had a dramatic story to tell. Her second marriage had been to an ugly but rich man with whom she lived in the lap of luxury in a chic arrondissement. We're talking Jacuzzi bathtub, split level atelier, full time housekeeper, designer clothes and wall-to-wall floors here. I thought the marriage would end because it seemed inevitable she would tire of him, but instead he turned out to be a gangster and a fraud. She put all her money into a joint account with him, he took off to South America and she was left with literally nothing but the family silver. NO MORE HUSBANDS, she promised. I don't understand why you do husbands anyway, I tried to say nicely. It always seems like a good idea at the time, she laughed. We spent a memorable day wandering through the métro with this silver, taking it to various auction houses, and still she kept smiling and laughing in that infectious Brazilian way. Incidentally the métro is the best and most varied source of musical entertainment in Paris, encompassing piano accordion, African drumming, harp playing, classical violin concertos, earnest folk singing and saxophone blasts.

In France, opera can be heard not only on TV but also in the most idiosyncratic of locations. Gabriella and her friend Thomas, a German cultural critic, took me up to Belleville on the rue Faubourg du Temple to see a performance of Mozart's *La Finta Giardiniera* at Le Tambour Royal theatre. In my new red Jean-Paul Gaultier stiletto thongs (red toe-nails in the dirt) I picked my way through the rubbish, doggie doodoo and expectorant, up an alley, into the ratty entrance and up the narrow stairs into a tiny, voluptuous theatre. The walls were covered in murals, the opera was accompanied by a grand piano and the heavy, red velvet curtains lifted to reveal the seven players in marvellous, eccentric costumes. Within minutes it was as if some friends were putting this on in your home. The French are very good at this – where else in the world would you find patrons for a tiny opera in the slums? This magical little theatre has been in existence since the turn of the century, and Maurice Chevalier made his début here in 1903.

On our way home from the opera we looked in on the Java dance hall across the road, where dark gentlemen in white suits and ladies *d'un certain âge* dressed up like *cocottes*, danced the waltz, the tango, the rumba and the paso doble. The place reeked of pastis and nostalgia. I was enchanted but my friends dragged me away to eat a couscous down the road at La Medina on rue de l'Orillon. This restaurant was an oasis of beauty in a desert of drabness with its walls covered from floor to ceiling in ornate blue and yellow Algerian tiles, engraved mirrors and photos of the singer Om Kalsoom. We gorged on the ritual of this North African dish, heaping first the couscous on our plates, then the vegetables, then the broth mixed with *harissa* (chilli paste), then the meat and fish.

Walking through the Marais one can still find tiny bars that have nothing in them save a few bottles of wine, a bar, a table with coffee and tea on it and an old lady. I stopped to get a hit of that amphetamine they call coffee and leaned up at the bar to mainline it. *Un café* in France means a short, sharp black and you don't get anything different unless you ask for it – the words cappuccino or flat white are unheard of; so, actually, is good coffee. You have to cross the border into Italy to get the good stuff. The waiter was rambling on and on about his financial problems so to shut him up I said I didn't speak French. 'Who cares?' he replied, 'I'm the one who needs to talk, not you.' So I let him talk on and on while my mind wandered. I studied my coffee studiously and thought about the global addiction to this strange-tasting substance. The French make terrible coffee generally, but somehow in the south I got lucky quite often – maybe because they're so close to Italy. In Marseillais cafés you find everybody – office workers, chic fashion designers, business people, construction workers, idlers, tourists; but most of all you find people who really, really, really like coffee.

The story of coffee reads like an archetypal mythical tale – it has heroes, adventures, travel, subterfuge, ordeals and finally the return of the magic elixir. Coffee is the elixir which so invigorated Mohammed that he was able to 'unhorse forty men and make forty women happy'. Like sex, coffee is very exciting – people have tried to ban it, they turn to criminal activity if they can't get it and they think they've understood the meaning of life when they do. Coffee is good for you and makes you feel better than you already feel as it stimulates digestion, regulates the cardiovascular system, increases awareness, improves concentration and memory and mood. Of course caffeine is bad for you if you take too much, just like wine, but if you figure out how much you can drink before enough is too much, you will only experience the benefits. Espresso (meaning 'made on the spur of the moment') coffee made with arabica beans is the *crème de la crème*. Decaffeinated blends can be as good as normal blends but the process requires very expensive equipment and top quality beans.

Kaffa in southwest Ethiopia is the original home of the coffee plant and Ethiopians still roast their own coffee and drink it in the traditional ceremonial way. The legend goes that an Ethiopian shepherd called Kaldi noticed that his goats danced all night after they had been eating a certain shrub, so naturally he wanted to try some of the 'magic berries' to brighten up his boring old job. Soon he was dancing all night too. He took the berries to a nearby monastery where they tried to do the same thing they do to sex – destroy it. The abbots chucked the berries in the fire – and guess what happened? The heavenly aroma of coffee was released in the heat. So they smartly whipped the berries out and figured out how to make a drink out of them.

A more likely story is that coffee was first eaten whole in the berry, then the beans were taken out, ground and mixed with animal fat and, repulsive as it sounds, eaten like that. In 1000AD the Arabs discovered how to make coffee as an infusion, initially using green beans in their raw state then figuring out, four centuries later, how to roast and grind them before infusing them. Magnificence can't be rushed.

The first coffee bars were the *qahveh khaneh* of the Arabs where men hung out, listened to music, gambled and indulged in intellectual activities. You let people talk to each other and pretty soon they'll be plotting to overthrow the government or getting strange philosophical ideas, so the coffee houses were banned a few times – but nobody took any notice, thank God, and the rest, as they say, is history. Arab women also loved coffee, and refusal by a husband to procure coffee for his wife was quite rightly legal grounds for divorce.

The Arabs held their monopoly over coffee for a staggeringly long time and it wasn't until 1615, two centuries later, that Europeans got a whiff of the exotic beverage. Those great traders, the Venetians, decided to be extra nice to the Arabs, and green beans left the port of Mocha in Turkey one fine day to arrive in Venice. Coffee shops, called *bottega del caffe* (soon abbreviated to just *caffe*), quickly sprang up all over the place – by 1759 there were 206 in Venice alone. Meanwhile an Indian pilgrim had smuggled seven coffee seeds through Mecca to Mysore in India, where he started up plantations. The Venetians held on like grim death to their monopoly of green bean importation into Europe but their old trading competitors, the Dutch, were the first to smuggle actual coffee plants into Europe. Believe it or not, they grew them in the botanical gardens in Amsterdam then whisked them off to be grown in their colonies of Java and Sumatra in the East Indies. Within a few years the Dutch became the principal suppliers of coffee to Europe. Strangely enough they didn't open coffee bars but drank it at home. The Dutch were also generous: in 1714 they gave a coffee plant to King Louis XIV of France.

They'd already been drinking coffee in the French court for a while and had invented the idea of sticking sugar in it, which no one had done before. And off coffee went on another adventure, this time to be grown in the French colony of Martinique. From then on it was all go – the Spaniards grew it in the West Indies, the English in Jamaica and India and the Portuguese in Brazil. In Brazil's ideal climate and soil, coffee grew like it had never grown before and the Brazilian plantations became the biggest in the world and remain so. Now coffee was a fire that couldn't be extinguished and it spread to Mexico, Venezuela and Colombia, currently the second largest producer in the world. Coffee reached the New World in 1660 in what was to become New York and when the Bostonians chucked all the tea into the harbour in 1773 at one of their rebellious parties, coffee became more popular and is still the national drink. It is now the second largest trading commodity in the world.

To make a good coffee you need more than good Arabica beans. Even with all the new technology in espresso machines, the skill of the operator is still of great importance. The espresso method of making coffee, which dates from the 19th century, is the king of all methods, because the greatest amount of noble substances – body, aroma and flavour – are extracted. A good *express* is the result of several integral components and if one is missing, the show is over. As well as a good coffee-maker person, there has to be a good mixture of beans, they must be ground to the right fineness in order to get the creamy stuff on top, they must be ground freshly for every coffee made, and the machine itself must be top quality and cleaned regularly. And a red ribbon must always be worn in the hair.

Most people actually drink coffee too hot. The water must be no hotter than 90°C and the cups must be warm and small – coffee is to be savoured, not gulped. You should be able to fling yourself into a café, order an express at the bar, throw it down your throat and walk out without having to call the burns unit. The colour should stain your tongue for half an hour after drinking and should taste a little bitter, a little sweet, with slight acidity and big flavour. You may be aware of tastes and smells like toasted bread, flowers, chocolate and fruit. Smell is a little-used sense these days as we don't need it for survival, so we tend to forget about it. I'm always getting into trouble in restaurants for smelling the food (for pleasure, not criticism). My advice is, start using your olfactory senses – it will teach you what is good and what is bad – and smelling freshly made coffee must surely be one of the greatest and cheapest pleasures in life.

Everywhere you go in Paris you pass stunningly plumed birds of paradise in the form of tall, regal African women, trailing their beautifully dressed children behind them. People with little dogs everywhere – in their cars, in restaurants, in their arms. It's only in Paris you a see a man in a leather jacket, tight black jeans and pointy cowboy boots walking his black poodle. And by the way, pedestrian crossings are not marked for the same reasons as in other countries – in Paris they are there to provide a clear target for the cars.

I managed to negotiate the streets to have lunch at Chartier, one of the oldest restaurants in Paris, where I ate a *pot-au-feu* with mayonnaise as they do in the south, instead of mustard. I inquired of the waiter if they took reservations for groups and he snapped, 'NEVER.' The couple at my table advised me to try again later so I kept talking and cracked a few jokes and by the end of the meal they took reservations. Exceptionally, you understand. He gave me the Chartier card and I asked if the fax number was on it.

'Obviously, Madame, otherwise why would I give you a card?'

'Thank you so much' (big smile).

'You're welcome, Mademoiselle' (little bow).

To call me Mademoiselle instead of Madame was being very familiar, and it signalled that I had won his heart. He added the cheap bill up on the paper tablecloth but admitted he did have a calculator that he never used. On my way to the métro I passed a prostitute having a loud argument in the street with a client. She was twice his size, hugely, frighteningly blonde, encased in latex and not interested in doing business. He was the size of a toothbrush and obviously had no limits in the humiliation stakes.

The translator of my book, Jocelyne, introduced me to an area I had ignored in my 10 years in Paris – the quartier St-Blaise in the 20th. It is a real secret in that it's quiet, harmonious, clean and spacious – an artistic quartier full of artists, sculptors and teaching ateliers. She took me to a magreb restaurant where you can eat only the formula, there is no choice. The feast started with bottles being put on the table – three sorts of pastis, gin, vodka, sangria with olives, little onions, pickles and chickpeas. This was followed by *brique à l'oeuf,* followed by a huge plate of lamb, *merguez,* chicken brochettes, tagine and couscous. We said we definitely couldn't eat anymore so they brought us huge piles of fresh dates, fresh fruit salad, cherries and a basket overflowing with fruit. The owner, who appeared to be a courteous man free of any cynical calculation, came and kissed our hands. I ask you.

On the way back to the métro I came across the Flèche d'Or Café, a big, seedy bar overlooking the railway lines. It was like something out of *Mad Max* or *Pulp Fiction* with huge motorbikes outside, a screaming chef and grindingly filthy décor. It's a popular joint for rock concerts and apparently a really good dance happens on Saturday nights. They had a system of toilets that I'd never noticed before in Paris but seem to come across often now – unisex ones. It's bad enough that the toilets are the revolting, squatting variety, but now we are obliged to watch men using the urinal too. Working on not looking anywhere one shouldn't look, blind with anxiety, one bangs into walls trying in great haste to find the women's place. Then you have to go through the whole thing again to get back out. Utterly desperate. It's already lucky for men we talk to them, now we have to share the toilet with them?

By accident rather than design, I wandered into another quartier I didn't know that well and fell into a wonderworld of ancient passages. I was on the rue des Petits Champs and at No 4 fell upon a very chic arcade called Galérie Vivienne. It was full of expensive boutiques, antique bookshops and *salons du thé.* Lucien Legrand's Atelier du Vin is there, supplying everything to do with wine – hundreds of different openers, glasses, bottles, carafes, ice-buckets, cellar books etc. There is a flower shop that sells only white flowers, a shop that sells only women's scarves and shawls and a garish novelty shop. At the end of the passage is the best shop of them all – Jean-Paul Gaultier: mutant, supercilious shop assistants who think they're Brad Pitt, high velvet hats, sparkling netting tops, lime green striped jackets, kimono-inspired coats and space-age jewellery. I memorised everything, gave the mutants an 'old-fashioned look' then walked out. Following Galérie Vivienne to its logical destination, I ended up on rue Vivienne, turned right, walked past the Bourse and somehow found myself in the passage des Panorames, lined on either side by restaurants with intricately engraved exteriors, bookshops and art shops.

Upon reluctantly emerging onto the Boulevard Montmatre at the other end, I was enchanted to discover another passage facing me – the passage Jouffroy. I had now moved into the 9th and the flavour was changing to become more down to earth and colourful. This passage was slap bang in the middle of quintessential old Paris and half way along was Le Chopin hotel. At the end of the passage I crossed the rue de la Grange-Betelière and went straight into the passage Verdeau, full of more bookshops, home-supply shops and a pretty restaurant with yellow walls. If I hadn't then got tired and gone home to Michèle's, I would have discovered another one – the passage de Deux Sœurs.

That night Gabriella took me to dinner at the *porte ouverte* (open house) of a sculptor friend of hers on rue Jean de Beauvais in the 5th. Francois Baschet was a pleasant, unpretentious man with a messy studio who spoke flawless English and, according to our German friend Renate, perfect German also. I later heard him speaking fluent Spanish with a Mexican journalist and Portuguese with Gabriella. Francois is fascinated by shapes and sounds produced by folded metal. Upstairs he makes bell towers, windmills, fountains etc, using the natural elements of wind and water to make music. Normally his porte ouverte happens every day except Sunday, at lunchtime. Anyone can turn up; a volunteer cooks the food, people leave a bit of money. Above the dining table was a cheeseboard suspended on a pulley system that moved along the table if you pulled on the strings. I left the party as the Mexican was singing mournfully, a painter was doing the dishes and some American writers were talking about how hard it was to get published.

The next day I went back to Montparnasse to have lunch at La Coupole. Immediately I sat down I was so flooded by memories of my old life in Paris, I almost drowned right there and then before I could even say *garçon*! I was placed, in spite of my zero status, at a very good table in the centre of the room where I could do social studies on the other customers. I ordered the menu of *fricassée de poulet, tarte aux pommes*, a carafe of wine and a coffee. The garçon, dressed in black pants, white shirt, black waistcoat and bow-tie and long white apron, carried the food on a tray on his shoulder from the kitchen to the maître d'hôtel. This smashing gentlemen, dressed in a black suit, white shirt and black bow-tie, reheated the food on a small silver burner at the central service area. The crumbs were brushed off my table with a little silver comb and the coffee came with wrapped chocolates.

After lunch I knew I had to do something I had been putting off since the day I arrived, so, steeling myself, I crossed the boulevard to rue de la Grande-Chaumière. I hadn't seen the atelier where I had spent those happy years as a chef in Paris with my old friend Willy Maywald before he died. As soon as I reached the beginning of the little street and looked up at the street sign, my heart began to thump and my eyes to sting. I can't do it, I thought, it's too hard and I can't breathe and all these people will see me weep. I leaned against the wall and closed my eyes. When I looked down at my bag my hands were trembling. Finally I moved slowly down the street to No 10, stroked the door and imagined I could hear the music of Nino Rota that he always played. I don't know how long I stood there but presently someone who lived in the apartment upstairs arrived home and opened the door so I followed them inside to the courtyard.

His courtyard. My courtyard where I drank whisky and ate little fruit tarts and he smoked, laughed and told stories. His garden table, chairs and sculptures were still there and nothing appeared to have changed although the house was now owned by someone else. The tears poured quietly out of my eyes, which seemed to have lost their borders. I sat on the ledge by the garden, the tears fell into my red basket and onto the steps and I thanked fate for having placed him in my path. The next thing I remember was being on a bus to the area where my restaurant had been on rue d'Arras in the 5th arrondissement.

As I walked down the street for the first time in years, one by one the shopkeepers and inhabitants came out of the building to shake my hand and talk to me. The printer told me Rose Blues had changed hands four times since I had sold it, and had never worked. '*Oh Madame Peta,*' they said, smiling, '*on ne mange plus bien dans le quartier. On est désespérés. Quand est-ce que vous revenez?* (There's nowhere good to eat in the quartier since you left. We're desperate. When are you coming back?)' My restaurant is now called Le Rive Gauche and I hope the food is more original than the name. The street doors to my old apartment building around the corner were now locked with a code and there was a new Australian bar next door, of all things. On I walked to the beautiful, magical Ile-St-Louis, down the main street, past the church where I went to the free Sunday classical concerts, stopping in front of La Charlotte en Isle, the chocolate shop of my friend Sylvie. My senses took me across the Petit Pont to the Shakespeare & Co bookshop on the rue de la Bûcherie off Boulevard St-Michel then over to the Centre Pompidou and Les Halles, where I ordered a *citron pressé* at the Café Beauboug and watched the world go by.

One warm evening Michèle and I decided to visit Lulu at her famous restaurant, L'Assiette, on rue du Château in the 14th arrondissement. Lucette Rousseau was a major inspiration and teacher in my gastronomic journey and a loving friend when I lived in Paris in the 1980s. I worked as her waitress when she first opened her restaurant, just to be near her and learn. She was a witness at my marriage in Paris and gave me her sapphire engagement ring as a wedding present. L'Assiette was exactly the same except that now there was a large sketch on the wall of one of her most faithful clients, Frédéric Mitterand. The menu was still written in hand by her, a lot of the same dishes were there, the dinner plates were the same and her boyfriend Hervé didn't look a day older. An addition was a temperature-controlled case containing Havana cigars, ostensibly for the customers but Lulu now smokes them instead of cigarettes. The prices were expensive so we just ordered mains. At that moment Lulu arrived from her apartment across the road, saw my name in the reservation book and screamed. I hadn't seen her for seven years and she looked great – a little more weight, which she needed, her hair now short, and black-rimmed glasses. I showed her my first book and she screamed again at the photo of herself. We managed to catch up a bit in the kitchen but she was busy, of course, so I sat down to see if she could still cook.

Two duck and foie gras terrines were placed before us, garnished with pickled cherries and tarragon branches. A present from Lulu.

'Already I'm impressed,' said Michèle, 'and I haven't lifted my fork yet. I can't bear restaurant owners who are mean and vulgar and penny-pinching. People don't know how to be hosts anymore. This gesture shows that Lulu is not only a good hostess but she really understands the restaurant business.'

The terrine was exactly what I would have expected – fresh, perfectly seasoned and delicate. For the main course Michèle ordered sole with miniscule potatoes. The sole was perfectly cooked and the potatoes tasted like the dream potatoes that my father grew in our childhood garden. I ordered black pudding with mashed potatoes, which sounds simple enough but was exquisite. It arrived in its copper frying pan, grilled on top and wrapped in a starchy white napkin. We absolutely couldn't consider dessert, but the lovely waiter insisted I eat one scoop of caramel ice cream. When it came time to pay, there was no bill.

'*Non, non,*' we said.

'*Si, si,*' he said.

'*Non, alors là, non,*' we said.

'You must surely know there's no point in going against Lulu,' he smiled.

This is why Lulu is still a great cook – she is not only utterly consistent and uses impeccable ingredients, she has a huge heart.

Michèle hates the word 'food' – it's weak and simpering and one almost spits it out; whereas the French word for food, *nourriture*, is a beautiful, expressive, sensual word that one can really get one's mouth around. She stood in the middle of the footpath saying nourriture over and over to show me all the permutations. She instructed me to invent another English word for food that showed that you actually liked the stuff. The fact is, we have many words for food already – nutriment, manna, edibles, victuals, grub, stodge, sustenance, nourishment, fodder, provisions, to name but a few – but none of them do the same as nourriture.

Another evening my translator Jocelyne and her husband Luc invited me to their home in Montparnasse. Way up on the sixth floor, their sunny apartment has a terrace with flowers and potted trees that even have birds landing in them. We ate a good summer meal of salads, fish terrine, sheep's milk cheeses and an amazing selection of little chocolate cakes. Jocelyne and Luc are a very civilised, interesting couple with a gorgeous, 11-month-old daughter with whom they are besotted, to their utter surprise. Luc is a gynaecologist who specialises in abnormal medicine and rides a bicycle to work. He found it very interesting that as the eldest child of a large family, resenting all the other interlopers in his mother's affections, he became a doctor whose main work involves bringing yet more babies into the world. When I told him that I was the eldest child of a large family who considered my siblings to be passing guests in my mother's affections, he found it even more interesting that I became a nurse who liked only maternity and delivering babies. He helps people who are basically beyond help, and is a passionate gourmet, recounting stories of the best restaurants, the best food and gastronomic excursions in Italy. He loves wine and like all French people has strong opinions on which ones he prefers. The French don't describe wines by the grape, they describe them by the province – a Bordeaux, a Gamay, a Brouilly etc. If they needed a transfusion, the French would rather have wine than blood – there is the story of the man who carried a card in his wallet that says GEORGES DUROC. JE SUIS COTES DE BEAUNE POSITIF.

After a good night's sleep in my linen sheets, I rose and got the métro to the St-Germain quartier. While I was having a prolonged argument with myself about some shoes I had seen at Maude Frizon and how could anyone pay that much money for shoes, I came across an old bistrot on rue St-Benoît where I had often eaten with my friends. Le Petit St-Benoît at No 4 serves traditional and family-style cooking, which the French love because they cannot forget the wonderful meals of their youth. The menu had the usual things and I chose a *suprême de poulet estragon* (chicken breast with tarragon), making the fatal mistake of asking the snail in an apron what it was served with. Slight sneer and unmistakable little tone of voice.

'*Mais, avec du riz, Madame. Le suprême de volaille à l'estragon se sert toujours avec du riz. Depuis toujours.* (But with rice of course, Madame. Chicken breast with tarragon is always served with rice.)' And only a stupid foreigner would have to ask. Slap! The whole world knows that this is how it is. I really wanted to ask her to replace the rice with vegetables to see if her heart would stand the strain, but as usual with the French, I just burst into laughter. There's a certain type of French woman, be she working class or upper class, who specialises in complete bitchery, calling it either brains or personality, and they get worse as they get older. They are specialists in the no-win style – you lose because you get to feel awful and they lose because they end up with pinched faces and liver crises.

Bistrots. In these cigarette-stained finishing schools of psychopathology, there's a time-honoured style of waitressing that uses the same rules of engagement as warfare, and the client is a fool if they can't play. Everyone is the enemy, *bien entendu* – if it wasn't for you they would be at home with their feet up. But even these bitches have their limits. Occasionally they smile a manipulative little grimace so that their faces don't completely fall off. It is a deeply ingrained habit of some (not all) French servers to ignore, snub, scare and, well, hate their customers. Even when I arrived in Paris to live in 1980 there were posters everywhere encouraging people to be nice to customers and tourists, but it's been an uphill slog for the poor *chéries* ever since the Revolution and progress is spotty – some people just can't take the culture shock of having to be nice.

In spite of being unimaginative dressers, BCBG (*bon chic, bon genre*) Parisian women have this way of wearing a scarf like no one else in the world. The scarf is normally silk (light and fine) and is wrapped around the neck loosely until there's none left. The ends are tied in a chic little knot to the side. They also all wear little white sandshoes, plain cotton slacks and polo shirts. One sees very few huge fashion statements in this rather conservative city. Maude Frizon has her shop on rue des St-Pères and makes the best shoes in Paris in my opinion. It would be better not to buy three pairs of ordinary shoes and spend the money on a pair of hers – they are beautifully made, really different and last forever. If you look after them, they go out of fashion before you wear them out. I gave my sister a pair in 1985 and they are still avant-garde.

Actually, if you want to be happy forever, walk along the rue des St Pères in St-Germain. I started at the Seine and walked up past the art and antique shops. ETRO had Japanesy/Chinesy/Indiany flowing, loose clothes with Western-style structured jackets over them; Sonia Rykel had clothes that would look good on a tiny, thin, pale, red-headed woman just like her; Yamamoto was slick; Versace was garish; Anne Fontaine sold only white blouses and shirts for women – crisp, pristine and cleanly Catholic; Yves St Laurent was conservative; and the unbelievably fabulous lingerie shops made me think, 'I could buy four books for the price of those knickers and they'd do me a lot more good.' A woman walked by in an incongruous Provençal skirt and I wondered if I was dreaming. What was she doing here in Paris when she should be on a horse in the Carmague? Then the shoe shops finished the tour off along with the best frock shop of all, which is Onward Accessoires near the St-Germain métro stop, because they sell all the big designers in the same shop.

Now about fashion. There's runway fashion, which no one can wear or afford except Saudi princesses who have to wear it under their chador, and six-foot mutant models with huge feet; and there's street fashion which you and I wear. According to people who know, the 90s fashion victim dressed for attitude, dressed to kill or at the very least maim, sexiness was hard and violent, power dressing was out thank God and contempt dressing was in. We're talking trashy thongs, spiky stilettos, patent leather straps, black leather, sex-shop styling, bondage detailing and fetish-inspired boots. Believe it or not, real fur was replacing fake fur and the fashion writers were saying dominatrix. I seem to remember using that word in my first book *Fête Accomplie* when describing fashion in the middle 80s. Are we so lacking in ideas that we are recycling those stupid giant shoulder pads, leopard skin prints, feathers, fishnet stockings and hot-pants? At least heroin chic is out. I mean how much purple eye shadow can you wear under your eyes anyhow, and do you have any idea how difficult it is to peroxide your hair and deliberately leave the roots black?

The name of the game in the 2000s is that there is no more name, every woman wears what she wants now, every-thing is in and everything is out, nobody has the controlling cultural authority to dictate fashion. The days of rules are out the glass ceiling – there is no length for a skirt, no width for pants, no height for shoes and no particular hairdo. It's all deconstruction and, quite frankly, jolly anarchy and it makes me nervous – it's all going to end in tears. How can a person who was brought up by *Vogue* in unflinching service to an impossible ideal that was completely arbitrary, unsociable and would never be seen on your home shores anyway, now be expected to adjust to the fashion industry kowtowing to the consumer? This is role reversal at its most confusing. Young Parisian girls wear ridiculously high platform gym-shoes or *baskets*, as they call them, and the boys who seem to be getting taller, wear tight black jeans and black T-shirts. Even though they fall over at the idea of exercise and appear to eat lots (unless perhaps they do it with mirrors), they remain slim and sexy.

Okay, so I bought a pair of Patrick Cox boots with sharp toes, missing ankles, laces and very high, toilet seat-shaped heels because I thought it would be fun to stand in them for five minutes on a Saturday night. I knew there was no question of walking in them, but even when I just sat in them, they had the most extraordinary effect on men. It's true what they say. Men are like lino – they just want to be walked on. The minute I walked into a room in France with these boots on, half the men lay down on the floor and said, 'Beat me.' They didn't even have to be asked. Not only France either because I wore them to an architecture conference at home and a staid old architect got down on the floor and licked them, for God's sake!

While I was in Paris, a well known French fashion magazine dressed a model in Christian Lacroix clothes, then asked people in the street four questions:

(1) Do you like these clothes?

(2) Would you wear them and where?

(3) How much do you think they cost?

(4) Who is the designer?

The model was dressed in a lime green, see-through lace top, blue lace gloves, red and black print flares and long flowery coat. Most people loved them, would love to wear them but only in private, grossly under-estimated the price and a third of them guessed the designer. Men liked the idea of their women dressing like this but women were much more realistic, knowing they could neither afford nor look good in such clothes in a million years. The most interesting thing was that (a) the clothes looked as though they came from a Salvation Army shop and (b) most people mistook them for Jean-Paul Gaultier.

On my way home I visited Arlene, an American friend from the old days. Artist, writer, poet, playwright and local personality, Arlene was born and brought up in New York and although she has lived in the 14th arrondissement for over fifty years, sounds like she just got off the boat. She was married to a well known French sculptor, knew Henry Miller and in the early 60s bought paintings from Hundertwasser in the Select for 8¢. She teaches French people English and they all walk around sounding like Brooklyn Jews. Spectacularly unattached to housekeeping, Arlene lives in a ground-floor flat that is literally stuffed – floor to ceiling, wall to wall, on top of tables, under stools, in the bathroom and hanging on every available protuberance. Like a mini fleamarket her rooms explode with hundreds of paintings she will never sell, books, jewellery, bags of firewood, junk, clothes, papers and *objets d'art*. In the main room there's room for only one chair, which I was told to sit on. Her double bed is so overflowing with the colourful contents of her life that there is just enough room for her to slide in and lie down. The windows are covered so as not to let any natural light in (she can't think properly in the light); the rooms are lit with lamps. The table was set with three colourful tablecloths and I was ceremoniously offered strawberries and sugar, cordial and little tea cakes. I was told to eat. Eat already.

She has written two esoteric books that no one understands; one 'deals with the paradisial or infernal couple in their journey from the outside world of appearances to the inner world of absence and void', and the other is a collection of poems and short stories about the holocaust. Arlene believes 'that the concept of purity of race, nationality and religion is a perversity: there is only one purity of intention and when justice is not allowed to express itself, vengeance takes its place'. When I went back to Paris four months later, Arlene gave me a copy of her *Memoirs of a Frog Prince* to read, with an illegible dedication. I was surprised how quickly I fell into this book – I inhaled it almost. I walked around Paris, reading it on the métro and in cafés, reading it in the places she wrote about. It was dirty realism, a style I admire but don't really have a taste for, but funny, desperate, unflinching, grindingly honest and reminiscent of Paul Bowles and Henry Miller.

Witty, opinionated, good-hearted and eternally blonde,

she took me on a tour of the neighbourhood where I had lived and worked for a while. The 14th arrondissement has been transformed by a star of postmodern architecture – the Catalonian architect Riccardo Boffil. The slightly rotting quartier now has a circle of fabulous classical, theatrical buildings. Some people call it fascist architecture but both the old and new residents love it. On one side is state housing and on the other, yuppie (pronounced yoopee in French). Rue de l'Ouest, a dump in my time, now sports flash restaurants, bakeries and clothing shops and B.O.F., the little restaurant where I had learned so much, is now filled not with flowers and pears in cassis, but with people doing their laundry. Rue Vercingétorix, where I had bought my bread, is divided in two by the central square. I have to tell you that this dear little street was named after a man who bartered his own freedom for the lives of his men, was surrounded by the Roman legions and taken to Rome to be displayed in Caesar's triumphal procession and then imprisoned for six years in the Tullianum before being strangled there. It doesn't pay to be a hero.

It was June, which is really the best month in Paris – the weather is great, all the new season's produce is well on its way, there is flirtation in the air and the best designer sales in the universe start at the end of the month. I hadn't seen a French market for a year, so on a warm Sunday morning I put on my running shoes and walked briskly to the nearest one on Boulevard Garibaldi. Spilling over with vendors all yelling their heads off, the market seemed to be moving all on its own with bemused shoppers and a stiff wind that kept everything trembling. I bought *artichauts poivrade di Hyère* (little purple artichokes in a bunch) and *asperges sauvages* (wild asparagus) – a fat bunch of very thin green stalks with sheaf-like heads. According to Elizabeth David this delicacy is not an asparagus at all, but a hop. I suppose it doesn't really taste of asparagus, but it is sweet and delicious anyway. Later on I cooked them for one minute and ate with them butter, salt and pepper, but they would be ideal in risotto or an omelette. I also bought *asperges violettes des Landes* (purple asparagus from Landes) and fat, white asparagus that I long for the minute I leave France.

At that point I ran out of money which I do often in Paris, and had to go and find an ATM. Markets only take cash, of course, and the only place you can get cash is from a bank. I am so used to paying for everything electronically that, like the Queen, I carry very little real money. If a girl gets desperate for lipstick or a gin she just whips out her little card. Try finding a cashpoint with cash in it on a Sunday in Paris. Eventually I did, after lining up with all the other desperados, and no sooner had I paid for the asparagus than I spied the every-kind-of-potato-imaginable stall, notably the tiny spuds I had eaten at L'Assiette with Lulu. There they were under the extraordinary name *grenaille de Noirmoutier* – shot (as in gunshot) from Noirmoutier – and they are only in season June and July. I briefly considered lying on top of them and asking the seller to marry me or at least provide me with grenailles for life, but pity for a man sentenced to live with a woman who ate only potatoes prevented me. I walked quickly past the *chevaline* (horsemeat department), and my nose dragged the rest of me to the huge stall selling grilled meats, sautéed potatoes, couscous, hams, salads and cooked vegetables. Huge chunks of pâté were being cut off giant terrines in bowls with very serious-looking knives. When I leaned over the wide counter to pay the fat jolly sellers, they shouted, 'Hey *roukine*, if you want to kiss me you have to come over this side.'

Although it wasn't really the season for mushrooms yet, there were lots of *girolles*, *chanterelles*, *cèpes* and *morilles* (morels). After my shopping, all carefully placed in a Frederick's of Hollywood 'an intimate experience' bag, I did what everyone does after the market – found a sunny chair in a café, ordered a *crème* and settled down to one of the best newspapers in the word, the *Independent on Sunday*. Reading this paper reminded me why I can't stand the *International Herald Tribune* any more. I had never noticed before how reactionary and right wing it was with its schoolmarmish, up-your-bum slant on news, and not even particularly well written – quite untenable.

That night, the French elections were on TV so I stayed in, steamed the grenailles and laid thin slices of cured raw ham over them, cooked the artichokes in white wine, olive oil and garlic and cracked open a very nice bottle of *vin gris du Var* (table rosé). In France they vote twice, once to get people out of the front door and into the polling booth, then a week later everyone who didn't vote gets a terrible fright when they see who is winning and they all rush out to make sure of the correct victory. Very bad filming in the studios – people don't know which camera is on them so they end up doing things they wouldn't wish to be seen doing like adjusting their clothing, fighting with opponents, picking their noses and laughing at the presenter.

French politicians are great orators and rather pompous on TV, unlike our new world politicians who try to be men and women of the people. A few weeks before the election, President Chirac had won the *bourbon chocolat*, the *asperge blanche* (the booby prize) for saying that since he has been unable to change his country's inequalities or deficits or social security mess, the French must change the way they think, that they must get a grip. The French are, as a nation, both satisfied and dissatisfied with themselves and when election day arrived they changed the way they thought all right and voted the socialists back in. *Fromage dur* for Chirac. In a colossal political miscalculation, he had called an early election that spectacularly backfired on him, right in front of my very eyes. There are quite a few more women in this government (10 altogether, which is unheard of) than in the previous, a move that was treated with great fanfare by commentators. In general in France, activism, feminism and political involvement are still fairly alien and are regarded with a critical and mostly uncomprehending eye.

In the 1990s there was a bit of cooking on French television but in short pieces during the day – rarely in the evening at prime time, and there is little telly chef star carry-on as in Britain and America. There are repeats of an old show of Maité, a plump countrywoman with a strong accent who teaches traditional dishes with the annoying 'help' of an older lady. She gets fifteen minutes every day in the late morning on France 3. One morning she made *rouget farci aux anchois* (red mullet stuffed with anchovies, wrapped in curly cabbage leaves and baked in a very hot oven). The older lady made some inane remark about how desperately unusual the dish was and Maité moved quickly on. The best food show, called *Grands Gourmands*, was on Saturday morning, also on France 3. It was presented by a dear man, one Jean-Luc Petitrenault who has written a bestselling restaurant guide called *Le Guide Petit Renault*. The day I watched he was doing the rounds of the best restaurants in Lyon – La Mère Brazier, Léon de Lyon etc, in his inimitable style of almost whispering to the camera and drawing the viewer in in a very intimate way, rubbing his hands with delight and *tutoie*-ing all the big chefs. At midday on TF1 there was a five-minute show called *Cuisiner comme un grand chef* (How to Cook Like a Great Chef)... (in five minutes of course), hosted by Joël Robuchon. They do much more refined recipes and have flash guest chefs. Then of course, there was Lulu who cooked a recipe every Friday on Canal+ on *La Grande Famille*.

She invited me to come with her to the studio where she films live. I turned up at her restaurant early to go with her and was offered a coffee by the entirely beautiful and polite waiter Jean-Paul, whose calm manner was exceeded only by his grace. There was a sad case from the quartier sitting in a corner sucking on a fag and inhaling the express Jean-Paul had made her. When she left he said, 'Make sure you put your cigarettes out properly.' Lulu has always looked after these people in the quartier. If it's not an old lady, it's a child or a drunk or someone lonely. A gauchist from way back, she genuinely believes we should all look after one other. She walked in all smiles, threw her weight around the kitchen for five minutes, then we jumped in her lavender Deux Chevaux and she hurtled through Paris, talking non-stop, smoking her cigar out the window, running red lights (she uses them only as a guide) to the Canal+ studios. We ran through the corridors (Lulu never strolls, she always runs) and as I trailed behind she shouted, 'Follow me, follow me, you followed me for four years, there's no reason to stop now.' She greeted everyone she came across as a long-lost friend, throwing her arms around them, running from room to room.

'This is my friend Peta. She's from New Zealand. It's thanks to me she even knows how to boil water. I taught her everything she knows. Now she writes books where she talks about her friends having never asked their permission which she has no right to do but as she's a redhead I'll forgive her but on the other hand maybe I will call my lawyer. *Bonjour chérie chérie.* This is my friend Peta. She's a New Zealander. *Nouvelle-Zélande.* You've never heard of it? Nothing happens there but it's very beautiful and everybody plays rugby and eats pies and Peta does a TV show on food and she's a big star so watch out and make sure she gets a good seat in the studio. *Salut, ma poule!*'

I then saw things I never thought I would live to see: Lulu, who's never let makeup defile her face in her life, in the makeup room getting powdered and blushed; Lulu, who's never worn anything but shirts and jeans, in the dressing room being draped in a sky blue cashmere twinset. TWINSET for God's sake. Lulu, who refuses to wear a bra,

---

Cuisses de Canard aux Vinaigre de Xeres
Duck Legs in Sherry Vinegar

Serves 4

4 duck legs
2 heads of garlic, halved
4 large red onions, skins on, halved
1 cup sherry vinegar
sea salt and freshly ground black pepper
chopped flat-leaf parsley

1. Preheat oven to 150°C. In a frying pan, brown the duck legs on both sides. Place in a baking dish.

2. Pour off some of the fat and brown the garlic and onions. Place them in the baking dish along with the duck.

3. Deglaze pan with the vinegar, add salt and pepper and pour over the contents of the baking dish.

4. Cover and cook in the oven for one hour.

To serve: Sprinkle with parsley and accompany with fresh pasta.

---

being tied into a black lace number. Lulu, who never goes to the hairdresser, being teased, primped and sprayed. The hairdresser with a ponytail down to his waist, trying to impose style on hair that has a will of its own.

'*Tu vois ce que je dois supporter pour faire cuire une cuisse de canard?* (You see what I have to put up with to cook a duck leg?)'

She went into great details with the hairdresser about what she was going to do on her holidays, most of which involved activities best suited to the bedroom. We ran into the large studio, Lulu said, 'Sit there, that way my mother can see you,' and I suddenly found myself part of the audience.

Each weekly show of *La Grande Famille* was based on a different region of France and this day it was La Creuse.

Footage of the area is shown, the presenters discuss it, guests from the area talk about it and Lulu cooks something suitable in a kitchen in the middle of the studio, surrounded by the adoring audience, dozens of cameras and lights and the crew. She was deliriously happy, of course, because she is that unusual combination of master chef and performer and she does it all live, without practice and with great control. One of the presenters, Alexandre, a ridiculously handsome, well-constructed young man (I want one for my show), danced around her being silly and annoying and making fun of everything – her accent, the food, the price of fish... Normally anyone who talked to Lulu like that would find themselves with a thick ear in about two minutes, but she played the game very well, industriously getting on with the cooking while imparting her particular view of life and food.

They were brilliant together. He grabbed my camera, jumped up on the table lined with presenters and newsreaders and began photographing them. Lulu chose to highlight duck from La Creuse. Her recipe: duck leg roasted with Xeres Vinegar (*see recipe, facing page*), garnished with roasted red onions and garlic in their skins. Alexandre did really funny things with the various ducks that were displayed – like wearing them, ventriloquising them, and lifting up their tails to see what was there – so viewers could see the different types. When the duck was cooked, Lulu threw parsley on from a great distance then threw her arms around the presenter. At each ad break everyone smoked madly and at the end, the crew dived on the food like wolves at the end of a long winter. Some behaviours are international. In minutes the studio was deconstructed, the cameras disappeared, a cleaner dealt with the kitchen and it was as if nothing had ever happened.

I was invited to L'Assiette for Sunday lunch and turned up with my red straw bag and camera to photograph Lulu and Hervé's eight-year-old son Rémy. I hadn't seen him since he was a baby. I was greeted by a little boy dressed as a cowboy just like his mother had been at my wedding – cowboy boots, jeans, jeans shirt, red necktie, cowboy hat. When I asked him where his holster and guns were he replied:

'*Tu parles.* They're hidden in the courtyard. I only put them on when I'm going out to fight.'

Lulu grabbed a huge, gesticulating crab and yelled from the kitchen, 'This is your lunch.' Ten minutes later, after an extraordinary philosophical conversation with Rémy, the crab arrived on a platter, chopped into big pieces. It was accompanied by various instruments with which to drag the reluctant meat from its carapace, a freshly made *aïoli* and *mesclun* salad. We immediately dived in with our hands while Rémy recited poems and explained why he didn't do as well at school as his mother expected:

'*C'est pas moi. C'est ma cervelle qui est toute melange. Je n'y peux rien, tu sais.* (It's not my fault – my brain's all mixed up.)'

I was joined by Sarah and Tristan, old friends of Lulu. Tristan is a painter of Spanish extraction, dark-haired and white-skinned with a penchant for Mafioso-style suits and purple shirts. Sarah is a photographer, tall, slim, olive-skinned, large-eyed, resplendent of tresses and thinks everything Tristan does, whether it be art, theatre or just opening his mouth, is absolutely marvellous. They look at each other as if they had met only the day before.

Very thinly sliced *Brebis des Pyrénées* finished off the meal, with lots of cigarette smoke, of course. The *brebis* or sheep's milk cheese is from the rugged Béarn region in the western Pyrénées and is made from whole raw milk. It is expensive because it is a highly controlled, genuine product with its own AOC (*Appelation d'origine contrôlée* – certified description), a short period of production and strict rules surrounding it. No ewe's milk can be made into this cheese until 20 days after lambing, coagulation must be obtained with rennet only and the ewes have to have grazed on summer pastures between May and September. Some cheesemakers won't let anyone touch their cheese until they are sold and even then it is a good idea to cut this cheese a while before eating to allow it to breathe. It's very hard to get in Paris because production is so small; it is almost exclusively sold and eaten locally. Brebis des Pyrénées is the most exquisite of fine, dense cheeses with a strong, lingering flavour like caramel and an aroma that fills your mouth.

Hervé came to take Rémy to the swimming pool but looked hesitant as the weather was changing. '*Mais non,*' said the little boy, '*c'est pas grave. C'est un autre pays là-bas à la piscine – il fait toujours beau.* (It's okay. Down at the pool it's a different country – it's always fine.)' After lunch we all went off to Tristan's studio to look at his paintings – most of them were huge, erotic, very powerful works with a light that seemed to come from behind somewhere. Penises and vaginas and bodies were painted fearlessly in orange, ox-blood red, black, yellow, terracotta, vermilion, electric blue and copper. When my intellectual art friends looked at the photographs they said, 'he'll never sell these paintings', but I really liked them.

Everybody knows that French intellectuals are totally un-suited to the task of thinking in any real and useful sense of the word. One only has to look at their dress sense to know they would be more comfortable in a cheap whorehouse, either as clients or staff, where they could really impress someone, than in austere halls of learning. They love hanging out in ill-lit corners of cafés talking about books written by foreigners from places no one has ever heard of or ever will again after they've finished. And it's not just *moi* who can't understand their writings – apparently no one can. According to a book called *Intellectual Impostures*, written by two Anglo-Saxon physicists, if French intellectuals seem incomprehensible, it's with good reason – they actually have nothing to say. They style themselves as self-appointed 'thinkers' who mix up a salad of modern scientific theory and garnish it with fatuously muddled ramblings on the nature of literature, philosophy and life. All this makes really brainy people burst into laughter, which doesn't go down at all well at Les Deux Magots. Clarity of thought has gone out the window and banality, pomposity and pointlessness have flown in. To intimidate rather than to elucidate is a form of intellectual terrorism, so the big question in the left-leaning magazine *Nouvel Observateur* was, 'Are French intellectuals impostors?' The French defend themselves by straightening their bow ties and explaining that French philosophy depends on interpretation and style and that, as essayists, they have produced the most brilliant strokes of thought from the 17th century onwards. But of course, they say, Anglo-Saxons drowning in facts, information and moderation couldn't possibly understand the subtleties of poetic metaphors, *n'est-ce pas?*

Another thing – I have never known a clean intellectual. They live in utter filth because (a) they can't see and only put their glasses on to steal other people's ideas, (b) they need darkness to maintain their negativity – light would lift the pessimism and (c) they actually consider themselves above house cleaning and personal hygiene. Whenever I smell body odour on a person, I just know they will be carrying a copy of *Crime and Punishment* in Latin in their grubby little pocket. Since the few marginally important thoughts they had as adolescents, all intellectuals really think about anyway is getting laid. In this respect they resemble all other humans because this is all anybody thinks about, but they consider themselves rather clever to have a brain. Having a brain is not clever – most of us have one (I exclude here any members of the far right political spectrum and rugby players) so there's no reason to show off about it. The only real use intellectuals find for their brains is figuring out how to steal other people's husbands or wives or seducing the underage babysitter. How many real jobs did Sartre ever hold down? In what way did he contribute to world peace? However, he succeeded in keeping the most intelligent and beautiful woman, Simone de Beauvoir, at his feet and in nicking lots of others. Hence the expression – never let an intellectual anywhere near your spouse.

Lovers kiss passionately everywhere in Paris, and doing it comes as naturally as brushing hair out of your eyes – on the métro, in bistrots, on the street, in parks. They are arguably the best kissers in Europe, but don't kiss in public as much as they used to according to worried observers. Supposedly in Paris you cheek-kiss twice, in the suburbs you do it three times and in the provinces it's four – which I find very time-consuming. There's also quite a bit of hand pecking that goes on from very classy quarters. My father actually kisses women's hands and all my friends are in love with him. If only men knew how easy women are to please. All we want is a little romance and we'll put up with ANYTHING. There are no rules for kissing passionately in public – if you're that close, who need rules – but these are the dos and don'ts of cheek-kissing etiquette:

DO:

Kiss the left cheek before the right.

Kiss someone your own age.

Kiss the cheek when you mean it.

Kiss the air when you don't.

Kiss a hand but only when it is offered to you.

There is only one reason to kiss a person on the mouth and it doesn't involve friendship.

DONT:

Open your mouth.

Kiss more than twice unless you are a *plouc* (country bumpkin) or Belgian.

Kiss your boss when you meet him or her for the first time.

Kiss someone if you have a cold (air kissing is thus permitted).

Worry about lipstick – real men don't.

Kiss Russians – they don't use birth control.

French women enjoy great courtesy from men in public, even in a big city like Paris. There is a gentle and amused air of flirtation between men and women that pervades all social interaction. It is not pushy or offensive, everyone likes it, everyone does it and it's very pleasant. You don't have to be fabulous to get what seems to be an automatic reaction. 'Now there's what I call a beautiful woman,' they say, or 'I wish I was that croissant you're eating,' or 'Look, the sun has come out at night.' My Brazilian friend Gabriella said it's much more exaggerated in Brazil; and in London you feel there's something wrong with you, as if you're invisible. My staunch friends say this behaviour is a tool of manipulation – if you can make a woman worry about the way she looks, she'll become dependent on male approval for her self-esteem. I say it feels good and if the comment is particularly poetic, I reward the man with a small, allusive smile.

They say men are like buses – you wait for ages then two turn up at once. In Paris the buses come frequently but where I come from you wait for ages then you die of old age. French men and women show how they feel all the time by their eyes, facial expressions and body language. Unlike Anglo-Saxons, they put their cards on the table immediately, have pretend fights over each other and if a total stranger decides to kiss you on the mouth, they sometimes do it. Fear of rejection doesn't seem to exist.

Life is dirty in Paris and even more so when it's hot – after a day in the métro and on the streets I had to shower twice and wash every garment every day and the water ran black. I've never had such clean clothes in my life. I may add that my Parisian friends thought I was exaggerating.

The French are excessively polite and impolite and have very definite behaviours at which they take umbrage. If there's one thing that drives them to expletives its a lack of *mercis* for services rendered or lack of *pardons* if you accidentally brush them, and if you forget them, you're *petit bourgeois, tu, mal élevé* and in extreme cases *mange-merde*. If you say thank you or excuse me it is noticed, recorded and acknowledged. Parisians park with two centimetres to spare between cars, then they leave the brake off and the car in neutral so other people can gently push the car backwards or forwards if necessary. That's politeness.

I walked over to the market at Edgar-Quinet near Montparnasse and it was a very different experience from the Saturday market. This was Wednesday and it was quiet. As usual there were lots of beggars – a lot more than when I lived here. In the 1980s you never saw beggars in the open markets. A boy pointed a toy gun at me and, grave-faced, asked for money, and a girl asked for a few of my cherries. When I gave her the whole bag a woman reproached me, saying, you shouldn't let them hassle you madame – they'll only resell the food. So what, I thought. It was lovely strolling through the market with lots of room. Even the sellers were slow and into having conversations. At every stall I heard sellers giving people recipes and advice on how to cook what they were buying. The fishmonger will say to cook something with shallots and cream in the oven and an elderly, dapper gentleman next in the queue will add his method – this happens all the time. There was a *charcutier* selling extraordinary salads made from the bits of animals not normally found outside third-grade horror movies of the chainsaw massacre variety, e.g. ears in vinaigrette, pork tongue in vinaigrette, trotters in vinaigrette, nose in vinaigrette. I recovered with my habitual *crème* in a nearby café but French coffee with milk is too weak for me. The only way you can get the equivalent of a double flat white is to order a *double express* with a tiny jug of warm milk on the side. Try to teach the French how to make Italian-style coffee, which is much better, and they go purple.

Gabriella and Thomas took me to an African dance performance at La Grande Halle de Villette, an old cattle auction house in the south-east of Paris which has been turned into a magnificent performance space. Afterwards we ate at a tiny Lebanese restaurant in a side street that only Thomas would know of. They had the best Arab pastries according to him. It was 11.30 p.m. but they were still serving so we ordered mint tea, cinnamon tea, red wine, and lots of pastries – cigarette-shaped ones full of almonds, flower-shaped ones full of pistachios and little rounds full of peanuts – melting flakes of honeyed exotica. On our way home at midnight we came across a trapeze performance lit by spotlights and accompanied by opera singing and cello playing.

Another sweltering, hot evening Gabriella took me to a tiny theatre called Guichet Montparnasse on a little old street called rue du Maine. It felt like Pigalle and inside the entirely black theatre were four short, hard rows of seats that took up the same amount of room as the stage. The performance was a gripping two-person show of clowns in a tragi-comedy, centred on a train platform, lettuces growing out of a suitcase and Russian folk songs. There were four spectators and we clapped wildly.

Later in the week Gabriella and I braved the Saturday

evening métro which is always full of particularly mad/drunk/foreign/musically talented/reckless people, to hit the wilds of south Paris, the 18th to be precise. Here in a colourful, proletariat neighbourhood, one eats very well at the restaurant of our friend Nillo. Hailing from the southwest, Nillo and his brother who does the service regaled us with their impossible accent, dry humour and delicious food. Whenever I am in Paris I eat there with Gabriella, and we all amuse ourselves imitating each others accents. We sit

---

Glace Nougat au Grand Marnier
Nougat Ice Cream with Grand Marnier

To make the nougat:
100g sugar
1 tbsp water
50g roasted, skinned hazelnuts
50g blanched almonds

1. Place the sugar and water in a heavy-based saucepan, and gently bring to the boil.
2. Throw in the nuts and cook until the almonds start to crack – about 5 mins. Pour into an oiled pan and allow to cool.
3. Break up into pieces with a knife then grind in a food processor until coarse.

To make the ice cream:
1 kilo vanilla ice cream
100g nougat, ground coarsely
50g chopped candied cherries
50g chopped candied orange
50g currants
Grand Marnier

Fold nougat, cherries, orange and currants into the ice cream and refreeze.

To Serve: Pour over a shot of Grand Marnier.

---

down, say 'feed us' and wait for the show to unfold. Last time I was there we got a salad full of foie gras, jambon du pays, gizzards and finely julienned raw leeks. Dessert was Nillo's nougat ice cream with grand marnier (see page 69). To make the nougat he cooks hazelnuts and almonds in sugar and a little water until caramelized, then grinds them up and stirs them into hand made Grand Marnier ice cream along with candied cherries, currants and candied orange. You receive it dripping with *crème anglaise* and warm honey. This time a bottle of Château de Pierriere was placed on the table along with a basket of sliced baguette. We asked for butter. Two hundred and fifty grams of butter arrived on a silver plate garnished with a derisory smirk. *Vichyssoise* – chilled potato and leek soup garnished with tiny dices of tomato and snipped chives – appeared in front of us. This is a classic soup that is rarely made these days and is quite stunning on a hot summer's night. Plates whipped away. Replaced by fresh foie gras wrapped in curly cabbage leaves and poached. It was served with a little bowl of what Nillo considers to be the best sea salt in France – *sel de Guérande*.

'*Tu peux changer la musique?*' asked Gabriella, in reference to the football commentary coming from the kitchen television. They bridled, as fanatics will.

'Just eat your meals. *Merde.* Did you see that? Did you see it?' the brothers yelled at the TV. 'Instead of whining, why don't you two come and watch?'

'We're not interested in your macho, dickhead, violent football,' we protested. 'We want music.'

'Music, music. You want music you can sing.'

So I sang. They stared at me, open-mouthed.

'We didn't know you could sing. You're good enough for the métro. Go and sit down and get out of our kitchen. *La suite arrive.*'

A fillet of bass resting on a lobster sauce, garnished with vegetable *confit*, invited us to eat it – all the flavours perfect, with nothing over-powering anything else. This is really the up side of French cooking. This is what people mean when they say they don't want change. Nillo has been cooking like this for years and, like Lulu, his style has never changed and there is no reason for it to. It is simple but made with utter understanding of the principles of cooking. It is conservative, unpretentious and consistent. Dessert was a tuille overflowing with fresh red berries, coulis, mango ice-cream and cream. There was no bill, all this had been made specially for us and we could have eaten it in the kitchen and watched *le foot* as well if only we had been cultured enough.

Nillo is quite an anarchist in the kitchen. He changes his dishes often, doesn't appear to be influenced by anyone else, if he doesn't like someone he doesn't serve them and if there's a good football match on, he's been known to refuse customers. He was head chef at the famous Archestrate restaurant in the Louis Carlton hotel but couldn't bear the snobbery and opened his own place so he could cook what he liked and serve whom he liked. Another evening I ate there with his wife Renate and it was the take-what-you-get deal as usual. We started with foie gras and fresh figs wrapped in filo pastry, went on to saddle of rabbit with *pappardelle* pasta, fried oyster mushrooms and chive sauce and finished with *tuiles* filled with a mixture of cream and pastry cream, topped with apples caramelised in calvados.

The day before I left Paris for the Dordogne, I was interviewed for an hour and a half on RTL radio by Nague, a well known radio and television personality. I had been told by one faction of friends that he was an unintelligent but very popular smart-arse that I would be able to run circles around, and by another faction, that he was charming, good-looking and great fun. He was all these things really – very funny and very confident. It was the sort of show where he does a lot of fast talking, lots of advertising, making fun of everybody, talking to the guest (*moi*), running a competition where the listener had to answer questions about my book in order to win a free holiday to Morocco and generally waking France up from 8.30 until 10 a.m. At song breaks he massaged my shoulders, flirted and exposed his abs when I got out my camera. And then he was gone. On the dot of 10, he stood up, put his jacket on, shook my hand, said *au revoir* in a very professional way and exited as fast as he had entranced.

Dordogne

THE PLAN WAS TO SPEND a week in Paris doing publicity for *Fête Accomplie* then head off to the Dordogne in the southwest of France to write another book in the bucolic peace of the countryside. I was obliged to spend almost three weeks in Paris, as it turned out, so by the time I got to the train station at Le Buisson I was almost beside myself. As fabulous as Paris was, I couldn't wait to get out of the heat and dirt and constant eating in restaurants. As I neared my destination the people standing at country stations started to look different – tanned faces, bare legs, relaxed air and slower movements. Country people on the train on their way home from perhaps visiting family in Paris were all set up with little feasts of bread, bottled water, biscuits, cheese and good, sharp pocket knives. They put their feet up on the seats on newspapers and set to telling stories and putting the political situation to rights.

The deeper you get into the Dordogne, the greener it gets and although you can't feel the heat through the air-conditioning of the carriage, you can see it shimmering. The train roared past a man tending his vegetable garden under a beach umbrella which he moved along as each patch met with his satisfaction.

I jumped off the train at Le Buisson into the arms of my friends Bronwyn and Lesley who were staying in an old presbytery at St-Amand-de-Belvès. Belvès is an ancient hill town with streets lined with Gothic and Renaissance buildings and the *bastide* in the centre still has pre-Revolutionary chains for hanging people. Nice work, if you can get it. Breathing in the good air, I watched the walnut and chestnut trees and wild red poppies fly by as we drove there. Paris was already just a memory.

The presbytery was attached to an ancient church which is now only used for special occasions like weddings and funerals. I arrived in the middle of all sorts of fixing-up goings on. Nothing seemed to work and the women were whipping the house and the workers into shape with their inventive French. The bee man came twice at 11 at night to take away a beehive that had formed on the house; he talked so much I thought the bees would leave voluntarily. The plumber came to fix the flood, the tile man came to make the new shower, the pool boys came to clean the salamanders, toads, frogs, bugs, mud and filth out of the swimming pool – but the electrician was being recalcitrant. He had promised several times in two weeks to come and *faire le nécessaire* – and just never turned up. Every time Lesley did the washing she got an electric shock, every time you turned on more than one appliance everything went dead, and very soon it was all going to end in tears.

'There's only one way to deal with French tradesmen who have an attitude problem,' I said, 'and that's to read them the riot act. It always works and moreover, they love and respect you for it. The last person they expect to tell them off is a foreign woman. They're convinced the English are stupid, the Americans naive and they've never heard of the South Pacific. Watch this.'

I got on the phone and put on the voice that I had learned from years of doing business in Paris. Monsieur the electrician was there in his blue overalls promptly at eight o'clock the next morning as arranged. We of course were deeply unconscious in our beds.

Every so often a worker would turn up at the presbytery unannounced in the middle of the afternoon and catch the women lying around in the sun the way God had created them, whereupon he would approach backwards from the edge of the property with his hands over his eyes saying loudly, '*Je suis là, Mesdames. Je ne vous regarde pas.* (I'm here, ladies. I'm not looking at you.)' The mayor's name was M. Personne or Mr Nobody, the grass cutter and grave digger was M. Manoeuvrier or Mr Manworker, the best *cabécou* (goats cheese) in the area was made by Mme Grosein or Mrs Bigbreast, and the electrician's name was M. Malaterre or Mr Badearth.

The 200-year-old presbytery was really well constructed to accommodate guests: there was a large central area combining kitchen, dining and living room on the ground floor, and at either end stairs led up to two bedrooms and a bathroom. One doesn't want guests on top of one. If they start dragging home *garçons* or *filles* from the local café, at least one won't be bumping into them on the landing. We sat down to a big salad followed by freshly cracked walnuts (it's what they live on down there and one of the four major products of the region) and cherries that Bronwyn and Lesley bought every day from the man next door who plucked them off his tree. Bronwyn had a thing about having to see the beautiful food they bought at the market every day, rather than have it hidden in the fridge, so big bowls full of spring onions, peaches, tomatoes, garlic, bread and raspberries sat like still lifes on the tables, along with the roses from the church wall. They had adopted an orange cat that they called Monsieur Reynard, and fussed around it like the mothers they are. M. Reynard enjoyed running and skidding across the whole length of the downstairs at dawn – an activity I soon put a stop to.

My room was white with yellow hand-blocked flowers on the walls, a large white bed and a window that looked out onto trees and the swimming pool. I closed the white shutters, slept like a baby and was awoken by birds at dawn. We went to a different village market every day – Le Buisson, Belvès, St Cyprien, Limeuil. Even if we bought only one asparagus, we went every day just for the pleasure of the social event, the people and the gastronomic hit. There was everything you could possibly make from walnuts – walnut oil, walnut cake, walnut bread, candied walnuts, walnut liqueur. There was every bird you could imagine – chickens, guinea fowl, capons, pheasants, pigeons, geese with their huge livers, quails and ducks. Lots of bunnies too. These markets were particularly marked by the revolting, ugly clothes and cheap shoes they sold. Cheap I can do if there's nothing expensive around, but ugly I find no excuse for. One day we bought the sweetest, most intense raspberries we'd ever tasted, white peaches, harissa, a roasted free-range Gascon chicken with its black feet on and armfuls of purple and white petunias.

Alexandre Dumas' *père* said, '*Il n'est pas un gourmet d'autrefois et d'aujourd'hui qui n'ait cent fois proclamé l'indispensabilité du fromage dans un dîner petit ou grand.* (There is no gourmet past or present, who has not a hundred times proclaimed the absolute necessity of cheese in any meal, small or large.)' All the cheeses were laid out in their splendour, the great speciality being the goat's cheeses, some of which were dried to the point of being no bigger than a small, flat disc. Bronwyn called the woman who travelled with her cheeses to every market the Cheese Dyke or the Cheese Pikelet – her word for lesbians. I called her *La Crêpe au Cantal*. There were gypsies with their dark skin and teeth full of gold and two singers dressed up in costume, ruining everyone's day with their atrocious singing. They were thrown out of each different part of the market they stood in to bray and thrum, and found themselves in front of the spice and herb stall.

'Get away from here – you are disturbing us. Not only do you sing badly but you don't know the music and you sing too loud,' yelled the spice lady.

'Don't you dare tell us what to do. We are greatly appreciated wherever we go. What do you know about music?'

'I know that no one will come near my spice stall while you are here.'

'Well you're not the mayor, you're not in charge here and anyway I'm allergic to your horrible spices. Do you hear me complaining?'

We had our favourite cafés for afterwards, one of which was the Hôtel de la Poste in St-Cyprien. This place had an English waitress and was frequented by English expatriates. The Dordogne is crawling with English people who have retired, or who have holiday homes there. Some French people say they are destroying the culture and integrity by introducing artificially high real estate prices and some say they have saved the economically depressed region with their pounds. The right-wing fascist politician Jean-Marie Le Pen says, 'What the English couldn't conquer in the Hundred Years War, they are buying up in the 20th century.' There was no evidence of animosity from the French locals towards the English that I could detect. They sit around in cafés in tawdry clusters, mumbling away benevolently in English. Across the road we watched the flower-shop owner whacking a little dog with her fly swat as it enthusiastically tried to hump her leg. Here we perched, clutching a Cantal cheese *d'un certain âge* and listening to English accents *d'un certain milieu* – then went home, made lunch, did gardening, wrote, lay around reading and falling into the pool when it got too hot.

St-Amand-de-Belvès was in the middle of nowhere and we were basically IT, along with a few other houses. Our nearest village was Belvès and our favourite café was Le Madelon on the Place de la Croix des Frères. The café used to be a dump but had been taken over by the children of the owners, who had never worked in it but had inherited it from the mother's grandparents. The daughter, Pascale, was beautiful like her mother with long dark hair tied at the nape of her neck with a velvet ribbon, large eyes, arched eyebrows, a strong nose and creamy skin. She wore miniskirts and orange tops and behind the smile were the eyes of a businesswoman. There was a photo of her primer class on the wall above the bar: she was the only child with a straight, determined face looking directly at the camera. Her brother Bruno was a slight, nice-looking young man, softly spoken and obviously not trained in the business. He had been dragged from his chosen profession into running the café, but seemed quite happy and determined to make a go of it. On Saturday nights there was live music of varying quality and it was always a pleasure to sit at the bar over *une vieille prune* (plum *eau-de-vie*) and chat with them.

Across the square was the best *boulangerie* in the area. Seven times a day on average, the boulanger in his white baker's cap made his perfect, crunchy baguettes and huge *boules* or round loaves right there in the shop. He made his own *levure* (yeast) and added two percent of artificial yeast, then laid the *baguettes* out to rise in wooden trays lined with cloth. Once risen, the bread was lifted off the trays with a big wooden paddle and placed in perfect rows onto a long, canvas oven tray. This was raised up on a trolley and slid into the huge ovens. Twenty minutes for a baguette and two hours for a boule. The bread was taken out of the oven by hand, brushed to remove the flour and neatly stacked. The damp, cloudy, warm day I was there talking to him, he said it was very hard yakker baking good bread with the humidity making it all soft. A lot of these village boulangeries don't even have proper tills – they write every sale down on a piece of paper and add it up at the end of the day.

The little post office at Le Buisson, a village that had nothing to recommend it, was straight out of a Pagnol novel. It was only open between nine and five but nevertheless closed for lunch between noon and two. There was a long queue with one person serving and about half a dozen out the back pretending they were on holiday. As usual the pace was harrowingly placid, tooth-grinningly flaccid, insanely pedantic. I wish doctors would make their minds up about euthanasia because it could be put to humanitarian use in French post office queues to prevent unnecessary suffering or death by starvation. I wished to send a pair of harlequin print pantyhose home to a friend. I finally got to the front of the queue. This is an extremely abbreviated version of the conversation:

'*Bonjour.* I would like a bubbly envelope to send this small item overseas.'

'We don't have bubbly envelopes. You'll have to go to the supermarket.'

'This is a post office. Why should I go to the supermarket?'

'Because we don't have any left.'

'Okay, is there some other way I can send it?'

Huge and thoughtful discussion with all the other employees who trailed out from the back. Where was my country anyway? Clock ticking on towards mid-day. Queue behind getting longer. Lesley giggling. Cicadas crackling.

'You can buy a box.'

'But it's only a pair of pantyhose. A box seems far too serious. May I have a big envelope?'

'*Ah non.* An envelope won't last all the way.'

'Please give it to me. I'll take the risk.'

'*Il n'y en a plus.* (None left.)'

Lesley doubled over.

'Okay, I'll take the box.'

'Are you sure you've put all the information on the box?'

'I've never been more sure of anything in my life. I'll have a second-class stamp please.'

'Yes, a second-class stamp is best – it won't take too long. Is the post *chez vous* as fast as in France?'

Lesley howled and had to leave. Smiles all round that the transaction has been completed with such efficiency. I found out later in Marseilles that there are prepaid cardboard envelopes especially for this purpose.

The naming and understanding of this whole southwest area is extremely complicated and one really needs to do a degree in history to understand it. The village of Belvès was in the area called the Périgord Noir or Black Périgord (black because of the truffles or the deep shadows cast by its oaks) with the city of Périgueux as its centre. Périgord (from the Gaulish Petrocorii) is the old name for Dordogne and both names are used in everyday conversation. What is now the *département* of the Dordogne was the county of Périgord until the Revolution. People who live in the Dordogne are called Périgourdin(e). There are other regions named after colours: Périgord Vert (green) after the trees, Périgord Blanc (white) after the stones and Périgord Pourpre (purple) after the wine.

One evening on our way back from a late afternoon walk around the ancient village of Cadouin, famous for its 11th-century abbey, we looked behind us in the car to see the most extraordinary sight – an electric orange-red sun sinking fast out of sight. The first time Lesley had seen this southern phenomenon she burst into tears, thinking it meant impending disaster. We paid respect to the part of the Dordogne flowing past Laroque-Gageac where the girls had almost drowned last year. This stage-set village is built right into an overhanging cliff with a little space for the road, and then there's the river. The golden houses seem to melt into the mountain as if they were a natural outcropping and if you peer up narrow steps here and there between the houses you can see the caves up top that the troglodytes lived in. The downside of living in a movie set is that big rocks sometimes dislodge and plonk down on the hapless good people. Just down the road was the macho, hulking, French, fighting castle of Beynac and across the river, its perpetual nemesis – the stark, arrogant, English castle of Castlenaud. These two, convulsed with hatred, hurled huge stones with catapults over the river at each other.

One of the most amazing things about the southwest is the palaeolithic (meaning the age when man only knew how to chip flints as distinct from now, when man knows how to rearrange your brain cell structure with the press of a button) caves with skeletons of Neanderthal and Cro-Magnon man and quite sophisticated carvings, engravings and paintings of animals, people and activities like hunting. Most of the natural attractions in the southwest – caves, mountains, rivers, Gérard Depardieu – were caused by erosion. Although the Neanderthals get very bad press because we all know people that resemble them, they were in fact as intelligent as us, large, rugged and not unlike Arnold Schwarzenegger BUT they literally disappeared off the face of the earth about 30,000 years ago. In spite of many rugby props you know, our ancestors were not the Neanderthals – it has recently been proven they have a completely different DNA. It seems the Cro-Magnons who came to Europe from Africa replaced all the other species including Solo Man in Java and Peking Man in China. This means we all have a recent African origin, contrary to the previous idea that the different races were vestiges of million-year-old cleavages in the human family tree. It now appears that our friends the Eskimos, the Aborigines, the Scandinavians, the Indians etc., only appeared in the last 50,000 years. Our DNA points to a common ancestor who evolved into *homo sapiens* just before the African exodus. So it turns out we are indeed all God's children under the skin because even though we don't look alike, we're all Africans.

The minute I arrived, the girls started talking about the Auberge de la Nauze, a restaurant nearby in the village of Fongaufier. A young chef called Etienne arrived there one day to fill a position as chef, fell in love with the young owner called Nathalie and now the two of them run it to the delight of everyone far and near. It was a typical country *auberge*, which are the best places to eat in this part of the country, as everything they use in the cooking is local and fresh. The layout was classic – a bar and room for the workers downstairs, flasher room with linen serviettes and tablecloths upstairs and terrace outside, a stone's throw from the river Nauze.

They serve a smashing cocktail in the Dordogne if you get sick of kir, called a *fenelon.*

Fenelon

1 shot cassis
1 shot walnut liqueur
Fill the rest of the glass with red wine.

The menu sported all the traditional dishes of the Dordogne such as *salade de gésiers tièdes aux noix* (warm gizzard salad with walnuts), *confit de canard aux pommes sautées* (preserved duck with sautéd potatoes), *mesclun périgourdin* (salad greens with slices of foie gras), dried duck breast, preserved gizzards and walnuts, *filet de sandre au vin de Bergerac* (fillet of pike in Bergerac wine). They used *cèpes*, pigeon, armagnac, *cabécou*, red berries and even made an *oeuf cocotte* or egg poached in a ramekin and stuffed with foie gras. THE classic salad of the Périgord is *salade de pissenlit* (dandelion-leaf salad) with fresh walnuts and a vinaigrette made from walnut oil and red wine vinegar.

We drank a Cahors with our meal. The food was amazingly good value. It is almost never worth it to order *à la carte*. The special menus are the same food, the same talented handiwork and a third of the price. They're also smaller servings, which is great at lunch time. We went back there another day with my English friend Jessica who lives nearby and partook of the worker's menu. We had a beautiful salad of *jambon cru, saucisson* (dried sausage), melon and lettuce with soft country bread, followed by steak with Roquefort sauce, stuffed potato, stuffed tomato and a bundle of beans wrapped in bacon. Dessert was fresh fruit salad. Absolutely unbelievable for the reasonable price. Yet another day, Jessica and I had lunch there in exchange for translating their menus into English. There was an interesting dish called *tête de veau bourgeoise à l'ancienne truffée – recette exceptionnelle du XVIIème siècle* (truffled bourgeois old-style calf's head – exceptional 17th-century recipe). You had to be a table of at least seven people to order it. I asked Jessica about this delicacy and she said she and her friends had tried it. I thought it was something like a *fromage de tête* or calf's head terrine, but no, it was actually a cooked, boned head with the contents removed, mixed with, among other things, foie gras and truffles, stuffed back into the head again and brought to the table steaming. The ears were pinned back and the eyes stuck on etc. They all gasped, felt slightly desperate but ate it, commenting that it was rather rich – and had nightmares for the next week.

Apart from the bucolic charm of the southwest with its little family farms and lazy lifestyle, the main reason to go there is the food. This is a land of rivers, valleys, woodlands, green limestone hills and prehistoric caves. Périgourdine cuisine is what a French person thinks of when they long for old-fashioned comfort food and a land overflowing with the good things of the soil. The Dordogne is a paradise of truffles, foie gras, poultry, fish, cèpes and *confit* (preserved meat), as well as the wines. The Périgourdins are so in love with their food and wine, you can't get anything else. You can forget nouvelle cuisine down there; you can forget any innovation since the 1800s – in fact, they say all the duck and goose fat and red wine are essential for a healthy diet and ravishing figure. Suited me. Every time I went out I ordered foie gras (it's best eaten with a glass of sweet Monbazillac), confit de canard and lots of local red wine – and never felt better. For the main part I avoided breakfast (one has to stop somewhere). They say some French still have pastis and Gauloises for breakfast, which I couldn't face – but it has some merit. There's no need to eat breakfast – it's just indulgence.

It was a very complicated road to Jessica's house in the middle of nowhere, going down roads sprouting bright blue wild chicory flowers, lavender, blue heather and tall yellow verbascum. 'It's just after a messy farm then *tout droit*,' she said on the phone. Technically speaking, *tout droit* means straight ahead, but for the French, or foreigners who have become French, it means straight ahead, turn left by the illegible hand-painted sign, turn right at the cherry stall then go straight. Fortunately all the neighbours knew Jessica or said they did, and we got lots of useless, contradictory instructions from them. In our quest we visited old ladies who tried to rent us rooms in their farmhouses and little old men in dark, medieval dwellings up stringy tracks with nothing but a can of potatoes and a 20-watt bulb to keep them company.

'Nothing's changed in Périgord,' remarked Bronwyn, 'they still live the way their grandparents did.'

'Actually nothing's changed since the wars of religion,' I added.

'Maybe the light's on a dimmer for atmosphere,' Lesley suggested.

'Oh, right, a dimmer for God's sake; they've only just stopped using candles.'

I hadn't seen Jessica or her partner Jean-Louis for eight years and of course they both looked more or less the same, but had multiplied into four: now there were two babies

– a beautiful brown-haired, green-eyed one who looked like her father and a beautiful blonde-haired, blue-eyed one who looked like her mother. The little girl Rosalie spoke English with a plum in her mouth like Jessica and French with a southwest accent like Jean-Louis. Jessica was also speaking with the southwest twang. The baby Lucy, cute beyond endurance, looked and spoke like Bubbles from *The Flintstones* – daa-doo-daa-doo. We went on a tour of the farm complex which was made up of the main house flanked by two other buildings, vegetable garden, chicken pen and lots of general Dordogne scenery. The three pale ochre buildings were surrounded by yellow and white roses, honeysuckle, purple buddleia, clematis and *indigotier*. No sooner had we set foot in the henhouse than Bronwyn slipped into her mother earth persona. There were '*cou nu*' (naked-neck) hens – very strange-looking things with lots of feathers everywhere except on a four-inch stretch of neck, making them look as though they'd just emerged from the fighting ring.

'Oh my God. Look at all these eggs,' she gasped.

'Yes, I know,' sighed Jessica, 'she's terribly broody. I can't get her off the eggs so there's millions of them. No doubt half of them are rotten.'

'The best way to get a chook over broodiness is to peg her upside down in a linen bag on the clothesline for a week,' said Bronwyn firmly.

'Oh I can't,' wailed Jessica, 'I just can't do that.'

Bronwyn and Lesley sloped off, leaving me in Jessica and Jean-Louis' large kitchen to contemplate my culinary future for the evening. Summer in the southwest started unseasonably early, in February, with everything bursting into bloom. We were in mid cherry season and a big pot of cherry jam sat on the stove waiting to be put in jars. As with all families, dinner happened in between running around after the little ones. Jessica said they were in a state because of my red lipstick, uncountry-like clothes and glamorous presence. I would say it was more likely they would be fascinated even by the mailman, so isolated were they. Dinner was a very sweet, most tender rack of lamb from the farm next door and sweet peas from the garden. Cooked on the barbecue, the lamb was like butter. Ever the rustic, Jean-Louis said, 'Peta, this lamb comes from our neighbour as do the peas. The peas were fertilised by the shit from the lamb you're eating – that's why they taste so good.'

'How kind of you to share that with me.'

'As you can see, we eat very simply,' said Jessica, 'but such is the taste when you grow it yourself, that you are reluctant to indulge in fancy recipes because you just don't need to. The real pleasure is in the flavour and quality of the produce.'

As with all French meals, there was cheese – Cantal, *chèvre* (goat's cheese) and Roquefort. Jean-Louis always used to leave his cheese out until it was really hard and smelly but Jessica had recently purchased a special aerated container to keep the cheese in the fridge. They whip it out an hour before dinner and everyone seems to be happy with this system so far. Dessert was Jean-Louis' father's *pêches de vigne* – small white peaches, so called because they are grown in between grapevines. More and more of a rarity, these delicious little peaches burst in the mouth like packets of sunshine. As is common in this part of the country, Jean-Louis poured red wine over his sliced peaches. The Périgourdins stick wine in their soup at the table also, which is called *faire chabrot*.

Jessica is the great-granddaughter of the English painter Augustus John; her great-aunt is Gwen John (a much better painter) and in fact she is about the only one in her family who didn't go to art school. The walls of her ancient farmhouse are covered in paintings by family and friends; dried flowers hang from the exposed beamed ceiling, as do huge baskets full of tea, walnuts, potatoes and dried lime leaves for herb tea, to keep them out of the hands of children. The lounge room is full of history, being the original part of the house, whose name, *Le Breuilh*, means 'stones' in *patois*. The walls, made from *pierre de Mauzens* (stone), are 65cm thick, and the only original window was an *oeil-de-boeuf* (bull's-eye) – a tiny hole above the old stone washbasin. Jessica has since added other windows. The original fireplace with the *crémaillère* (rack for cooking) is still in action, and next to it is the *potager*. This is a stone slab with two square sunken holes, in which hot embers were placed. Pots of cooked food were put on top to keep warm until the occupants got home from the fields for lunch. Jessica found piles of linen and antique nighties and even a flint tool in the house when she bought it. Out the back in the storage shed were shelves of wine and her preserves – pork and chicken pâté, cèpes, bigarreau cherries in eau-de-vie and quince and grape jelly.

In the morning Lesley and Bronwyn turned up late to pick me up.

'We're late because we were looking for your lipstick – we were terrified that you had stayed over and found yourself without.'

We all went for a walk in the forest to look for *girolles*. In the spring and autumn one can find *trompettes de la mort* (trumpet of death mushrooms), which are not as fatal as they sound, chanterelles and the fabulous cèpes that fetch big bucks at the market. We set out with hope in our hearts and plastic bags in our fists, pausing on the way to pick wild cherries – smaller and sharper than normal ones – and admire the stags that wandered onto the path. Bronwyn took a lovely photo of us picking cherries in which everything was in the photo but our hands picking cherries. You know what it's like when you're doing something special and elusive and you just know deep within you that every other person will find a girolle except you. It's like fishing – the fish jump onto everyone's line but yours. You know you're deeply flawed and don't have the talent God gave gravel to find a mushroom, then you see something pale and yellow and almost luminous hidden in the leaves. Self-esteem soars. You are clever and hawk-eyed and salt of the earth. You're not just a trumped-up city girl in a lace frock after all.

We did quite a bit of wine tasting in Dordogne. Of course, the world's wine trade congregates down the road in Bordeaux for France's biggest wine fair, Vinexpo. People from all over the world come to sell their wares. In 1999 the exhibition staged its first wine fair devoted exclusively to the Americas. France is slowly, but very slowly dragging itself into that scary world of change, noticing the skillful winemakers of the New World and getting their heads wrapped around a new attitude, according to Claude Tattinger, the bubbly man and president of Vinexpo. Sales of imported wines have leapt, something unheard of 15 years ago. In 2000 in Bordeaux, a grand jury of wine experts decided that the best Chardonnay in the world came not from Burgundy, the grape's traditional home, but from the California winery of Robert Mondavi. The best Cabernet Sauvignons are likely to come from Australia, New Zealand, Eastern Europe and South America and the Rhone's Syrah grape is more internationally known now under its Australian name, Shiraz. Obviously France still sets the world standards and the top *crus* (growths) are still much sought after at up to US$600 a bottle – and that's while it's still in the cask!

However, there are oceans and lakes of other ordinary and perfectly good wine produced in France. Who's drinking it? Not the French, *mes chéries* – the Agricultural Research Institute surveys reveal that wine consumption has fallen from 126 litres a head in 1961 to below 50 litres a head today (which is still quite a lot actually). Please sit down for this: water has replaced wine as the favourite mealtime drink! Today just 27 percent of Froggies drink wine, against 45 percent who choose bottled water. The rest drink hard liquor and soft drinks. I suppose it's an improvement from the 17th century when they tied their children to chairs while they went out into the fields to work all day, giving them bottles of half wine and half water to keep them quiet. But it is not only fashion that has changed French drinking habits, it is also legislation. The government controls the advertising of alcohol in an effort to battle disease. Even the innocuous 'Drink Less But Drink Better' advertisement for a recent Bordeaux wine was shut down by the courts. The previously huge consumption of wine was also responsible for all the maniacs on the road, and now that the government is coming down on drunk driving, wine consumption has gone down by 15 percent. There are also social changes in the fabric of society – young people don't drink like their elders did – but one thing hasn't changed: the French still mostly buy their own wine. Only two percent of wine bought there this year came from outside France.

I whipped down to Provence for a change, and during my absence it rained non-stop in the Dordogne. Traveling from the south back up to the southwest by train is a fascinating journey because one sees the climate and countryside changing before one's eyes. At around Carcassonne it gradually became greener, softer and cooler until arrival at Le Buisson station, where it was cold and raining. The stationmaster was having an altercation with his computer, speaking to it as if it was replying, insulting it and finally telling it it was over and storming out of the office, slamming the door. When I got to the presbytery Bronwyn and Lesley were huddled around a four-inch-square heater with three layers of summer clothes on, suffering from cabin fever and low humour. One good thing about being back was that I woke up to the sweet soft music of St-Amand birds singing, instead of Marseillais traffic noise. Another good thing was that the garden was coming along nicely, especially the herbs, tomatoes, chillis and capsicums. The eggplant was a bit slow and the letti were being eaten by slugs, snails and maybe a

bunny. The sweet peas were about six cute little inches high
and would soon need to be tied up.

Instead of staying home and being rotten, we went off to
the market at Lalinde, where we bought *Brebis des Pyrenees*
(sheep's cheese from the Pyrénées mountains), well-aged
Cantal all dark around the edges the way I like it, and Piotet
(a cooked cow's milk cheese). There was always a stand selling
dripping, grilling, mouth-watering chickens and quail which
I found devilishly hard to walk past. The problem with
these markets is that you want to buy everything – which of
course you do, then you can't eat it all. An army couldn't eat
what we bought. And then in a few days it would be gone.
I chose three quail from the young man sticking them onto
the spit then expertly whipping the cooked ones off and into
an ovenproof bag.

'*Jeune homme,*' I commanded. Every older man in the vicin-
ity stood to attention then burst out laughing. '*Je voudrais
trois de vos cailles, s'il vous plâit.* (Three of your quails,
please.)'

'*Oui, Madame. C'est pour tout de suite ou plus tard?* (For
now or later?)' This was obviously something he said to all
foreigners, assuming you are too stupid to know there is no
later, as the markets all close at 12.30.

'*Oh, demain ça ira. Je ne suis pas pressée.* (Tomorrow will
do. I'm in no hurry.)'

Double take. Look of comprehension crosses face.

'*Elle est drôle, celle-là.* (She's witty, this one.)'

'*Je voudrais des oignons avec, s'il vous plâit.* (I'd like some
onions too, please.)'

'*Oui, ca me plaît. Vous me plaisez. Sinon, tant pis. Si on ne
se plaît plus il faut aller à la pêche, Madame, n'est-ce pas?* (Yes,
it pleases me. You please me, too. Otherwise, too bad! When
people stop liking each other we might as well go fishing,
right?)'

'*N'est-ce pas.*'

The weather was unremittingly sodden. Every day Bronwyn threw her hands up with a tragic look on the face and said, 'If this continues I'm going to London tomorrow; at least they have culture there' – and every day she was still with us. Bad weather is like bad sleeping – you never do anything about it because you always think you're about to fall asleep any moment. I came equipped to spend three years in France just in case someone made me an offer I couldn't refuse, so the girls were wearing my cardigans and jumpers. In the drizzle we visited eighth-century churches, vineyards, fighting châteaux, romantic châteaux, burnt down and reconstituted châteaux, restaurants, more churches and the most beautiful villages in France. We drove along country roads with people on bikes dressed in the regulation blue overalls, beret and sometimes slippers, old people walking bent over with sticks, and French drivers overtaking on corners, on double lines and into oncoming traffic. The locals said the unheard-of weather only happened every 200 years and would change with La Lune de Jésus, which was due on the 5th of July. In a church with a walnut wood Jesus, I asked for some sun.

'But you are a recovered Catholic,' said the Jewish Bronwyn.

'It doesn't matter. You never recover. If I ask for a sunny day and get it, it will prove I haven't recovered yet.' One day, after a bit of creative parking on Lesley's part, the front chassis of her new rented car started to fall off. We took the car to the local garage and discovered it had been stapled on with plain office staples. '*C'est malheureux*,' said the mechanic, shaking his head. '*Ça, c'est la France.*'

We visited La Ferme de la Porte, the goose and duck farm of Mme Gaultier at Beynac, to watch a *démonstration de gavage* (force feeding). Foie gras is literally the enlarged liver of a duck or goose, one of the oldest of French gastronomic extravagances. The Romans forced figs down them and the Périgourdins do it with maize. One can't help but uncharitably notice that there is an enormous amount of foie gras consumed in France, let alone what they export, and not an enormous number of ducks and geese wandering around. There are a lot of eastern and central European and Israeli livers coming into France, so with the big producers, one can't be absolutely sure one is getting the real thing. The only way to be sure is to buy it yourself, raw, from the farm and cook it yourself. Jessica always does this and of course only ever eats it between October and April. If you're eating foie gras in the summer it is preserved or it is imported, which is very good but inferior. When you've eaten it fresh from Périgord and cooked whole in a terrine, you will find it hard to go back to slovenly gastronomic habits.

The most common way of preparing foie gras in Périgord is to gently separate the lobes, never cutting them, then gently remove the membranes and pull the veins out. This is easy to do because the liver is as soft as butter. Then you marinate the liver in a little port, cognac, salt and pepper overnight and if you're rolling in it, stick in some truffle slices. The terrine is covered and baked slowly in a low oven around an hour at 90°C, or some people wrap it in a tea-towel, tie the ends and gently poach it. To buy *foie gras entier* (in one piece) is the most expensive. After that there is *bloc de foie gras* which is reconstituted, then there is *mousse* which is puréed with other things. Personally I think the value-added products are a waste of money – I'd rather save up for the entier.

So there we were *chez* Mme Gaultier and there she was in her smock and gum-boots ready to go. We were led into a room full of ducks, geese and straw. You have to keep in mind this is all done by hand – that's why it's so expensive. She grabbed the bird and put it in a box from which the neck protruded (they used to sit lightly on the bird with the head and neck sticking up between their legs), sat on the box, inserted the metal tube attached to a machine full of maize into the beak and turned the machine on. With her other hand she massaged the bird's neck to help the grain go down. It's all timed so the bird gets just the right amount. Seeing *gavage* does put you off your stroke a bit, and of course you hear terrible stories about ducks having cirrhosis of the liver and being so fat they can't walk, but these birds didn't look unhappy and were walking around almost queuing up for their feed. Mme Gaultier said it was very important that you treat the birds well and that it's always the same person who feeds them, so it's not traumatic – upset birds do not produce good meat. And of course they use everything else on the bird – the legs and gizzards are confit, the breasts are fried or smoked, the neck stuffed and they also make pâté with pork. Even the fat is sold to cook potatoes in.

One soft day, as the Irish say, we turned off the road at Fosses-et-Baleyssac at a sign that said *Château Les Rambauds – dégustation et vente*. Southwest wines are divided into two groups – Bordeaux, which has 40 appellations, and Haut Pays. In France a lot of vineyards are called château, which doesn't necessarily mean their house is a château – it could be a very ordinary building. If you love wine the trick is to buy it from the producer or *vigneron* at a fraction of the price you would pay at home or in a restaurant.

Ancient, golden-coloured chickens wandered around the yard, someone's bloomers and kitchen smocks were on the line and vineyards surrounded the house. We rang the bell and an adorable little old man appeared dressed in blue overalls over an old jumper, the lot being held together by a wide leather belt with an ornate buckle. M. Darcos smilingly got out the *méthode champenoise*, the white and two reds. We immediately bought the sparkling to celebrate the eventual return of the sun, didn't taste the white and opened the 1993 and 1994 Bordeaux Supérieur. It was surprisingly smooth and slightly fruity and cost so little no one could argue with the price. You could hardly buy a bottle of lemonade for the same price, for God's sake, so for us this vineyard was the happy discovery of the trip.

The prices were written down on a piece of cardboard and the bill added up on an old envelope. Like all winemakers he loved talking about his wines, regaling us with information and history. His grandfather had bought the property, and his diploma from 1872 was still on the wall of the tasting room. He had sold the property to a friend *en viager*, a system they have in France whereby the elderly person without descendants sells their property before they die in exchange for a lifetime annuity. The buyer pays a deposit and keeps paying a monthly amount to the old person until they die. Sometimes the old person stays in the house or on the property, either with the new owners or without them, and sometimes they move into a retirement home. In any case it's a lifesaver for the seller and if the person dies soon after, it's a very cheap deal for the buyer. I would watch my *pain au chocolat* for poison, personally.

In July and August provincial France throws itself into festivals, fairs and concerts. Every single village and town has a yearly fête to celebrate itself and its patron saint: there are classical concerts in churches, jazz festivals, *bals* or village dances with old-fashioned music for the oldies and horrendous, tinny rock groups for the youngies, folklore events and circuses. On the first weekend of July the walled bastide of Monségur near Entre-Deux-Mers hosts a jazz festival. In the Middle Ages all this area belonged to the Bénédictines who constructed lots of Romanesque churches, then it was devastated by the Hundred Years War, afterwards populated by northerners, or *gavaches* as the Gascons called them, speaking the *langue d'oïl* or old French. The descendants are to this day called *gavaches* or *gabots*. The arcaded central *place* with a 19th-century covered market made a perfect concert hall and when we arrived the village was abuzz with activity, setting up food tents, testing the sound equipment and praying for good weather. Local officials stood around proudly smiling, all the villagers were beside themselves with excitement and local jazz bands played outside cafés. We had a not very good dinner at the Grand Hôtel then strolled across the road to the concert, due to start at 9 p.m. (French time, not world time).

At 9.15 the public started straggling in and at 9.30 the concert began. This year it was a local singer as warm-up, then an American spiritual jazz singer called Liz McComb. Liz was a fairly big woman in white who sang in the no-prisoners-taken-gospel-style, thumping that piano and yelling that song out. She had two topics – good and evil. God and the devil. The message was simple but profound and was repeated over and over again. With her bassist, drummer and guest organist she jumped up and played the piano standing up, chanted, gasped, swooped, caressed, menaced and loved us with her raw, powerful songs. The best one was an African song where the music stopped and she went into a sort of trance, African dancing around the stage. It was an emotionally shattering show and she did it for two hours straight. At 12.30 we staggered outside into the night for some hot *chichis* (or *chichiffregi* – a sort of long doughnut, very light and drenched in fine sugar). After a long break the second part of the show commenced.

The Spiritualettes. Bronwyn, Lesley and I liked the name and decided we would call ourselves the Amandettes from now on. The lights went off and seven huge black mamas in red dresses struggled up the steps onto the stage. We all clutched each other in alarm. Would they ever get off the stage again, let alone live to see another day? They were varying in vintage from middle-aged to very old and were obviously veterans of the gospel-singing game. Sing that song for Jesus! They launched into all the old favourites like 'Rock My Soul', 'Amazing Grace' and 'How Great Thou Art' in seven-part harmony. For us it was all a bit dated but the Froggies loved it and went wild. They love a late night, especially when nothing happens in the village from one jazz concert to the next. We finally left at 1.45 a.m. for the two-hour drive home and they were all still at it, singing their heads off, joining hands and praising the Lord.

Almost every day we went on an adventure. The golden Renaissance town of Sarlat-la-Canéda, called Sarlat, is the architectural diamond in the southwest. It is a protected and restored national treasure under the state law Loi Malraux. Every shop we walked past was selling foie gras and truffles so of course we bought some. In such a stunning (and expensive) town you wouldn't expect to find great food as it would be too much to have the two in one place, so we asked our gastronomic sleuth Jessica to guide us. She advised Chez Marc and Le Relais de la Poste. We chose the latter. One really had to know this place was there, as it was hidden up a side street and had a secret terrace a few doors up that couldn't be seen from the street. They had set menus and the style was nouvelle cuisiny/refined. I chose the cheapest menu and ate a delicate tomato salad wherein the tomato had been skinned and fanned out on a bed of lettuce. The main was *émincé de boeuf* (sliced beefsteak) with jus, scalloped potatoes, ratatouille, grilled tomato and carrot and courgette ribbons. Lesley and Bronwyn ordered the more expensive menu and were served soup followed by marinated raw salmon, red mullet with vegetables, a huge cheese platter loaded with goat's cheese, blue cheese, Cantal, Brie and Vacherin FOLLOWED BY a dessert of grilled red berry *sabayon* in a tuile. We drank a Cahors and had expensive coffee, which is of course where they make their money, but it was still ridiculously cheap for the quality.

Eventually the sun did come out – two days after the predicted Lune de Jésus – and we took it with us to the romantic and elegant wine town of St-Emilion. As you approach this world-famous area you begin to see hectares and hectares of grapevines, some with their ancient, low stone walls. A few of the vineyards had ornate graves in the middle of them, housing winemakers who couldn't bear to be separated from their beloved land, even in death. Very good for fertilizing the soil, I should think. We parked in the centre of St-Emilion and across the road was a *grand cru classé* (classified great growth) vineyard right in the middle of town. Arising magnificently out of it was all that remained of the Grandes Murailles – the great city walls built in 1287 and destroyed by a pillaging army in 1337. It's a shame about all this pillaging and plundering and raping because what we find so beautiful and touching in these ruins is a result of appalling historical suffering and viciousness. St Valéry is St-Emilion's patron saint of vintners and for some dodgy reason he is also known to get new brides pregnant. They wipe their hankies on him. No, look, that's what it said in the book and I won't even bother to go down that road.

We did a tour of the vineyards, driving up and down and across hectares of pure gold, knowing that all the secrets of St-Emilion are underground. No one really knows why grapes grow so well there – there is no special micro-climate and the soil is complex but not to die for. There is a lot of clay, hence the dominant variety (over 60 percent) is Merlot mixed with Cabernet Franc (they call it Bouchet), Cabernet Sauvignon and Malbec. One of the secrets of the quality is that St-Emilion wines have extremely strict controls and the estates are small. There are only two premiers *grands crus classés* (first-rate great classified growths) and they are Ausone and Cheval-Blanc. Below that are nine *classés B*, followed by 63 *grands crus classés*. The humblest are the simple St-Emilion appellation contrôlée. All these wines are blind-tasted regularly by the Jurade of St-Emilion to see whether or not they still merit their status.

The élite vineyards of St-Emilion don't lower themselves to do tastings for individuals (unless you're rich, American and flash the chequebook around) so we went on a guided tasting to Château Grave Figeac. This six-hectare *grand cru* vineyard has very illustrious neighbours bordering it – Cheval Blanc on one side and the Pomerol appellation on the other – so even though it doesn't have the official status, its 30-year-old vines are actually grown in similar sand and gravel soil. The vigneron, Jean-Pierre Clauzel, took us around his vineyard, into the *chai* or storeroom and eventually to the shop. M. Clauzel was a happy, relaxed man, incapable of giving a simple answer to a question, to the chagrin of the translator. He loved it when people showed interest in his beloved grapes and method – in other words, his life. It was the beginning of July so the colour of the grapes was starting to change from green to the classic red-purple. When we were there they were just blushing; within a week they would be deeply embarrassed. The workers were pruning leaves, tying vines up, doing the 'green harvest', which is sacrificing certain bunches of grapes for the benefit of others and ploughing weeds back into the soil. From now on the grapes would be sprayed every 12 days (no chemical herbicides).

M. Clauzel harvests his grapes by hand, which is more expensive, but he considers the human hand better than any machine could ever be. He employs students whom he describes as lovely people, but you need two for every normal person because they party all night and don't work very hard. The wine is aged in oak barrels, filtered with egg whites, and professional bottlers come to the property to bottle it. He produces only two wines – the Grave and the Pavillon – and they have that well-balanced combination of the powerful Cabernet (35 percent) and the soft Merlot (65 percent). M. Clauzel doesn't use *négotiants* and what he doesn't sell in Central Europe, he sells through private sale in France.

The first delicacy I spied and exclaimed happily at as we wandered around St-Emilion were silver trays of dark brown, moulded pastries sitting on tables outside many shops. I couldn't believe my eyes. I had first tasted *cannelés* in New Caledonia when I was filming my television food show there. They were made by a French *pâtissier* from Bordeaux, the origin of this speciality. The other speciality of the area is the horrifying and justly feared *lamproie* (lamprey fish). This thing has no eyes, is as ugly as sin due to the fact it's an evolutionary throwback, and sucks blood. Legend has it that Roman tyrants fed slaves to lampreys if they displeased them, and Henry I liked them so much he died from overeating them. In my opinion the best thing to do with a lamprey is pray for its soul and turn your back; but if you wish to eat it the Bordelaise make a stew of it swimming in their wine and its blood. I got this recipe from an old Périgord cookbook and I swear this is really what you do. To make *les lamproies au vin du sud-ouest*, first take a beautiful live lamprey. Nail it upside down to the wall through the tail. Once it's feeling a bit dizzy grab the body with a teatowel-wrapped hand and with the other hand make an incision in the head with a sharp knife to bleed it. Make sure you place a bowl underneath to catch the blood, go away and vomit and come back in two hours. Cut off the poisonous dorsal cartilage so that if you haven't yet died of fright you won't die of paralytic spasms, and dip the lamprey in hot water to facilitate ripping the skin off. Make a sauce from red St-Emilion wine, a roux, leeks, onions, garlic, bouquet garni, salt and pepper, and stew it for two hours. Cut the lovely lampreys in big chunks and stick them in the sauce to cook for forty-five minutes. Add a pinch of sugar or a square of chocolate to make it more palatable, then just before serving, stir in the blood to thicken. Serve surrounded with fried croûtons.

St-Emilion is very touristy so you really have to have inside information on where to eat. Bronwyn and Lesley

knew of a simple but honest wine bar called L'Envers du
Décor on rue du Clocher. Their wine list was six times longer
than the menu with bottles going up to 380€ each, which of
course we ordered. The real story is that we drank a very
good, reasonably priced Château Penin Bordeaux Supérieur.
The standard southwest bistrot fare that we ate included, of
course, foie gras and confit de canard, with the most divine
French-style wedges. As I scraped the last possible suggestion
of foie gras off my plate the waiter said, 'Keep your utensils
please.' Look from me. Shrug from him. 'Well at least we
smile when we ask,' he purred.

'*Oui, oui, ça va,*' I snapped.

The market in the river port of Bergerac (medieval name
Brageira) in Purple Périgord is on Wednesday and Saturday.
Ever since I had read that poetic sad story of Cyrano de
Bergerac I had wanted to see this town. The rustic market
circling the church was full of fresh hazelnuts in their
pretty green coats, huge black figs the size of pears, grey
shallots (the best), melons, prunes, fresh and dried flowers,
cornichons (baby cucumbers for pickling). It was the end of
the berry season but there were still lots of strawberries
(including tiny wild ones), blackberries, blueberries and
red and white currants. Also, because of the rain followed
by sunshine, every kind of mushroom, especially cèpes and
the slightly less tasty pine cèpes, had burst out of the forest
and were laid in baskets and rows everywhere. The tiny
sweet *bouchot* mussels were piled up in mountains and huge
pans of the ever-present saffron-coloured paella wafted past
our noses. Bergerac wine is quite ordinary but it makes the
perfect accompaniment for foie gras – the sweet Sauternes-
like Monbazillac wine. Dying of hunger on the way home, we
decided to stop at a *routier* (trucker's restaurant) for lunch.

Routiers can be fantastic. The food is cheap, copious and
good; they are no nonsense, full of huge truckies, and you
take what you are given. I love that. I love walking into a

restaurant and saying, 'Feed me.' I am telling you this story to warn you of the perils of spontaneity. This was one of the rare times when we really blew it. The menu was take what you're given for the price and thank God you're alive. Fine.

First course
Dishwater with leeks, turnips and huge chunks of bread floating in it

Second course
Dog food and donkey salami and potato salad

Third course
Blanquette de veau or veal elbows, undercooked in wallpaper paste with catatonic macaroni

Fourth course
Soap cleverly disguised as cheese

Fifth course
Dessert and fruit. Unidentifiable

The veal was so tough that Lesley dragged out the dental floss in the restaurant to dislodge five-inch chunks from her teeth. I was astounded she had such a thing in her handbag. Condoms I can understand, because these are modern times and one never knows – but dental floss? These were the permanent, non-negotiable contents of Lesley's bag: maps, fan, sewing kit, measuring tape, corkscrew, all the car papers, spare keys, passport, tissues, television ID card, French dictionary and anything that belonged to Bronwyn. The lardous cook came out to add insult to injury by proudly asking us if we were happy with the food. How could you be so far removed from reality to ask such a question? Was he on drugs? Every time he came to the table he said, '*En France on parle français*.' I don't think he was a racist pig but I did want to slap him after the third time. The one saving grace was the bottle of red wine with the stars around the top plonked on the table. We drank far more of it than necessary to kill the pain of the food.

The Dordogne is famous for its *tempêtes* – dramatic and frequent lightning and thunderstorms which appear out of nowhere and are usually followed by a beautiful day. One late Wednesday afternoon as I was writing in my white room upstairs with a tempête as the foreground, the church bell began ringing. The little church attached to our presbytery seemed part of our private domain and the bell had never rung before. Who was ringing it and why? It went on for a long time.

'Someone's dead,' said Bronwyn ominously. Sure enough, an old lady from St-Amand-de-Belvès had finally gone to meet her maker at the age of eighty-three. The next morning at 8.30 a.m. I was almost knocked out of my bed, the closest to the bell tower, by the bells ringing their dirge again to tell the countryside of the death. That evening the message was repeated, echoing across the fields and hills around us. Various people turned up at the church to clean it and fill it with flowers, and as it was usually locked up to thwart vandals, I took the opportunity to have a look inside. It was a simple but pretty building in the characteristic mustard-coloured stone, with a main altar and two tiny side altars. The altar table, covered in white lace, was a huge flour millstone that had been dragged in by two oxen some years before.

Next morning at 8.45 the bells rang to signal the start of the funeral service, so I quickly got dressed and went down to sit in the back row of hard backless seats. The church was filled with village people and the woman's family, all dressed in their sombre best. The young priest, imported from somewhere down the line to do the service, gave a nice sermon, considering he didn't know the deceased, who was relaxing in her coffin, covered by a black cloth with purple cross. He mentioned that it was now *interdit* for civilians to carry coffins; it had to be done by a professionally trained person. As a true Frenchman for whom rules are a simple excuse to take a flying leap, he said he was pleased to see the family were ignoring that rule and carrying the coffin themselves, which was only correct. The deceased's four best friends started the procession off by holding the black cloth by the four corners and setting off towards the cemetery. Followed by the priest, the hearse and finally the mourners, this grey procession slowly wound its way down the road in the morning silence and mist to the pretty little graveyard. All the while the bell was ringing slowly and sadly. It was the most wonderful sight and I was desperate to photograph it but just couldn't bring myself to violate the scene.

One of the biggest festivals in France is the 14th of July, the day the Bastille prison in Paris was stormed by the people during the Revolution. When I lived in Paris I always hid at home on this day to avoid the noise, drunkenness and crackers-up-the-frock syndrome, but Bastille Day in the country is altogether a different story – a much softer, more gastronomic affair with genuine conviviality. For days the central marketplace at Belvès had been revving itself up for the huge communal dinner and bal. One day long rows of tables with hundreds of chairs appeared. The next there were red, white and blue streamers hanging from the rafters of the 15th-century *halle* covering the marketplace and more tables and chairs were added. That night there was a tempête, so the day of the 14th, up went plastic covers on either side of the roof, a stage for the band was built and all the flowers on the wrought-iron balconies bordering the square were in full bloom.

Bronwyn, Lesley (who said she couldn't eat anything on the menu) and I arrived early, all scrubbed up, and reserved seats for our friends right in the middle of the feast. The mile-long tables were set with white paper, white plates, knives, forks and wine glasses. Our friends arrived late, which is just on time for the Froggies, after having had 'a few cocktails'. One of them had just read my first book *Fête Accomplie* and was thrilled to find Jessica in it; another was thrilled to find he'd already previously met me at Jessica's place; with a few more glasses of wine I found that I too was thrilled. If you know three people in a village in France, you know everybody because, like all villages, they do nothing but talk about everyone else. We all immediately became intimate friends with everyone within bread-throwing distance. Next to me was a couple from Paris who had a family home in Dordogne. He wore a T-shirt that said 'I like work, I spend hours thinking about it'. Across from me were two Dutch boys who immediately got out their own Château Plastique and spent the evening smiling befuddledly at us.

Greta, a jolly Belgian woman who spends a lot of time in Dordogne with her dapper English husband Ray, was telling a true urban myth. A woman goes into a cinema to watch a film. At half-time she nicks next door for a quick coffee. She has bought a Kitkat in the cinema. The café is crowded so she has to share a table with a man. She makes no eye contact with him but suddenly he breaks off a piece of the Kitkat and eats it. She is horrified but pretends to ignore him, eats some herself. He breaks off another piece and eats it. She still makes no eye contact with him but now she's really pissed off, finishes her coffee and when she stands up to go, sticks her finger in his coffee, swirls it around and makes a face at him. She goes back to the theatre, opens her handbag to get her ticket and there is her Kitkat in her bag. Ray maintained the best thing he ever did was to marry Greta. Quote: *Being married to her is like being on holiday – it's fun and expensive.* Unquote.

Bottles of water were placed on the tables and we got our wine before anyone else due to high-up contacts with the chef (imagine cooking a meal for 500 people!). Ray told me to cease drinking so much water as it would rot my Wellingtons.

Suddenly there was a drum roll and we rose as one to sing the *Marseillaise*, the battle hymn of the republic. Every nationality seems to know this song and every person who sings it seems to come over all queer and thingy. In spite of this, when we asked around the table, no one could give the correct date for the year of the Revolution. Finally the Parisians gave it – 1789. This song is called the Marseillaise simply because it was first heard sung at a banquet by a soldier from Montpellier posted to Marseilles. It was actually composed in an overnight writing binge in Strasbourg by Claude Joseph Rouget de Lisle, a soldier and songwriter. My friend Emmanuel maintains he can find the tune in a Mozart concerto written long before – and anyway, everyone knows it is an old German folk song.

Revolutionary France had declared war on Austria and the *Chant de guerre de l'armée du Rhin* (war song for the Rhine army) was hastily composed for the departing volunteers. It was sung by various soldiers going south, whence it found itself in the dulcet vocal chords of Francois Mireur at the banquet. Revolutionary hearts quickened to this rousing and passionate chant so it was taught to Marseillais soldiers soon to leave for the defence of Paris. Now called the *Chant de guerre aux armées des Frontières* (War song for the Border Armies), the song was sung by these soldiers all the way up to Paris with mounting passion and conviction. When the Parisians heard this electrifying, revolutionary war song coming from warm, southern voices the effect was instant and they called it the *Chant des Marseillais* (Song of the Marseillais). Soon after, they stormed the Tuileries and, on July 14th, 1789, the Bastille – at which point La Marseillaise became France's national anthem. *Voilà.*

Le Tourin
Onion and Garlic Soup

Serves 6

4 tbsp duck fat
500g onions, very finely sliced
10 cloves garlic, finely sliced
2 litres chicken stock
1 *bouquet garni*
sea salt and freshly ground black pepper
500g peeled, quartered tomatoes
3 eggs
1 tbsp red wine vinegar
6 thick slices *pain de compagne* (rustic country bread)
100g grated emmenthaler or gruyère cheese

1. Melt the duck fat in a heavy-based saucepan. Cook the onions gently until they are translucent and pale golden (this might take 20 mins). Add the garlic and cook for another 5 mins.

2. Add stock, bouquet garni, salt, pepper and tomatoes, bring to the boil and simmer gently, covered, for half an hour. Discard bouquet garni.

3. Separate the eggs into two bowls. Beat egg whites then whisk into the simmering soup. They will immediately form threads. Whisk the egg yolks with the vinegar and add a ladle of hot soup. Turn the heat off and stir this mixture back into the soup. Taste for seasoning.

4. Grill bread on one side, turn over, place grated cheese on top and grill. Place in the bottom of soup plates and ladle soup over.

Note: The Périgourdin usually tip some red wine from their glass into the soup and I see no reason why you shouldn't tip in a shot of cognac.

Large bowls of delicious country soup *le tourin* (see above) with bread floating in it were brought around by the volunteer servers and ladled out into our plates. With the last dregs, the Périgourdin guests did *chabron*, mixed in some wine and drank from the plate. They told me the REAL *tourin* is a great delicacy and better than what we were eating – the classic Bordelais onion, garlic and tomato soup thickened with egg yolks. A variation of it is *le tourin au vinaigre*, or *l'ouliat*, which is made the same way but without tomatoes. At the end put in a little vinegar. Put the egg whites in to cook with the soup at the last minute, cut into little pieces and sprinkle over the soup. Large wooden trays full of bread were carried around on the server's shoulders and handfuls plonked on the tables. The foie gras was served on little toasts, Lesley wouldn't eat hers so the rest of us dived on it. The Parisians looked on in horror.

'*Mais comment ca se fait qu'elle ne mange pas du foie gras?* (How come she doesn't eat foie gras?)'

'She doesn't like it.'

'But, how could anyone not like foie gras? *Ce n'est pas normal.*'

'I agree, but she is perfect in every other way.'

Meanwhile 499 other people, including children, were munching away in ecstasy. It was a beautiful dark blue night, we were surrounded by antiquity and the main course was about to be served.

We wiped our plates with bread for thick slices of pork with a mushroom sauce. When this was gone the beans arrived. Didn't wipe the plates for the green salad so we could mix it in with the juices from the pork and beans. A little ball of bread landed in my hair. No way of knowing where it came from. The only honourable thing to do – throw one back in the same direction. Four tables away it hit a gentleman right on his bald patch. The French (especially the bourgeoisie who grew up in boarding schools and never got over the pleasure of throwing food) love this game and often do it on special occasions. On New Year's Eve they throw whole rolls. Obviously all the other tables joined in wholesale until a woman waved a white serviette and things calmed down. The next course was cheese followed by a *choux* filled with pastry cream. Our wonderful young stationmaster from

Belvès made the rounds of the long tables with bottles of champagne.

As coffee was being served, the band struck up an old-fashioned *javanaise* and people took to the dance floor in droves – mothers with their babies, fathers with daughters, very old ladies with their grandsons, couples, teenagers. The bread-thrower patiently wound his way through the tables to ask me if I danced as well as I threw bread. The band played a good mix of old and new, rock and jazz, black and blue. More and more tables near the dance floor were folded up to make extra room. The French do a particularly fancy, athletic form of jive, called ceroc (*c'est rock*) in other countries. They learned it from the Americans after the war and have made it their own. The bread thrower would let me dance with a few other people then come back again for an enthusiastic fling through the crowd. I have to say for a little bald banker from Paris, he was a bloody good dancer. At this point the sterling servers sat down at a big table and had their well-deserved dinner. We left at 1.30 to take Greta and Ray home before they fell over but apparently the bal went on until five which is customary. Most local people would have got up again at eight for work the next morning, a Tuesday.

It had been wonderful and entertaining staying with Bronwyn and Lesley but all good things seem to come to an end; the owners of the presbytère were approaching fearlessly from the north to reclaim their property and the girls were girding their loins to continue their journey south to Portugal. We briefly considered weeping, got over it, said our fond farewells and I went off to stay with Jessica and Jean-Louis for a week. I have a marvellous vision of Jessica the blonde bombshell striding through Le Bugue in a miniskirt and espadrilles, a baby on her hip and a little child by the hand, both in bright sundresses – surely the three prettiest girls in the town. Jessica's children were a neverending round of ice creams, idle threats, extravagant promises if they would just behave for one minute, merry-go-rounds, hysterical non-dummy-finding crises, them stuffing things in one end of their bodies and waiting for them to come out the other end, kissing them passionately, getting three-day-old paddling pool water out of their mouths and almost weeping with pleasure when they decided they liked you enough to rest their little hands on your arm while telling you their little stories.

Aside from getting used to children running loose (it being a farm and all), I also had to get used to the flying population (it being a farm and all) and the noise of the bloody rooster at the crack of dawn (it being a farm and all). It's quite a trick of concentration writing with two hands on the laptop while simultaneously using those two hands to get flies, wasps and bees out of your ear, out of your pastis, off your hair and out of your life. I was fortunate enough to be lodged in the self-contained guest house complete with lace curtains, antique mirrors and high brass bed with monogrammed heavy cotton sheets. These sheets were from the untouched trousseau of the sister of the previous owner who had never married. I lay on these sheets of disappointment and it didn't take much to imagine what that poor woman's life had been like. The brother hooned around the neighbourhood on his bike having liaisons with married women while the sister wept over love letters and infertile proposals of marriage. Jessica had found beautifully written love letters between her and a man who wanted to marry her but the brother had forbidden it, forcing her to stay home and be his housekeeper. Men. Can't live with them; can't shoot them.

I went into the ancient town of Périgueux which, being first and foremost a market city, was my kind of town. Without planning it I turned up on market day – but in fact every day is market day; it just gets bigger on Wednesday and Saturday. I decided to be desperately organised because for once I was blissfully on my own, so set out with the guide book in my hot little hand. I got about a quarter of the way through my tour and what with conversations about the price of fish here and my pathological inability to walk past a foie gras shop there, three hours had gone by and I had to meet my ride home. I had been told by an affectionado of the Dordogne and previous lodger at the presbytery, of a regional restaurant in Périgueux called Le Vieux Pavé. This person is so in love with the Dordogne that before I left home he remembered and told me the exact time to the minute the train to Le Buisson left Paris and arrived at its destination. He said the restaurant was owned by an elderly couple – Monsieur *derrière les foumeaux* in the kitchen and Madame *dans la salle* in the restaurant. I came across it by chance and to my chagrin there was a big FERME sign on the door. Not just closed for the day but closed forever. I walked a little further to enquire in the bar next door. A very nice, motherly, plump lady confirmed the restaurant was closed and would I be needing a drink? I ordered a *panaché* (shandy) to deal with the heat and rested my elbow on the bar. There was a very old woman in the corner engaged in an interminable monologue with a young man and an old man in a beret taking his vieille prune to keep the blood nice and thin.

'I have come from the other side of the world,' I told the woman behind the bar. 'My friend told me the food at Le Vieux Pavé was very good. Do you know what happened to the couple?'

She smiled sadly and said. 'That person was me, Madame. We didn't want to stop but my husband became very ill and we had to close down three months ago.' She told me her name was Mme Maurence.

'I'm so sorry,' I said. 'So this bar was part of the old restaurant?'

'Yes. I had to keep it on so as not to disappoint the regulars – and, you know, I love my job and am happiest behind the bar and helping people to enjoy themselves. I didn't want to stop and neither did my husband but hard work did him in. I am going to the hospital to pick him up today, but I don't think he'll ever work again.'

'Did you have the restaurant for a long time, Mme Maurence?'

'Oh yes. We've been in the business for 42 years altogether. Six months after we married, we opened our first restaurant in Paris serving Périgourdine cuisine. My husband is a very good chef and we were successful because we were serious and we loved it. What is your interest in food? Are you a chef?' she asked.

'I had a restaurant in Paris in the 5th,' I replied.

'Where?'

'On rue d'Arras.'

'Our restaurant was just around the corner,' she smiled with delight at the coincidence.

Mme Maurence moved down the bar to serve other people and I waved goodbye to wander around the markets in the various marketplaces.

The best markets are in the Puy St-Front district or old Périgueux, where all the artists and merchants used to live. Everywhere in France there is massive restoration going on, and Périgueux is no exception. It is a very beautiful town full of Renaissance facades, ornate staircase towers, turrets, secret courtyards behind big doors, Gothic windows and fabulous half-timbered townhouses. Everything that was ruined by man is now being repaired by man. Maybe I was just in a good mood but the Périgourdins seemed very friendly, relaxed people to me and the markets had the same air – there was a lot of exhorting one to buy, but gently. Every day there's a fruit and vegetable market at Place du Coderc and around the corner on Place de l'Hôtel de Ville. Place du Coderc used to be a field for keeping pigs and executing naughty people.

The Place de la Clautre has a slightly bigger market on

Gateau aux Noix
Walnut Cake

Serves 8

For the cake:
2 slices of white bread
150g butter
100g sugar
4 eggs, separated
grated rind of one lemon
150g walnuts, ground
pinch of salt
25g sugar
23cm cake tin

1. Preheat oven to 150°C. Toast the bread in the oven until dry then grind it up in a food processor.
2. Grease and flour cake tin and line base with baking paper.
3. Cream butter and 100g of sugar then add egg yolks one by one, beating in well.
4. Stir in lemon rind, breadcrumbs and ground walnuts.
5. In another bowl whip the egg whites and salt until stiff, then add the 25g of sugar and beat for another minute.
6. Fold the egg whites into the cake mixture and pour into the tin.
7. Bake for 45 mins to one hour. If the cake browns too much, cover it.
8. Remove from oven and cool.

For the icing:
100g chocolate
30g butter
Two dozen walnut halves

Gently melt the chocolate and butter together. Spread icing all over cake and decorate the rim with the walnut halves.

Wednesday and Saturday. The Place St-Louis is called Foie Gras Square as in late autumn and winter, amateurs come from all over to buy fresh raw foie gras and black truffles. These markets were exceptionally pretty and full of farmers selling little bits of this and that from a wooden table – a few onions, a black-footed Noir de Périgord farm chicken, plucked and sitting on the inevitable tray of ice cubes, three giant cèpes, a dozen brown eggs in a basket and a box of broad beans. There were melons everywhere as it was the season for them, and still lots of berries and walnut cakes by the armful. Actually the best walnut cake in the area is made at Fouquet's pastry shop and tearooms in Le Bugue. It's more like a tart really and similar to pecan pie – crunchy and caramelly and not detestable with a dollop of walnut ice cream. Once you've licked your ice cream off a baby's fingers that have been stuck in your tart then stuck in your face with 'doo-da-doo-doo-doo-da-Pe-ta', you can never go back really.

I liked Périgueux and wanted more time there, so I got a ride in with Jean-Louis a few days later. He makes music videos from a studio in Périgueux.

'I'll take you in, Peta, but I'm very busy and can't show you anything, so I'll drop you off somewhere and pick you up at the end of the day. Okay?' he said in the car.

'Okay,' I said, not in the least disappointed because I know Jean-Louis and I just waited patiently with my hands folded neatly in my lap. Deep, dark, country areas are full of eccentric people. We passed the farm of the man who shot Greta's dog; passed the family who live in the forest with no modern conveniences and ten children; passed the house of the woman who has twelve children supposedly by twelve different men; passed the naked man with fifty dogs. As we neared Périgueux he said, 'Well, maybe we'll just quickly pop into Barnabé for a look. This place is really something ... wait until you see it.'

I smiled and knew the day would pan out exactly the way I wanted it to.

We followed the river Lisle until we got to the Boulazac district just before Périgueux, drove to the end of rue des Bains and there was Barnabé, right on the river. Jean-Louis had told me it was a place where you could get drinks and snacks, and had a camping ground and golf course attached. What I found before me was a majestic white and burgundy building with a large terrace full of tables and chairs overlooking the Lisle. Although it was originally built by the owner's father in 1936, it was redone after the Second World War which explained the distinctly late 40s early 50s architecture and interior design. Inside there was a huge round ballroom/concert space, unfortunately full of pool tables, the original telephone booths, rounded alcoves with wooden window-seats, tall plants, wood finishing everywhere. There was a beautiful chestnut bar in the grand dining room, the original tables and chairs and an antique chestnut and brass *tireuse à bière* (a cabinet for serving beer on tap). In 1956 the daughter, Mme Foussard, and her husband took it over and now their son works there as well, organising jazz, traditional and classical concerts. Jean-Louis produced a marvellous CD of old-time accordion music, rounding up people from all over the Dordogne who used to play the dances, weddings, clubs and concerts in the 20s, 30s and 40s. The very successful launch was held at Barnabé.

It seems such a terrible waste for this distinguished dream of a palace completely intact from another era, to be used only for icecreams, pizzas, coffees and drinks. Mme Foussard told me it was the oldest (and surely most glamorous) camping ground in the department; they never advertise, and all their business comes from word of mouth. She didn't even have a business card to give me for the correct address.

'We have many faithful clients,' she smiled as she handed us our expresses over the bar. 'People have been coming here for years – sometimes even people from New Zealand

and Australia who came with their parents when they were children turn up and everything is still the same.'

'Come with me,' said Jean-Louis, 'I'll show you the camping ground.'

To get to the camping ground one had to cross to the other side of the river in a little white and red barge that one pulled across by a wire rope. At the other shore one walked through a white and red archway with BARNABÉ written on it and there was the camping ground. It was romantic beyond words, you felt you were in the country and yet a five-minute ride down the road and you were in the centre of Périgueux. A tourist coming to Périgueux would never find in any guidebook the information that, if they were to just go down to the Barris bridge which leads into town, cross it, turn left and stroll along the river for 15 minutes, they would find this charming scene. French people make lots of jokes about how now that I've discovered a certain place, the whole world will know and it will be ruined. They think this is a very good joke because everyone knows that no one from the other side of the world comes to France and I only found my way there by chance ha ha.

We jumped in the car and Jean-Louis said, I'll drop you off at Fébus to show you where it is and we'll meet there at the end of the day.'

'Yes Jean-Louis,' I said, knowing exactly what would happen. He had told me Fébus was one of his favourite hangouts for eating, drinking, misbehaving and sometimes staying the night in one of the rooms upstairs when it was too late to drive home. He also told me the *patronne* was a bawdy woman with *beaucoup de gens sur son balcon*, literally translated as having a lot of people on your balcony, meaning big breasts. We walked into a lovely courtyard on rue Judaïque, off rue Notre Dame near the cathedral and there was the Fébus, a colourful, slightly shabby bar/restaurant with lots of character and tables spilling out onto a terrace and into the courtyard. It's open all day as a café/bar and serves meals at lunch and dinner.

Jean-Louis sauntered in with a huge smile on his face.

'*Peta, je te présente Bernadette*,' he said proudly, holding his arms out. And there she was, exactly as he had described her – a generous body encased in tight bellbottoms, see-through black blouse, platforms and tiny white apron. Her dark, hennaed hair was swept up in a French roll held in place with two big bulldog clips. Everything about her was voluptuous, from her dark eyes to her red lips to her big voice. Needless to say we had to order a café just out of politeness, and got into conversations with other people at the bar. Bernadette was in a bad mood, which only made Jean-Louis tease her more. He likes women who give him a hard time and provokes them until they do, as Jessica (who's no slouch in the strong character department) would readily attest to.

'We're angry today,' Bernadette said to me, 'so the food will taste accordingly. Taste these mussels and tell me if they're too spicy.'

'*Donne-lui des moules à goûter*,' she screamed to the kitchen. Her waitresses were all big buxom women, making her look positively anorexic.

'They're very good,' I said, 'but not really spicy enough.' Her eyes widened. 'Just kidding.'

One of the waitresses wore beautiful necklaces and rings which she said she had bought to reward and console herself for having survived either a financial, health, professional or personal crisis. She pointed to a new BMW outside, saying it was her latest gift to herself. I didn't wish to be treated to her life story but did wonder how a waitress could afford a BMW.

The menu was of the scribbled-all-over-the-blackboard variety and included tapas, dishes of the day, cosmopolitan influences, made-up stuff and chilli con carne which Bernadette had been serving for about 20 years.

'In terms of food, we make what we feel like – it's a living cuisine. We're not stuck in the old ways and we don't make food that's only fit for a picture frame.'

Suddenly there was a loud clacking of tap shoes. It was midday, the CD had burst into Spanish singing and Bernadette snapped into Spanish dancing behind the bar. Of course Jean-Louis had piles of work to do but I convinced him he was working by helping me with my research. He said nothing but I could tell he was very attracted to this idea.

I like Jean-Louis a lot, would hate to be married to him but he is great as a friend – funny, seductive, deeply Périgourdin, wiry good looks in a rustic-never-comb-your-hair sort of way and an extremely good raconteur. When you have a friendship with a couple, either they come as one unit or they come as two and you have a different relationship with each one. The latter was the case with Jessica and Jean-Louis – and of course its much more interesting that way. The only way you can pull this off without getting into trouble, is never to repeat what the other has told you. Arlene told me this secret a long time ago. It's quite simple and works if you stick to it – that way both people know they can trust you. Jean-Louis belongs to the macho school of fatherhood – that is, he is fabulous with the children, playing with them and inventing stories for hours, but less fabulous with the other side of parenting, i.e. washing, cleaning and handiwork. He's one of those fathers whose children will grow up and remember his larger-than-life personality, roguish charm and cèpe-hunting expeditions.

After we left Fébus Jean-Louis said, 'I'll just drop in to Le Printemps to pick up something. This is a typical Périgourdin workers' bistrot which you should really try out – they have reasonably priced set menus.' We drove over to rue Louis Blanc and immediately ordered apéritifs, as was only correct at midday – Jean-Louis a Pernod, and I a Salers. This gentian liqueur is made near a village called Salers in the Auvergne.

It is a long, hard process of digging up deep gentian roots by hand with a special instrument as there is no machinery yet invented that can do it. One drinks it straight or with an ice cube. Weaklings add water. I looked around at the tacky paintings, clay-pigeon shooting trophies, neon lighting and revolting retirement-home-pink walls and couldn't help but wonder why it was called Le Printemps (Springtime). This bistrot was in a working area and no tourist would ever wander in there by mistake. It was started by Thierry Vidalen's parents and he and his wife Marie-Laure eventually took it over. Half an hour later, hunger had imposed itself on us so we were forced by circumstance to sit down and eat. By now the patron had found out a very exaggerated account of my raison d'être from Jean-Louis. He tried to get us to sit in the flash room next door with the proper tablecloths and lamps on the walls but I said no, I wanted to sit at the long table with the workers in the main room. This he couldn't understand.

'She doesn't want special treatment,' said Jean-Louis.

'But ladies don't sit in here,' replied Thierry, flustering.

'Don't worry. I'll make sure she behaves.'

So down we sat. Red wine plonked in front of us onto the plastic tablecloth. It was the usual tiny five-course menu so we chose and waited with anticipation.

The soup was the same soup you get in all the bistrots – watery broth with vegetables and bread floating in it and you drink as much as you want. This classic country soup is considered with great affection by the Périgourdin. Personally I don't see the interest in it at all. Jean-Louis always pours his wine into the dregs, which does improve it slightly. Next was a red cabbage salad with ham. Thierry literally ran around the restaurant on his own, serving, pouring drinks at the bar, clearing the plates, making coffee and doing the bills. There were three people at the other table who had been there drinking since we arrived – a fat woman with long white and black hair like Cruella, a middle-aged man and an old woman. Marie-Laure did all the cooking and all the washing up by hand on her own. To visit the toilet you climbed upstairs and to wash your hands you went downstairs.

The next course was a delicious *blanquette de veau* with potatoes. This was how a veal blanquette should taste – tender, subtle, creamy and properly seasoned. It was getting towards two o'clock and two late workers walked in. They calmly cleared the table, stacked the dishes, wiped the tablecloth and sat down. 'Now we can get to work,' they said. Jean-Louis loved all this and his eyes were sparkling as he downed the special Bergerac wine Thierry had put on the table as a gift. The three drinkers in the corner were warming up nicely, especially the quiet old lady who suddenly got out her personality and started throwing it around a bit. We finished off our wine with a perfectly good *tarte au citron* unadorned with such distractions as custard or icecream. We were so full there was no question of cheese as some friends of Jean-Louis came from the flash side of the bistrot to have coffee with us. Only at the end of the service did Thierry permit himself to light up, have a coffee and sit down for two minutes. He brought with him a bottle of amber-coloured liquid in a large Perrier bottle – 14-year-old *calvados*. This is very common in restaurants where you know the patron. If he likes you, you usually get offered something at the end of the meal. New World restaurateurs could be a lot more friendly in this regard.

After lunch Jean-Louis finally went to his studio and I continued my tour of Périgueux. Walking down the pedestrian rue Limogeanne, I came across an authentic cheese shop which sold only farm and raw milk cheeses. Written on their business card was this: *La Renaissance multiplie ses sourires dans la Limogeanne. C'est le coeur gastronomique de la ville. Au numéro 9 dans la cave voûtée, les fromagers de la*

Ferme Périgourdine affinent avec passion leurs fromages pour votre plaisir. (The Renaissance unfolds its smiling past in the Limogeanne. This is the gastronomic heart of the town. At No. 9 in the vaulted cellar, the cheesemakers of Périgourdine Farm mature their cheese with passion for your pleasure.) I got into a conversation with Mme Michelle Thieullent, whose temperature-controlled shop had every good cheese imaginable from all over France. As the Dordogne is not milk country, there are no really good cheeses produced there. She told me rue Limogeanne used to be an entirely food street because it didn't get sun and thus was always cool, and in the days before refrigeration this was a great advantage. Then big supermarkets started opening and the small artistic shops were destroyed, so unfortunately it's mostly other shops there now. In next door's cellar at No. 7 the best partridge pâtés in the land were made by Antoine Courtois, the 18th-century caterer. His initials AC are still in the centre of the wrought-iron impost on the door.

A lot of the narrow streets in Périgueux still feel very mediaeval with their large uneven paving stones, small low doors and very narrow steep alleyways secreting their way off them. One can imagine the intrigues that went on. Then again some of the stairwells are so wide, horses could and did get up them. Names tell stories everywhere in France e.g. Ecorneboeuf Hill (*écomer* to break the horns, *boeuf* ox). It was so steep that the oxen used to slip and break their necks. Rue du Calvaire is a steep street the condemned had to walk their last walk up, on their 'road to Calvary' to receive their punishment (lopping off of head).

I met Jean-Louis at Fébus at the end of the day and we went off to see a man about a car. We arrived at a farmhouse, the car was there but the farmer wasn't, so the contact person who lived down the road decided we should all trudge through the fields to find him. I, of course, was suitably dressed in a Jean-Paul Gaultier number and my Robert Clergerie 'most

expensive sandals in the world'. We could see the farmer in
the distance as we went trudge, trudge, trudge. Presently we
were joined by two men in a van who had previously given
us directions. They were concerned about my get-up and
offered me a ride. I was kindly given the front seat and the
boys jumped up on the back bumper. It was thus we arrived
at said farmer – only it was the wrong farmer. They all fell
about at the hilarity of this and good-naturedly we continued
bumping through the fields to the next farmer bringing in
bales of hay on a huge tractor. He and his farmhand stopped
work, everyone descended from the car and the first farmer
turned up to put his tuppence in. Now there were six men
standing in a circle in the middle of a field in the evening
sun earnestly discussing a car. Only the car wasn't for sale
anymore as someone else wanted it.

Jessica, who felt that her brains had temporarily been turned
to mush by motherhood, has always been very well read.
Her house was full of books and every so often she would
wander in to my domain to give me a book that I must just
read a few pages of. She would hover near my laptop with
her large eyes and bee-stung lips and say, 'You know, lots of
farmhouses around here don't even have one book in them
– can you imagine that? She ordered the excellent Granta
books, the latest one being on ambition. Her back catalogue
showed there were lots of collections on travel writing, so I
resolved to add even more weight to my overweight luggage
and buy some when I got back to London. Margaret Atwood,
Lawrence Durrell, Nabokov, Thomas Hardy – they were all
there begging me to stop working and start reading. It was
hard enough to work as it was. My mother sent me an email
saying, 'You seem to be doing a lot of living, dear, but are
you doing any writing?' which made me sit up very straight.
Even my old boyfriend in London called periodically to
check up on me. So touching, really. The only person who

had unconditional faith in me was my editor who knows I've never missed a deadline in my life.

Almost every day the neighbouring farmer would wander up to Jessica's house to pass the time of day and have a few glasses of red. M. Kleber was a kind-hearted man with an accent as thick as porridge with rolled Rs and old-fashioned phrasing. He didn't have grandchildren but wouldn't have minded some. He was always dressed in old pants tied up with a thick belt, old shirt, beret and either what looked like slippers with rubber soles or gumboots. The ruddy, weathered face had a cigarette permanently attached to the bottom lip, a few days' growth and a variety of teeth here and there. The idea of taking a day off was completely foreign to him, and his wife Hortense had never gone further than the village, let alone to a restaurant or the cinema. He could easily polish off a bottle of red in the course of a conversation then go back to his *bêtes* and work for the rest of the day. He was the source of Jessica's good meat and the pears she made purée out of and the peas she shelled for our dinner. When I left he came out of his *champs* to say goodbye. I told him I was going to Cordes-sur-Ciel and of course he had no idea where it was. When I mentioned near Toulouse his eyes opened wide and he said, '*Eh – mais vous n'êtes pas encore arrivée.* (Oh well, you're not there yet.)' Completely adorable. I took a photo of him with glass of wine in hand which he insisted I show to no one – 'Everyone will think I'm an *ivrognard* (pisshead).'

Periodically I called my bank for a financial forecast, I would be depressed for a day then smile bravely through the panic. At these moments I always said to myself, 'That's it, I can't take this artist's life, I can't take the insecurity, if it wasn't for money my life would be heaven on earth, I'm going back to a real job where there are no surprises.' A day later I would say, 'It's all worth it just to be able to write. I'm not dead or in prison yet, nature has mercifully removed the fear of pregnancy, security comes from within, I must continue for the sake of the ordinary people who may never get to make their living by drinking and eating.' Bruce Chatwin called it '*horreur du domicile*', this need to be nomadic that is both a compulsion to wander and a compulsion to return. All human beings have the wandering characteristic genetically inherited from vegetarian primates, just as they have an emotional need for a base or port which comes from carnivores. But a nomad is not a person who wanders aimlessly from place to place; *au contraire*, it is a person who follows prescribed paths, someone who is following a calling, be it professional, spiritual or pastoral. By definition a wanderer is usually poor, as luxury hampers mobility and you can't have both. You can't have an ornate house, silver goblets, social commitments, overindulgence AND freedom, movement and understanding of other cultures and climes. An insatiable lust for gold has ruined many a nomadic tribe.

Pascal said that all man's unhappiness stemmed from a single cause, his inability to remain quietly in a room. We seem to need change as we need the air we breathe, for without it our brains and bodies rot. Encephalographs of travellers' brains show that change stimulates the brain rhythms, bringing a sense of well-being and a purpose in life. I know that if I stay in one place for too long I get tired, irritable and apathetic, and yet as soon as I voyage I feel stimulated, alive, open and much more tolerant than normal. Chatwin said that 'traveling doesn't only broaden the mind, it makes the mind. Deprived of the danger of movement we invent artificial enemies, psychosomatic illnesses, tax-collectors and worst of all, ourselves. Adrenalin is our travel allowance. Drugs are for people who have forgotten how to walk.'

The Saturday before I left Le Breuilh Jessica and I got all scrubbed up, she put on the lipstick I had given her eight years ago and we went out to dinner at a country restaurant called La Metairie, seven kilometres from Les Eyzies at the foot of the Château de Beyssac. The décor was zero but the food was one-star quality at least (without one-star prices) and they also sold regional products like walnut oil, wine and foie gras. Once again it was run by a young couple with a baby and another one on the way, and it was full to overflowing. Jessica knows her local wines well so she ordered half a bottle of white Château de la Jaubertie as an apéritif. Jaubertie is the best of the white Bergeracs and this one had a gorgeous crunchy apple bouquet and managed to taste dry and fruity at the same time. To her it tasted of grapevine flowers and went perfectly with the little dish of melon balls that accompanied it.

I ordered the famous tourin soup to see what all the fuss was about although I would much rather have had the tomatoes stuffed with ratatouille topped with chèvre. I make big sacrifices for the sake of art – but it was worth it. This one was a garlic tourin with the egg white stirred in so that it was in fine filaments through the soup and croûtons were served on the side. Jessica lapped up her *boudin* (black pudding) deep fried in filo pastry with walnut salad and smoked duck breast. We got serious with our red and ordered a *grand vin de Bordeaux*, a Medoc. Nineteen-ninety-four wasn't a great year like 1995 so it's often a good idea to drink such a wine young. It was a risk worth taking because it was not too heavy with lots of personality and went perfectly with the rather refined *navarin printanier* (spring lamb stew). Coffee came with a little plate of mini pastries – cannelés, lemon tarts and madeleines. Somehow we got to the local discothèque afterwards and danced off everything we had eaten.

Provence

BRONWYN AND LESLEY were going to Provence to visit friends so, in the spirit of adventure that comes only with a chauffeur-driven vehicle, I decided to go along. We broke camp at dawn and as Lesley competently slipped us away from the Dordogne towards St-Rémy-de-Provence, I knew I was getting there because the land became drier and browner, the accents changed when we got out for ice-creams, and olive oil replaced cream and fat in the snacks. The day I suggested making mashed potatoes with olive oil instead of butter to my friends in the Dordogne they all jumped back in horror. The fat in which the food of a region is cooked is the greatest shaper of its cuisine, and above everything else, the olive symbolises Provence. You hardly ever see butter in Provence but you do see acres and acres of silver-green olive groves. Man and nature are in very close harmony here, the place is swamped in oil and the people have sleek brown skin, slim bodies and shiny hair. They seem to be jumping out of their skins with *joie de vivre*. Their diet is mostly vegetarian with lots of fish, especially salt cod and anchovies, as well as artichokes, tomatoes, aubergines, garlic, courgettes, fennel, capsicums and lots of spices and herbs like saffron, basil, rosemary, nutmeg and dried orange peel. In Provence they say that a fish is an animal that is found alive in water and dead in olive oil.

It was the middle of June when we arrived in that most

spellbinding of all the provinces in France, so the heat was pleasant but not searing. My first indelible place of residence in Provence, if you call one night in a *chambre d'hôtes* (bed and breakfast) a residence, was at No. 17 Avénue Van Gogh in St-Rémy. Olive trees and rosebushes heralded the entrance. Maggie (85 years old), her husband Elie and her sister Louise (90) run their old family home as a *pension*, with the help of their son André and his wife Martine. Bronwyn and Lesley had become friends with them when they lived in St-Rémy for a year and they all fell into each other's arms with gasps and moist eyes and exclamations. We sat in the cool, dark dining room drinking pastis and catching up. Maggie and Louise spoke Provençal together and when Michèle (my translator friend) found that out later, she said, 'You're crazy not to have recorded them – almost no one speaks that language anymore. When they go, that's the last time you'll ever hear it spoken fluently.' Louise told me about the famous and much loved Provençal poet Frédéric Mistral, born in 1830. He was desperate for the ancient language of the troubadours not to die out so he revived it by only ever writing in it, making sure it was taught in schools and extensively chronicling all the traditions and recipes. There is even a society devoted to him called the Félibrige. I found a very old and highly respected cookbook called *La Cuisinière Provençale* first written in 1910 by J.B. Reboul, reprinted 16 times and still selling. In the first edition Mistral wrote in Provençal:

> *Mi coumplimen e gramaci pèr aquelo edicioun nouvelo de vosto Cousiniero Provençalo, qu'avion déjà sus noste fougueiroun e que rejougnerai dins la biblioutèco dou Muséon Arlaten. A la bono ouro! vivo aquéu libre goustous, que fai veni l'aigo à la bouco e qu'es mai utile segur que li tres quart d'aquéli que fan gemi la presso! ... tant soulamen, à l'edicioun setenco, oublidès pas i' apoundre li noum prouvençau.*

131

Maggie and Louise's family has been in St-Rémy since 1440 so they consider themselves to be *des vrais de vrais*, the real thing. They all had strong Provençal accents, hearing problems and huge hearts. In the kitchen were jars of *lou cachat*, the wonderful marinated goat's cheese which is quite strong but good spread on thick slices of country bread. I was shown up the stairs to my *chambre*, a huge room with two double beds, piano, bathroom and windows opening out to a view of the Alpille hills that Bronwyn was so in love with. The cicadas were singing and *le vent de dame* was blowing, a soft wind that only comes in the evening and only in summer. I spent the next 24 hours wondering why I couldn't stay there forever.

Lou cachat is best made in an earthenware jar but is just as good and very pretty in a glass jar.

Lou Cachet

6 bay leaves dipped in olive oil
6 semi-soft goat cheese rounds
cognac or eau de vie
coarsely ground black pepper
3 sprigs of thyme
3 small sprigs of rosemary

1. Put 3 bay leaves in the bottom of a 2-cup-sized earthenware or glass jar.
2. Press a layer of goat cheese on top. With your finger over the top of the bottle, sprinkle over a little cognac, grind some pepper and place a sprig of thyme and a little sprig of rosemary.
3. Repeat this layering 2 more times, reserving the remaining 3 bay leaves for the top.
4. Leave for at least three days in a cool place, but not the refrigerator. Eat it spread on toast or bread.

That evening we left the folks around their television set and strolled down the road into town to a pretty restaurant in St-Rémy – le Bistrot des Alpilles on the Boulevard Mirabeau. Everyone in Provence drinks rosé so we ordered a St-Rémy rosé and settled down to teasing the staff. We all ordered *artichauts à la barigoule* – a stew of fresh little purple artichokes, thyme, lemon, olive oil, lardons and lettuce. *Barigoule* (from the Provençal *bérigoule*) used to mean mushrooms or artichokes drowned in oil and roasted over the fire but has now come to mean the delicately perfumed dish I found before me. Our waiter was a delightful man who loved being teased and adored the girls' schoolgirl French. They had told me all about the great speciality of the house, *gigot à la ficelle* the woodfire-roasted lamb, so we all ordered it with barely suppressed saliva making our tastebuds hurt. At the far end of the restaurant was a huge open fire with legs of lamb hanging by string (*à la ficelle*) in front of it. When a customer ordered some, it was cut off – rosé, medium or well done – and garnished with sliced, gratinéd potatoes and grilled tomato. Everything in Provence is garnished with grilled tomatoes. This lamb from the Alpilles, the best in Provence, was tender, sweet, aromatic and really tasted of lamb.

Like all exceptional cuisines, southern French food is a result of the various cultures bombarding them or passing through. The Greeks arrived in Provence by boat to found Massalia (Marseille) in 600BC, bringing with them olive trees. When the Romans marched in they called their entry point Olivula, and the area Provincia (Provence), creating some of their greatest cities – Nîmes, Arles and Orange. Roman remains, some of them intact, are to be found all over the south of France. They had a very pungent, unusually spiced cuisine and loved chucking all sorts of mad things together in a way that was quite different from the rest of France. *Anchoïade*, that strong anchovy paste, comes from them, along with drinks made from aniseed (pernod, pastis etc) and mustard seed pastes. Provençal people love eating lots of little vegetable appetisers or even whole meals of little things like the *grand aïoli*, cooked vegetables and salt cod with garlic mayonnaise, a habit brought by the Spanish Moors.

A good restaurant near St-Rémy in the countryside is Le Bistrot du Paradou, where you pay a set price and take what you're given; you must reserve on a Friday because they serve a grand aïoli. Last year when I was there Jean-Louis was behind the bar as usual, his wife was in the kitchen and the waiters' charm was excelled only by their good looks. We were served, in a rather perfunctory way, a plate of little ravioli in tomato sauce, followed by roast lamb, an indifferent cheese platter and a lovely peach tart. The decor is enchanting – stone walls, ancient red and black tiled floor,

---

Le Mauresque

1 shot Pernod or pastis
1 shot *orgeat* or almond syrup
ice cubes
water

Provençal Punch

3 bottles of rosé
500ml cognac
3 oranges cut in half and stuck with six cloves each
1 grapefruit in thick slices
1 split vanilla pod
1 cinnamon stick
200g sugar

Marinate ingredients overnight.

exposed beams, bistrot tables, a well stocked bar and risqué photos on the walls. As is only correct in the south of France, the clientelle smoke cigarettes and cigars all through the meal and men at other tables flirt with you long distance.

Speaking of Moorish influence, there's a wonderful summer cocktail they make called *Le Mauresque*. Another good one is the *Provençal Punch* (see recipes page 134).

Nice joined the House of Savoy in 1388 and stayed Italian until 1860, making their food full of pasta, pesto, pizza and polenta. This is where the *Pissaladière* (see recipe on page 136) comes from – the word comes from *pissala* (fish purée).

The original Provençaux made the olive oil that the world now craves even better than the Greeks did. A real *amateur* will be able to tell you which olive grove his oil comes from, just as a wine expert will tell you what grape a wine is made from just by smelling it. At night the ashen-green leaves and gnarled branches of the groves of old olive trees seem rather magical and macabre. They shiver and whisper eerily in *le vent de dame* that comes down in the moonlight. Like grapevines, olive trees demand very little of their mother soil; they care nothing for conventional beauty; they are like strange gifts in the desert, bearing bitter fruit made heavenly by man. Olive trees can be very old, in fact they are the oldest of humankind's cultivated crops, and the edible olive, *Olea europa*, was grown in Crete in 3500BC. There are actually 50 species of olive, but only one bears useful fruit – and I've eaten at least 3700 of the useful ones. There are trees that are 700 years old, but although they're called immortal, they can be destroyed by unusual cold.

You can get a lot out of an olive tree – you can make soap from it, use the pulp for fertiliser, use the pits for lubricating oil, make salad spoons and bowls from the lovely tight-grained wood as well as the obvious fruit it produces and the oil that fruit makes. I got given a pair of olive-wood spoons

Pissaladière

For the dough:

1 tsp honey or sugar
1 cup warm water
1 tbsp dried yeast or 25g fresh
2 cups (270g) flour
1 tsp salt
olive oil

For the topping:

3 tbsp extra virgin olive oil
2 kg onions sliced into thin rounds
4 large garlic cloves sliced thin
2 sprigs of fresh thyme, finely chopped
20 anchovy fillets
20 black olives, pitted
freshly ground black pepper
baking tray approx 36 x 22cm

1. In a medium-sized bowl, mix together honey, warm water and yeast. Leave to start bubbling – about 10 minutes.

2. Mix in sifted flour and salt. Add more warm water if necessary to make dough fairly sticky. Turn out onto a floured surface and knead for 5 minutes.

3. Oil the bowl, place dough back in, cover with a damp tea towel and leave for an hour to double in volume.

4. In a large frying pan heat oil and throw in onions, garlic and thyme. Cook on a low heat until onions melt into a light, golden colour (about 30 minutes).

5. Make a 'pissala' by grinding 5 of the anchovies and 5 of the olives to a paste with a bit of olive oil in a mortar and pestle. Alternatively, smash with a fork.

6. Turn dough out onto floured surface, punch down, add a flat tsp of the pissala, knead a little and roll out into a square or oblong shape about ½ cm thick or even thinner. Place on an oiled baking sheet.

7. Preheat oven to 200°C. Mix rest of pissala with onions and spread this over dough. Grind on some pepper and sprinkle a bit of fresh thyme. Make a lattice of anchovy fillets, filling the spaces with olives.

8. Bake the pissaladière for about 25 minutes. Cut into oblongs and serve warm or at room temperature.

by a friend in contrition after a fight and will henceforward never be able to use them without thinking of him – which I suppose is exactly what he wanted. An olive-wood salad bowl should be made out of a single piece of root and never be washed (neither should the spoons). You cut and rub garlic around the inside before you make the salad then wipe it after use; the olive oil from the dressing impregnates the wood, ensuring a better salad each time. The finest 'fresh' olive oil is a murky, dense, green liquid that is almost opaque, and that's how the olive growers eat it, as it is fresher and fruitier in flavour. Most consumers who, lets face it, wouldn't know their oil from their face cream, prefer the colour to be clear and filtered. Slightly more informed people like you and me know that there should be a velvety, firm texture to a good olive oil and the colour can be pale green or lemon. The highest quality oil is made from green unripe olives, pressed once without the help of heat or chemicals, resulting in an oleic acid level below one percent. The best, best, *best* way to enjoy olive oil is to take toasted bread, rub on a little garlic, pour on some oil, add sea salt and freshly ground black pepper, close your eyes and eat.

Breakfast in the morning was on the vine-covered terrace, where Maggie served us bread, croissants, poached eggs still warm from the chicken, marmalade, homemade quince jam of which she makes 110kg every year, and tea. Bronwyn and Lesley are completely in love with St-Rémy, so they rushed me around all their favourite places. First I went to the *coiffeuse* and became a natural redhead again, then we walked around the town, down boulevards shaded by plane trees, across pretty squares with fountains, up and down the cobbled alleyways and along its rosemary and thyme-scented streets. I missed the market day, unfortunately, but everyone told me it's one of the loveliest markets in Provence. The square is hung with red, white and blue flags and the colourful stalls burst with all the fine fruit, vegetables and flowers for which this market-gardening area is famous. I did not miss the Souliado shop, however, where I became the proud owner of a traditional blue Provençal shirt with tiny red, yellow and white flowers on it. If I found my way to the Camargue I knew no horse or bull or cowboy could refuse me, so authentic did I look.

Along with their sunny disposition, the southern French are very mañana, mañana and will never die of overwork – as was encapsulated in the hours written up outside the *cordonnier* – I open when I open and I close when I close. I went in to the little shoe repair shop and there were notes stuck all over the mirror saying CLOSED FOR THE DAY, ready for use at the slightest provocation, usually having something to do with bullfights or fishing. I showed my stiletto shoes and explained they needed heeling, a five-minute job. There was no one else in the shop, we had a 10-minute discussion about how difficult the job was, he wrenched the worn plates off the heels, looked at the clock, threw his hands up in the air and said '*Mais, Madame, je ne peux pas les faire tout de suite.* (I can't do them immediately.)'

'*Pourquoi pas?*,' I asked.

'*Il est presque midi et demie. Je ferme jusqu'à deux heures et demie maintenant et j'ai tout ça à faire cet après-midi.* (It's almost 12.30. I close now until 2.30 and I've got all these shoes to do this afternoon.)'

'But you've already taken the plates off. It would take two minutes to nail new ones on.'

'*Hors de question. Pas le temps.* (No way, I don't have time.)' So saying, he shoved the now unwearable shoes back in my hands and shut the shop.

People feel very passionate about the Alpilles, this series of low limestone hills that rise abruptly between Avignon and Arles and border St-Rémy. Mysterious and eerie in any light, these hills seem to be papered in silver and imparting secrets to those who are in their thrall. In the daytime the arid crags bleached white by the searing sun are a great place to have a picnic. The lower slopes are spread with olive and almond trees, sometimes Cyprus and pines, but basically it's rock and scruffy bushes, not the greatest place to place your posterior but one must suffer for the sake of beauty, as my mother always said. Even a city girl like moi can get prickles where God never intended, so quite frankly the best part was after our picnic when we picked the wild Provençal herbs that grow all over the hills. That's one of the reasons the merino sheep grazed on the Alpilles taste so good – they eat marjoram, thyme, rosemary and savoury all day.

The sun ensured Provence became a land of painters, some indigenous and some immigrant, attracted to it by the extraordinary luminous light. Cézanne was born there. Renoir put the rosy light he found in Cagnes-sur-Mer into his paintings. Gertrude Stein spent lots of time there talking in circles, as was her wont, Nostradamus was born there, Picasso lived there, as did Matisse who came down from the north. Vincent van Gogh spent the last year of his genius life there . . . and I would like to spend the rest of my humble little life there, but not in the same lodgings as poor Vincent. We drove past pure Van Gogh country – yellow fields full of sunflowers, mauve fields full of lavender, blood-red poppies and wild irises speckling the roadside and olive groves. The buildings are in perfect harmony with their environment, specifically the traditional Provençal *mas* or whitewashed, low, stone farmhouses with red roofs and varying shades of blue shutters, clinging close to the earth. And everywhere it is dry and hot – not unlike Greece in fact.

We visited the lodgings of poor Vincent at the St-Paul-de-Mausole mental asylum. It's a lovely place to stay if you are ill or need a rest, and the Romanesque cloisters by the little 12th-century church are gorgeous – columns carved with plants, animals and masks and overflowing with flowers. In May 1889 Vincent committed himself there and embarked on the greatest artistic output of his life, wandering around the nearby fields, observing life in the hospital, creating self-portraits – more than 100 drawings and 150 paintings, exploding with light, in one year. Then he left, went to Auvers, couldn't stand the torture of schizophrenia any more and shot himself. When you look at the fields of sunflowers and think of his paintings, so hallucinogenic in their colours, you feel like weeping. The light in Provence really is inebriating – unique in its brilliance, clarity and luminosity. The sunsets are searing pink and electric orange and the nights are deep purple/blue.

My friends Frédéric and Kathryn, who live in Auxerre, were holidaying nearby at Châteauneuf-de-Gadagne and had invited me to visit. They arrived to pick me up resplendent with sunburns and smiles. Tall, French, dark-haired Frédéric was dressed in blue with sandals, and small, blonde, fair Kathy from New Zealand in a white skirt with big red roses and white sandshoes. Frédéric is everything a girl needs in a

Quince Paste

2 kg quinces
sugar

Rub the down off the quinces with a cloth and stick them, as is, in a large ovenproof dish. Cover the dish and place in a low-heat oven until they are soft, then core the fruit and slice them without peeling. Purée the fruit in a food processor, weigh it and add the same amount of sugar. Boil it up in a preserving pan, stirring constantly with a long wooden spoon (boiling sugar is hot, hot, hot). It is ready when the paste starts to caramelise and pull away from the pan. Remove the pan from the heat and keep stirring until the paste has cooled down. Ladle it into shallow containers like jelly-roll tins. The next day, place the tins of paste in a warming oven or on the lowest possible temperature of the oven for a few hours until it has dried out. Cut the paste into whatever shape you like – in the south of France it is usually cut in little oblongs. Keep it in a paper-lined cake tin.

man: funny, attentive, a marvel with his hands which always seem to be far from their correct place – and married.

'*Bonjour ma vieille. Il y a Jean-Marie en Bourgogne qui m'ont demandé de te culbuter dans l'herbe.* (Jean-Marie in Burgundy has asked me to romp in the hay with you.)'

'*Merci*, Frédo. How kind of Jean-Marie to think of me so.'

Kathy is the perfect wife for him. She smiles sphinx-like, is almost always calm in contrast to his emotionality, and is quietly capable. We all sat on Maggie's terrace drinking cool sparkling peach wine and nibbling on *pâte de coings* (quince paste). Quince paste (see recipe opposite) and *marmelade* are very popular in Provence – in fact the word marmelade comes from the Portuguese name for quince, marmelo. In concocting the marmelade, the skin and pips are used to make the base (jelly-like syrup), in which the sliced fruit is then cooked.

As we drove along I said I had all sorts of plans for things I wanted to do, and Frédéric said very clearly, 'We are doing nothing, we are going nowhere, we are exhausted. If you want to go somewhere – drive yourself. By the way, that's your room up there.' He pointed to a castle turret on the top of a hill. Very funny, I thought – until I got there. They hadn't mentioned that they were staying in the château of Châteauneuf-de-Gadagne. The view from the terrace was of poplars with birds in them, rosemary bushes, then the pretty little village with its pale yellow houses and ochre or blue shutters. The earthy red and mustard-coloured houses in Provence come from one of its most important products – the mining and treatment of ochre. This iron ore is a mixture of argillaceous sand and iron oxide which, after washing, filtering and drying, is cut into blocks. Once dried, the blocks are crushed and again sifted and sometimes baked to deepen the colour to give that orangey-red look. Below the village in the distance lay the picturesque Luberon mountains.

The château had been divided into three apartments, one on the ground floor and two up top and because of the steepness of the property there was a lot of privacy with a swimming pool, garden, rough tennis court and terrace on the lower level and the same on the upper level. Frédéric and Kathy had rented the ground floor, which had originally been the guards' quarters, stretching the length of the château. The apartment itself was nothing short of luxurious with its huge living area graced by engraved archways, antique furniture, *fresques* on the stone walls, beautiful paintings and plush carpets throughout. At one end was a *Côté Sud* (up-market decorating magazine) bedroom with en suite and salon, and at the other end another large bedroom. There was another bathroom, a bedroom upstairs, and all was graciousness and elegance. Next to the château was a church whose bells rang every hour all day and all night right next to my bedroom, I was to find out. I sat down and said, 'Bring me my Pernod immediately *s'il vous plaît.'*

To my delight Frédéric's sister Bénédicte, her consort Alain and brand new baby Louisa were also visiting from Marseilles for a few days. Béné is a raven-haired beauty with a voluptuous mouth and stunning dark eyes who has found herself the man of her dreams and now she not only makes television documentaries, she makes dear little babies. We all thoroughly approve of Alain, who is the curator of the African and Pacific Art Museum in Marseille. He is a large-boned, patrician-looking man; urbane, relaxed and jolly good company. Also he has a deep voice. One can't really go past a man with a deep voice, can one?

Frédéric and I sat on the steps made of old millstones going down to the swimming pool and sipped Côtes du Rhône rosé while Kathy did something gratiné with courgettes, Alain slept and Béné fed the baby. Dinner was courgettes with Nîmes olives marinated in garlic and basil, *merguez* (spicy red Moroccan sausages), sweet grated carrot salad with olive oil and lemon juice, *saucisson, jambon de Parme* and cheeses.

The next day I bought some *morue* (dried salt cod) to make a grand aïoli and put it to soak in milk and water for 24 hours, then looked around for a good market. Upon enquiry we were told about a night *marché agricole* in a village called Velleron, 3km from Isle-sur-la-Sorgue. Every evening except Sunday and Monday, from 6 p.m. onwards, the local farmers lay out their rustic produce from the backs of their trucks and vans; since they don't weigh anything, you can't buy two tomatoes – you have to buy a minimum of a kilo, or the whole box. This was the market of my dreams and it was cheap – a real farmers' market where the vegetables still had the good Provençal soil on them, fruit was still pulsing from being plucked off the tree, tomatoes were still attached to their vines and smelling sweet and acid, and hand-pressed olive oil could be appreciated by the spoon. Everyone was very friendly and an air of happiness and festivity prevailed. The accents came thick and fast and I couldn't stop imitating them. The garden strawberries so dark they're almost black and you want to inhale them instantly; the tiny *ratte* potatoes that look like a box of warts but taste like firm chestnuts; the bunches of garden flowers; the gypsy with the handmade baskets; the stalls of marmalade and jam; the hillocks of little violet-purple artichokes that are hard to find anywhere else; the courgettes with their flowers attached; all sorts of wild mushrooms; and the baskets of dried lime leaves for tea. I loved this market with its warm-hearted people, and Frédéric almost had to pry me away with a crowbar. My red basket was so full you could only see my hair over the top when I held it in my arms.

On our way home past orchards of lime trees we rewarded ourselves with a *pastis* at the Café de France in Isle-sur-la-Sorgue. This chic café is under the trees right next to the church on Place de le Liberté, and because we were charmed, a jazz band started up as we arrived. Isle-sur-la-Sorgue is an arty, hip town, famous not only for the beauty of the River Sorgue embracing it with its arms and the avenues lined with plane trees, but for having the best antiques fair in France. Experts and amateurs come from all over France and the world to shop in this sunny town where the sky is almost always pure blue and the people naturally gay. Of course our life revolved around food. Dinner was courgette flowers stuffed with mushrooms and ham by Frédéric and Kathy, ratatouille and barbecued T-bone by Alain, nothing by Béné except mother's milk for Louisa, nothing by me – far too busy floating in the swimming pool; washed down

---

Courgette Flowers Stuffed with Fish Mousse

Serves 4

16 courgette flowers

For the stuffing:
4 slices white bread, crusts cut off
100ml milk
500g firm white fish fillets
300ml cream
1 tbsp pastis or aniseed-flavoured alcohol
1 tsp sea salt
freshly ground black pepper
½ tsp freshly ground nutmeg
grated parmesan cheese

1. Soak the bread in milk.
2. Cut fish up and place in food processor with all the other ingredients. Blend until very smooth.
3. Remove pistils from flowers then spoon in generous amounts of the stuffing. Tuck in the ends and lay flowers side by side in a large steamer.
4. Steam for 10 minutes and serve with grated parmesan.

with a red from the Châteauneuf-de-Gadagne vineyard of Domaine Deforge. Dessert was strawberries, red currants marinated in wine and sugar, green figs, wild cherries and orange melons washed down with the sunset. Honestly, I was pooped afterwards. When I suggested a walk they all looked at me as if I had just said I had an incurable disease – a combination of disbelief, pity and confusion.

Alain loves cooking and reeled off some of his favourite dishes, the hands down one being the startlingly grisly *Pieds et Paquets*, a Marseillais speciality of sheep's tripe and feet. When you mention this old-fashioned dish to Marseillais they faint with pleasure just at the name.

To make the *paquets* (packets) you stuff minced salt pork, mutton fat, garlic and parsley into tripe and sew it up. Then you get your *pieds* (feet) and cook them in a big pot in bacon, stock, white wine, tomatoes and vegetables with the packets on top, for six or seven hours in the embers of the fire. You'll know when the feet are cooked because the bones will fall out. For the finishing touches you discard the bones, add a little butter and flour, some egg yolks, a bit of cream and lemon juice. You make this dish for a Marseillais man and you have him for life.

It's very hard to get the growers not to whip the flowers off courgettes for some reason, but in Provence they understand about such things.

Speaking of flowers, you can also cook with the carpets of lavender you see all over Provence. You can make lavender ice cream, flavour honey with it, perfume sauces with it and cook fruit in it. For the ice cream, make up a regular *crème anglaise* infused with lavender (see page 146).

Over the course of 24 hours I had been changing the milk and water the morue was soaking in several times in preparation for the grand aïoli. It's actually a better idea to soak this extremely salty fish in dribbling water all day then poach it in fresh water or stock and herbs. Grand aïoli is one

Lavender Ice Cream

500ml milk
6 sprigs of English lavender
100g sugar
8 egg yolks

Combine milk (infused with lavender), sugar and egg yolks. Strain the lavender out then churn in an ice-cream maker or pour into a container, cover and freeze. When it's half frozen, take it out and stir well, then refreeze. Repeat this process twice before letting it set hard.

Pears in White Wine and Lavender

1 bottle of white wine
3 tbsp Poire William (pear liqueur)
thinly pared peel of a lemon and an orange
half a vanilla pod split open
2 tbsp black peppercorns
six English lavender heads
5 tbsp lavender honey
3 bay leaves
1 cinnamon stick
6 peeled pears
2 tbsp lavender petals

In a large pot combine wine, pear liqueur, lemon and orange peel, vanilla pod, peppercorns, lavender heads, honey, bay leaves and cinnamon. Bring to the boil and gently simmer pears in this mixture for about 10 minutes. Remove pears and reduce syrup by hard-boiling to two-thirds its volume. Strain, pour the syrup over the fruit and decorate with lavender petals and some of the strained solids like the cinnamon stick, some peel and peppercorns.

of my favourite dishes and they eat it like mad all over the Mediterranean. This one was made with the products of the *marché agricole*.

Grand Aïoli

There is nothing more I can say about that heavenly, golden, glistening triumph – aioli – that hasn't been chanted by every other cook before me. It is a great carrier – you can add all sorts of herbs, spices and ingredients and it adds light and happiness to almost everything except sweets.

Serves 6

6 big cloves of garlic, chopped
½ tsp sea salt
2 egg yolks
1 tsp Dijon mustard
500ml extra virgin olive oil or ½ olive and ½ vegetable oil
juice of 1 lemon
warm water

1. Mash the garlic and salt together with a mortar and pestle.
2. Stir in the egg yolks and mustard with the pestle, then gradually add the oil drop by drop.
3. When half the oil is in, add a little lemon juice and warm water and continue the stream of oil, stirring with the pestle until all is incorporated. Alternatively, make it with an electric beater or food processor. You may add more salt or lemon juice to taste.

Note: If it curdles, throw in an ice-cube and beat like mad. If that doesn't work, take a clean bowl and crack an egg yolk into it. With the hand beater, gradually add in the turned mayonnaise.

For the accompaniments:

- 1kg morue (dried salt cod): Soak morue in frequently changed water for 24 hrs. Trim off any bones and skin and poach until just cooked in milk, water and bouquet garni
- Heat 24 snails in stock for five mins
- Boil 12 baby artichokes whole until just soft
- Boil 12 whole carrots until al dente
- Cut 12 tomatoes into wedges
- Hard-boil 6 eggs and halve

cont.

- Cut 6 fennel bulbs in half and boil until al dente
- Boil 600g green beans until al dente
- Boil 12 small waxy potatoes until soft
- Boil 12 small courgettes until al dente

To serve:
Place the bowl of aioli in the centre of a large platter and arrange all the other food – warm or at room temperature – around it.

I insisted Bronwyn and Lesley participate in the farmers' market at Velleron and they were charmed. We pored over the cheese stands that sold homemade *brousse* – a type of *fromage frais* (unripened cheese), quite sour and salty and good with spring onions dipped into it. The word *brousser* means to beat or stir in Provençal. This cheese is made by beating the curd before it is drained into plastic cones about 9cm high. It used to be called *fromage frais de corne*, as it was poured into sheep's horns. There were other sweeter, milder fromages frais in their little pots with the liquid running out the bottom, great with lavender honey or quince jam. *Banons* – little chèvres wrapped in chestnut leaves that have been soaked in eau-de-vie and attached with raffia – were there. This mountain cheese made in the village of Puimichel is a real treat because it takes on the colour and aroma of the leaf as it ripens. There were heart-shaped fresh goat cheeses, *faisselles* – fresh goat cheese made by draining the curd in a *faisselle* (basket), and big pots of thick *crème fraîche* begging to be married with grilled vine peaches. *Gardians* are little fresh cheeses made either from ewe's or cow's milk, sprinkled with pepper and *herbes de Provence* and decorated with bay leaves. You could spend your life just tasting all the different cheeses in France, never mind anything else.

As if they were meant to be side by side, the onion stand next door sold *Simiane* or new onions, *Lezignans* – the sweet, giant spring onions, and the prized grey shallots. There were stand-up bunches of end-of-season white asparagus, huge bunches of *glaïeuls* (gladioli), fresh almonds, live trout, plucked pigeons and beetroot (almost always sold cooked in French markets). A rough couple, purple-faced from alcohol and happy as pigs in shit, sold me what they called a grey truffle. It was the size of a baby's fist and smelled and looked like a truffle except for the colour. It tasted really good for a second-class truffle. I took it everywhere with me for the next few days and shaved or thinly sliced it onto pasta and scrambled eggs. My bag smelled of it, my pocket knife smelled of it and every food it touched was blessed by its earthy taste.

I called my friend Amanda and her teenage son Piers who had rented a flat up the tree-lined road in Aix-en-Provence for a few months.

'Darling hello, *bonjour* and *comment ça va?*' came the dulcet, laughing tones of the only woman I know who has driven into her restaurant on a motorbike, dressed in nothing but a black corset and fishnet stockings. 'When are you coming to see us?'

'On Saturday.'

'Great. I'll come and pick you up.'

That evening my hosts said actually Friday would be more convenient. Fine. Next day they said Saturday morning would be just as convenient. Fine. The next day Friday was more convenient again. Fine. It turned into a big fight, which was when I got the olive spoons. I was slightly relieved when a vision of azure blue and sunflower yellow wolf-whistled down to the swimming pool at us from the ramparts.

'Hello darling! Bloody hopeless instructions. I've been turning in circles for half an hour.'

'How ghastly. Take your clothes off immediately and jump in the pool,' I cried, hugging her voluptuous form ebulliently.

Amanda introduced herself to everyone then stripped off talking non-stop, leaving nothing but her curly blonde hair clipped on top of her head with purple bulldog clips, lots of blue eyeliner, blue mascara, pink lipstick, dangly earrings and an all-over tan. For the rest of our time together, I never saw her without this makeup. She even wore it in the swimming pool. She even wore it in bed. She especially wore it at the market, and combined with her outrageous student French and big blonde good looks, caused a riotous reaction from all the male stallholders. I sensed that Frédéric and Kathy's mouths were open so I didn't look too closely in their direction. They kindly provided cool drinks on a tray.

We said our farewells to Frédéric and Kathy, lugged my heavy suitcase into the car and set off for Aix. Now the thing about Aix-en-Provence, well one of the things, well actually the only gastronomic thing worth its sugar is the almond and melon paste sweetmeat called *calissons*. When spotted – and it isn't hard in Aix as they're sold in fancy *confiseries* all along the Cours Mirabeau – these almond-shaped delicacies must be consumed immediately. They melt in the mouth like a compliment on a bad hair day. One mustn't save them for a special occasion; as in Provence, *life* is a special occasion, if you'll pardon the violins. As I wrote this I was sitting tapping at my laptop in Amanda's dining room in Aix surrounded by loud visitors, food cooking, corks popping off rosé and red wine bottles, her bunny hopping and the neighbour's cat whingeing. But back to *calissons*, which have been made in Aix since the 1500s. The Aixois have had years of practice at these things, centuries in fact, and they're so good they have an appellation contrôlée, just like wine. At A La Reine Jeanne at No 36 Cours Mirabeau, five generations of the same family have been ceaselessly at it. Provence produces the best almonds in Europe and they even sell them fresh in the markets. You crack them open with your teeth, peel the thick outer layer off and sink your teeth into the soft, delicate nut.

Quite unlike dried almonds – a much more subtle taste.

Amanda and Piers had decided to spend a year in France and were renting a small flat just outside Aix in St Marc Jaumegarde. It was a large property called Le Petit Prignon, with sprawling grounds and a good-size swimming pool. The proprietors, Josette and Pierre Peignier, never used the pool because the water was far too cold, sunbathing was for the birds and exercise for losers. They thought Amanda was mad to swim all those lengths every day. They lived in the big house and were very tolerant of all the noise that came from the visitor's apartments, but Josette did put her foot down when Piers announced he was going to spend the night in the garden shed with two of his French friends (never mind the fact that I was already in there). Already she thought it very eccentric that a foreign writer preferred to sleep in a shed than in the overcrowded flat, but 14-year-old boys who might smoke God knows what or burn the place down or worse, was more than she could accept. Josette also accepted the pretty beige and cream rabbit Amanda and Piers bought at the market to save it from the stew pot. It lived mostly in the bathroom but did promenade in the flat, as it quickly figured out how to open the bathroom door. I have to say it's very strange to have a bunny nibbling your toes while you're having a spiritual experience on the toilet.

Amanda was unable to travel lightly at the best of times but why anyone would encumber themselves with bunnies, huge antique tea makers, fleamarket purchases, crockery and 3600 earrings and necklaces was beyond me. Books, thick jumpers in 30 degree heat, shoes, lipstick and the entire bathroom cabinet I can understand, but the rest, no. Most of us are more endearing for our vices than for our virtues, however, and Amanda's vices were so much fun, she hardly needed virtues. Every morning she took Piers to school, where he was a big hit not only for his beauty and gentle personality but for his foreignness. What he didn't learn in the classroom he learned in his extracurricular activities. The girls loved his pidgin French and introduced him to the delights of French manhood (everyone knows a bed is the best place to learn a language), and I would say it's a year of his life he will never forget. After dropping Piers off, Amanda then trotted off to the gym, a building whose doors I refused to darken, while I investigated Aix.

This stunningly elegant and aristocratic town is an intellectual and academic centre, teeming with people and cars on market days, three times a week. I became fond of Les Deux Garçons café on the Cours Mirabeau, where I often had coffee in the 18th-century surroundings, once the rendezvous for artists and writers. I imagined Cézanne and Emile Zola sipping *citron pressé* next to me.

All the street names are in two languages, French and Provençal, and the footsteps of Paul Cézanne are marked on the pavement. Cézanne was born there and if you look at his paintings you can see what Aix and the surrounding countryside is like, with its soft, vibrant light, shimmering shadows and luminous colour. The main avenue, the Cours Mirabeau, is probably the most beautiful street in France, like the Champs Elysées was before McDonald's and car showrooms – wide, completely shaded from the Provençal sun by huge plane trees and café awnings, expensive and desperately fashionable. It is a city of fountains and you hear water dribbling everywhere – there are even fountains all the way up the middle of the Cours Mirabeau. The Aixois are good-looking, well-oiled, tanned people who ooze chic and patrician confidence. They are a pleasure to watch as they saunter by in designer striped T-shirts, short shorts, painted toenails, Issey Miyake sunglasses, linen pants, a days growth and little dogs on leashes. The Cours begins with a large, pretentious fountain called the Rotonde and is surrounded by boulevards, squares and pedestrian streets. As it's very touristy, the designer clothing shops are fabulous and the restaurants are terrible by and large. One thing they do do well everywhere in Provence is real pizzas with their thin crispy bases, half-moon shape and sparse but intense toppings.

Amanda (in France they call her A-MON-da with longing in their voices) joined me to hit the *marchés*. Like me, she and Piers loved markets just because they existed; and Aix is really spoiled for them – you can't see the town for the *foule* (crowd). There is a fruit and vegetable market everyday at Place Richeime, plus on Tuesday, Thursday and Saturday there is a big market complete with clothes, bric-à-brac, meat and fish at Place des Prêcheurs, a flower market at Place de l'Hôtel de Ville and a *marché aux puces* at Place de Verdun. Finding a market in Aix is like finding an elephant in a telephone booth. Markets in the Dordogne are almost staid, dull affairs next to Aixois markets, partly because the produce is not the same and partly because the regional personality is so completely different. Provençal markets are dazzlingly colourful, exotic and energetic, pregnant with glorious bright flowers, every coloured capsicum, marinated sardines, salt cod, huge slabs of tuna, green and yellow courgettes, *anchoïade*, thirty kinds of olive, braids of garlic, hessian bags full of spices, madder-coloured tomatoes, black grapes, erotic figs split open for all the world to see and baby artichokes, so good you can eat them raw. And refrigeration *à la provençale* – farm chickens and guinea hens sitting on trays of ice-cubes in a glass case. Southern people laugh a lot and make a lot of noise. They're very strong-willed and assertive in a positive way, flirtatious and engaging. They yell at you from one side of the market to the other to come and buy their rabbits. You can't just quietly buy your stuff; you have to talk, tell jokes, argue about the price, complain, pretend you're at a party and even sing.

To prove that the French will eat everything on an animal, bird or fish, in his regular food column in the *Figaro* newspaper, chef Joël Robuchon started in on tuna. They eat a lot of tuna in the south – in *tartare*, grilled on vine twigs, fresh in *salade nicoise* and medium rare like steaks. The thing he really lamented about tuna was it was hard to get hold of the guts to cook, because they're emptied at sea. What happens at sea is the *tripes* (intestines) are cleaned with sea grass and washed with sea water, then blanched in boiling water. They are cooked with carrots, clove-studded onions, bouquet garni, salt, pepper, a chilli pepper, white wine and water. Three hours later, you block your nose, lift the lid off and throw in a glass of rum. Have a glass yourself to recover and after another 45 minutes, your delicious meal is ready. At this point I would jump off the boat and swim home, but there you have it – there's naught like folk. Joël Robuchon loves it.

Amanda had been invited to a party in Lyon so we made a huge platter of *crudités* (raw vegetables) and drove up on a Sunday morning. We raced past Montélemar and poked our tongues out at the smoke pouring from the nuclear plant chimneys. I was wearing my blue Souliado shirt and the-most-expensive-Robert-Clergerie-sandals-in-the-world and Amanda was weighed down with three kilos of lead mail in the form of a silver trinket necklace and bracelet, huge rings and a huge gold and silver watch that had everything on it but the family yacht. The blue eyeliner was on, both underneath and on top, lollypop-pink lipstick, tight, low-cut stretch top, blue leggings, red fingernails and heat-rollered curls. We arrived at her friends Ginette and Patrick's house on the outskirts of Lyon, to find a garden party in full swing. Amanda made a huge entrance then went off to change into something more comfortable, saying, 'I have to wear something outrageous. They expect it of me, darling – I have a reputation to uphold.' She emerged draped in a red handkerchief dress and vest that covered approximately nothing – and we're not talking stick-woman territory here, we're talking Mae West. I felt like the plain makeup assistant.

It was drizzling, so the food and wine was spread out on three long tables set up in the open-plan lounge and dining rooms. All this, in spite of the fact they had been up until three that morning at a wedding. Nothing prevents a party in France. Ginette welcomed me like a long-lost sister and introduced me to everyone. Lyon is the gastronomic centre of France in traditional terms and they do not consider themselves to be Burgundian, either in cuisine or wines. They drink Côtes du Rhône and eat Lyonnaise. We sat down after drinks and everyone, six people to the west and six to the east, set about giving me the names of their favourite restaurants in Lyon that I had to try. Everyone was smoking. The lunch was not Lyonnaise but a mixture of dishes everyone had contributed. We started with *taboulé* with shrimps in it, pasta salad and our crudités. I had made an aïoli which everyone lamented didn't have half enough garlic in it. The second course was a crab flan with paprika mayonnaise made by a very attractive woman whose husband was being distracted by Amanda. This was followed by a roast leg of pork with a strange chutney and rice. The cheeses were a *régal* (treat), with a Spanish version of a Comté called Manchego after La Mancha, brought by Ginette's Spanish sister and brother-in-law; a creamy *Bleu de Bresse*, a cow's milk *Saint-Marcellin* and a *Chaource*. Saint-Marcellin is a mild, acidic, slightly salty cheese from the Rhône-Alps which can be eaten right from fresh to robust and dry. If you're lucky you can find *Le Pitchou*, an artisanal speciality made by marinating Saint-Marcellin in grapeseed oil with herbes de Provence.

Someone had contributed a bottle of Crozes-Hermitage from the Braconnes vineyard, so I stayed close to it. This provoked the crab flan's husband to wax lyrical about wines and housework, one of which he got right and one of which he got wrong.

'There are two wines that have marked my life – a Condrieu which was paradise and a Bourgueil that I could fall in love with, but not necessarily take to bed.'

'So you're a romantic,' I said. 'A place for everything and everything in its place.'

'Yes, I suppose so. For example, my wife knows about food and I know about wine. My wife looks after me and I work. She loves doing housework but I find I do it better.'

'*Vraiment?*' I said, feeling little pins coming out from behind my eyes. 'How fascinating.' Even then, he couldn't sense the danger.

'*Oui.* I like to do it occasionally and I do a much better job.'

'If women only had to do housework occasionally, I'm sure they also would find they like it.' Finally his hackles rose to meet mine.

'*Bon.* We'll change the subject, shall we?'

'Some cherries. Monsieur?' I smiled, passing over the ripe, yellow fruit. There were also a selection of *clafoutis* (cherry flans), very appreciated in France at this cherry time of year. A clafoutis is simple to make and it's essential to leave the stones in the cherries. Just as meat has more taste cooked on the bone, so do fruits cooked on the pip, so to speak. With the help of a ladder, climb to the top of the cherry tree and pick the blackest, ripest ones. Once on terra firma put about 500g cherries in a shallow, buttered baking dish. Make a batter by sifting 30g flour and a pinch of salt into a bowl then add 60g sugar. Beat in four eggs one by one, along with 600ml milk, then beat in another two egg yolks for good measure. Strain this mixture over the cherries and whack at least four tablespoons of kirsch or cognac on top. Bake the clafoutis in a moderate oven for about three quarters of an hour or until golden and puffy, then sprinkle with sugar and eat warm or at room temperature. Some people also make clafoutis with apricots, plums and prunes.

After lunch there was coffee, which is always black in France ... and a knees-up, of course. I sang a few Piaf songs, out came the accordion, someone sat down at the piano and soon the whole place was dancing in the sunshine splintering through the rain. We were to be lodged chez Maurice and Françoise, other friends of Amanda's, so we left our things at their place and followed them on a tour of Lyon by night. Amanda has known them for years and talks about Maurice as if he were Mother Teresa and Pavarotti rolled into one, which of course he is. A more hospitable and social creature than Maurice has rarely been created, and someone more in love with Lyon must surely be hard to find. Fit, good-looking and silver-haired with sparkling blue eyes, he is a consummate guide/*gourmand*/*bon vivant* and deeply knowledgeable about his region. Old Lyon is very beautiful at night and Maurice knows all the nooks and crannies. The idea was to stay the night and drive back to Aix and Piers the next morning, but Françoise said it was out of the question to leave Lyon, the gastronomic centre of France, without her making a special lunch for us.

Even though Lyon has the reputation of being the *je ne sais quoi* of the eater's realm, there are those who say the food is élitist – in other words, the only people who can afford it are the very bourgeois population who live there. They also say it's hearty rather than graceful, lacking a little in imagination and spirit, and liver-destroying in its richness. Well they've got all those crowds of cows – they have to do something with the cream. The Lyonnais are well known for turning a simple chicken into a cholesterol assault of cream, truffles, Madeira, sweetbreads and butter. Françoise was a typical Lyonnais cook in her deep belief that guests would starve to death if not fed enormous amounts of food, but she had a light hand and made traditional dishes her own by adapting them to her particular style.

At 8 a.m. the next morning there was a call from a

journalist to interview me. Sarah-Kate Lynch said she had spent the last three days calling all over France to find me and this was her last phone call. If I wasn't there she was going to write a story about all the interesting people she had talked to and how she couldn't find me. She called Paris and got transferred to Marseilles, got snapped at by Michèle who told her to call my editor who gave her Bronwyn and Lesley's number in Dordogne. She had a creative conversation with the French floor-layer at the presbytery who told her to call back. Bronwyn gave her Amanda's number in Aix. Piers answered the phone and gave her Maurice's number. As I was asleep during the interview I had no idea what I said until someone sent me the article a month later, distinguished by a dreadful photograph. When my French friends saw it they screamed, 'How is it possible that they would print such a revolting, unflattering photo of you? And why would they do it – don't you have any control over what's printed?' The story was very good and I used to get upset about bad photos but it is such a regular occurrence that I don't care anymore. One gets over vanity remarkably quickly when one is terribly brainy.

After breakfast Amanda and I continued our tour of Lyon with Maurice, arriving home at lunch time to find Françoise resplendent in a blue and green dress, her blonde curls combed and red lipstick shining, the kitchen window thrown open and freshly cooked artichoke hearts cooling on the sill. If Maurice was the consummate guide, Françoise was the consummate cook. Baking smells embraced us, the long dining-room table was set formally for eight people and drinks were served with *taramasalata* (fish roe purée) and warm blinis in the sun room. Ginette, her Spanish sister Huguette, Huguette's husband Carlos and Maurice and Françoise's daughter joined us for what they call there *kir Bocuse* (champagne and raspberry liqueur). Maurice and Françoise make it with their own fortified raspberry wine from their homegrown raspberries. You marinate equal quantities of red wine and raspberries together for 48 hours, filter the juice through muslin and weigh it. Add the same weight in sugar, boil together for three minutes and pour into wine bottles. Out the back there was a veritable market garden full of vegetables, fruits, berries and flowers, a rabbit hutch which Amanda walked quickly past, and cascading grapevines.

The table was set with an embroidered cloth and a Juliénas was poured into etched glasses to keep us alive until the first course arrived. Steaming *quenelles* were brought in, sitting in a sauce of tomatoes, olives and *chanterelles*, and the silver cutlery scooped them up into our eager mouths. Maurice uncorked a St Joseph white to go with this. Quenelles are a sort of cooked pike mousse in the shape of little footballs, a great Lyonnais speciality. The most famous of Lyonnais cooks, La Mère Brazier, who died in 1977, gives a recipe for quenelles. In her typical bossy manner she starts off by saying its almost impossible to make good quenelles by hand and you would be much better off buying some from a specialist shop where they know what they're doing. Failing that, if you really want to know, they're made from milk, flour, butter, pike flesh, eggs, nutmeg and salt and pepper. Normally they're warmed up in a creamy mushroom sauce or sometimes a *sauce américaine* with bits of lobster in it. La Mère says quenelles won't wait. They expand when reheated in their sauce so, like a soufflé, everyone must be seated and ready to eat. None of this 'the customer is right' nonsense – although I have to say, that's a bit unfair on my part. La Mère Brazier was famous for doing her quenelles again from scratch if the customer wasn't at the sliver of readiness, to make sure they ate perfection.

I told the saga of Sarah-Kate finally finding me in a strange house with people I didn't know, which provoked lots of telephone-calls-in-impossible-situations stories from around the table. The best came from Carlos, an airline pilot who was a fighter pilot at the time. He was on holiday skiing in the mountains, did not wish to be contacted, had not left a number and was miles from civilisation. When he was out on the slopes one day, alone in the middle of nowhere, an employee from the nearest town skied down to him, gave him a cellphone and said, 'It's for you.' The moral of the story being – if someone really wants to get hold of you, they will. If they don't, they won't. Carlos, a rather conservative serious man, was undergoing a happy transformation with the wine and loved saying my name. He never called me Peta but always Peta MAA-thee-aas because he liked it. He spoke a little English and no French so Huguette patiently did a lot of translating. When he found out I was writing a book about France he insisted I call it *Libros Vivientes de Peta MAA-thee-aas* (The Living Book of Peta Mathias). In exchange for this title and anything I might say about him, he wished 50 percent in royalties. I could see how the guy became a fighter pilot but informed him that as I only got 10 percent myself, I would be impressed if he got more.

The next course was a green salad. Sitting on it were warm slices of pistachio, Lyonnais sausage, warm chicken sausage and the artichoke hearts filled with foie gras. We all gasped in admiration and nodded willingly to the 1978 Medoc from Château Patache d'Aux that Maurice had dragged out of the *cave*. He said it had no thighs but a nice dress. I could relate to the dress part. With the help of the Médoc, soon invitations were coming thick and fast.

'You have to come to Florence with us.'

'You have to come and stay with us in Spain.'

'You have to come to Beaujolais with us.'

'You have to come to Turkey with us.'

The third course was little *ratte* potatoes that had been safe in their soil only hours beforehand. They had been quietly sautéing away in the kitchen, talking to themselves. That's what's so brilliant about the way they eat in France. They're capable of serving up potatoes on their own as a separate course just because they're so good. I looked at Amanda enjoying life as is her wont, and wondered how on earth she was going to drive to Aix after all this consumption. The cheeses were served with a Cahors from Domaine de Lavaur, at which point Carlos suddenly jumped up, threw himself to the other end of the table and gave his dark-haired, dark-eyed wife a passionate wine kiss, announcing that she was the best thing in his life. She screamed with laughter and said she had never ever seen him behave like this – it must have something to do with Peta MAA-thee-aas and A-MON-da.

'He never meets women like you and it's obviously having a good effect on him. We have a *pied-à-terre* in Madrid that we keep for guests and you really are welcome to come and stay there,' said Huguette, tears of laughter rolling down her face.

'Yes, yes,' cried Carlos, 'I'll take Amanda for a ride in my plane (scream from Amanda) and I'll take Peta to my wine cellar. It's time she wrote a book on Spain, starting with my wine cellar. *Libros Vivientes.*'

Ginette said that within three hours of meeting her, Patrick said 'I want to marry you – you are the woman of my life.' This provoked big discussions on the secrets of relationships, sweetened by Françoise's apricot and almond tart and Maurice's sparkling dessert wine – a Cuvée Impériale from Clarette-de-Die. Carlos spied an exercycle in the corner of the room so leapt on it to prove he wasn't drunk, inevitably got his balls caught and everyone congratulated Huguette on having an easy night that night. Maurice did a few headstands to prove he was still young and fit as Françoise, still convinced we were starving, brought out a bowl of strawberries, red currants and strawberry purée, all the fruit of their garden. Carlos was now at the table again with five empty glasses in front of him and getting more and more abstract. He said, 'If I was eating the last meal with the best friends, I would eat the fruit of the last dream.'

'What?'

'I would like to die happy surrounded by wine and women.'

'Someone give this man a coffee,' I said.

With coffee things sobered up and conversation turned to politics. French people are very worried about their lost 'golden' youth who have become a generation in torment. They say the script doesn't change, no matter who is in power. In spite of *la belle vie* for some folk, a chunk of today's young people (most of them not lacking in education or qualifications) are already lost to unemployment, nihilism, drug addiction, poverty and despair. General *chômage* (unemployment) in France is approximately 10 percent and youth unemployment is a shocking 22 percent. The economy seems to have stopped creating new jobs and the French are stuck in this jobs-for-life mentality. It costs a lot to hire someone, it is almost impossible to get rid of them and everybody expects the government to look after them. They get paid as much on an unemployment benefit as they do for working. All is not well, I tell you, and that's why Maurice and Françoise's huge garden will be useful when the revolution comes. At least in 1968 the people took to the streets; in 1997 they seemed to be too depressed to get out of bed. In 2006 they once again rose up. In an effort to reform their out-moded welfare state traditions, the government proposed changes in job laws wherein employers can hire a person under 26 and fire them without explanation during the first two years of employment. This was supposed to be a common-sense measure to ease joblessness but several million Froggies went berserk, rioted and eventually the government had to back down. Outside commentators gravely warn that the French are blind to their own decline. To this the French say bollocks, the economy is far more flexible and successful than critics say, the infrastructure and education system are top notch and France has vast political influence as a founder member of the EU, the G8 and the UN. The French are terrified of liberalism and globalisation but they're not isolationist. The problem, according to some commentators, is that French polititians know the work force has to be opened up to competition but they have a Bonapartist streak, making them impose important changes too quickly and with insufficient consultation. Changes are doomed without the seal of democracy.

We reluctantly said goodbye and braced ourselves for the drive back to Aix. After about half an hour Amanda started nodding off so we swapped seats and I drove home with her sleeping peacefully, no doubt dreaming of Spanish nights. The next day Amanda's friends arrived, having been told there was plenty of room for them all in the apartments at Le Petit Prignon. She had rented the little flat downstairs and there they would all happily cohabitate. Except that's not quite what happened . . . but more about that later. The visitors seemed unusually subdued upon arrival but that was soon remedied by a quick sortie to the supermarket. They came back with enough alcohol for a week and got rid of most of it that night.

I made a huge aïoli and invited Josette and her family from the big house. Josette, who is a natural, warm and unaffected person, allowed me to cook in her big kitchen; their children set up a long table on their terrace overlooking the pool and it seemed as though Pierre had just been waiting for this moment. An academic, he improved greatly with a glass of wine in his hand and the company of uninhibited people. New World people like to have a good time, can cross social barriers quickly due to their relatively classless system, and let down their façades much more readily than the French. This encourages the Froggies to do the same and they feel greatly liberated for it. Even jet-lagged, the visitors were sparkling and laughing their heads off, fearlessly communicating in their pidgin French. We decided that Josette and Pierre should be paying us for the joy and fun we were bringing into their lives.

What the visitors hadn't realised was that they were not only going to be sharing rooms but sharing big beds in some cases. This is jolly good fun when you're in your twenties with a backpack. It is not so jolly when you're middle-aged and used to lots of space, both personal and physical. I was very happy to go down to what I considered to be my luxurious writing shed at the bottom of the garden. It was clean, there was a bed, a lamp, birds and frogs talking to each other and total, blissful peace. It's amazing how much we need peace, quiet and space to stay sane. Within days some of the visitors moved to a hotel to get some sleep, everyone clarified they had different tour priorities and none of them were the same, and Bunbuns the bunny ate Eve's new straw sun hat so she cut the crown off and gave it to him for breakfast. Everyone reacted to being in a foreign country, unable to speak the language, suffering from overwork recently left behind and being overwhelmed by the exoticness of it all, in different ways. Some became passive and dependent, some became hysterical, some laughed and some did yoga. I left a few days later fearing the worst, as they had yet to do Tuscany together, but Amanda informed me in our regular emails that once they adjusted, everything had worked out very well.

One hot morning, Josette was putting the garbage cans out for the collection and looked up to see four people walking past on the other side of the road, all dressed the same. She stood there in her dressing gown with a look of utter astonishment. I waved.

'*Bonjour Josette, vous voulez venir avec nous?* (Do you want to come with us?)'

She peered. '*Oh, mais c'est vous. Je croyais que c'était un cirque ou des Indiens qui passaient. Q'est-ce que vous faites?* (Oh, it's you. I thought it was a circus or some Indians marching. What are you doing?)'

'*On marche.* (We're walking.)'

'*Pourquoi?*'

'*Pour être en forme.* (To stay fit.)'

'*Mais pourquoi vous marchez si vite?* (Why are you going so fast?)'

'*Josette. Vous voulez venir ou pas?* (Do you want to come or not?)'

'*Bien sér que non. Quelle idée!* (Of course not. What an idea!)'

After our fast walk we piled into the two cars between the nine of us and set off for the red village of Roussillon-en-Provence, designated as one of the most beautiful in France. And it really is red – the soil, the trees, the earth, the hills, the houses – everything is turned red by the ochre vein this village sits on. Roussillon is like a magic fairyland where 17 different shades of red ochre tint every house, alleyway, winding stairway and ancient gateway. In spite of it being very touristy it must be the most breathtaking village I've ever seen – like a painter's palette, a sunset in stone, a village drenched in blushing passion. As you walk through amber, saffron, magenta, gold, red, pink, rust and coral, you can't help but gasp at one of the few examples of mankind building in perfect harmony with nature. The ochre quarry is called *falaises d'or et de sang* (cliffs of gold and blood). The mythological explanation for the colour is much more exciting than the technical one. The blood that stained Roussillon came from a woman's broken heart. In grief she threw herself from the top of the castle and the ground below was forever stained with her blood. They did that a lot in those days – there are screeds of medieval stories of barbaric love triangles and for some reason the woman always jumps off the ramparts as a problem-solving device.

We walked up the hill and lunched at the Résidence des Ramparts, a strict boarding school cleverly disguised as a restaurant and lodge, to lull us to the danger ahead. The décor was charming with red walls, blue doors, pretty tables and a terrace that had a panoramic view out onto the Luberon mountains. The *patronne* had been jettisoned from some hemlock-ridden part of Germany to try her talents on tourists, too weakened by hunger to defend themselves. The only reason I didn't unleash my tongue on her was because Amanda looked like she was going to take up the cudgel and although all's fair in war and love, I didn't feel two to one was cricket. When I saw how lightly Amanda let her off, I regretted my reticence. We waited a long time in an almost empty restaurant to get the menus, during which time Amanda used the cellphone. Error. The mistress, with a look of white horror, metaphysical whip in hand, explained this was a place of calm and tranquillity THANK YOU VERY MUCH in such a way as to silence the whole village for 10 minutes. Twenty minutes later the wine arrived and we placed our orders. We would have gone through the Hundred Years War to get a bit of bread, and begged many times, but attitude in a blue suit was a long way from that kind of frippery.

As there was no one else serving I said, 'I bet you anything she's also the chef and now she's gone to put her apron on to cook the food.'

'No,' they all gasped, 'don't be ridiculous.' But that is exactly what happened.

The overcooked pasta when it finally arrived 30 minutes later was made with a heavy German hand, lots of floury wallpaper glue and thick leathery mushrooms. When I thought of all the perfect pasta dishes I'd eaten glistening with lightness, colour and flavour, I wanted to weep. Certain members of the group ate it up and declared it delicious.

Then I thought of the gloop I had eaten as a nurse at Auckland hospital and realised what this meal reminded me of– formaldehyde, bedpans and layouts on night duty. When I put it in my mouth the consistency and flavour exploded in a symphony of marsh fog and forest mud. As is consistent with all sadomasochistic parlours, the mistress asked us to pay for her services, wouldn't accept credit cards and had no cash change. Amanda gave her a polite lecture on running a business while I wondered if I would break my you-must-not-slap-the-staff rule. On the way out I used the toilet and the seat was painted with thorns. I will never forget Roussillon.

I recovered at our next stop, Gordes, by buying a bottle of the best olive oil in France, that of Maître Cornille from his mill in Mauzanne. The approach to Gordes is paved with lavender fields and stony slopes and although it's not far from Roussillon, this village is stone-coloured because the red ochre only happens at Roussillon. The village winds up and up through a series of ever-tightening curves into the Provençal sky on ancient ramparts and within the walls the play of light in the steep, narrow streets is irresistibly beautiful. These streets, cobbled with river stones laid on edge, are called *calades*. The best parts of Gordes are the extraordinary walls of flat stones, all laid on top of each other and on the outskirts there is a village of *bories* – mysterious huts in the shape of honey pots, made entirely of these stones.

Another visit on our Amanda's-tour-of-Provence was through vineyards, olive trees and sleepy villages to the ruins of Les Baux. The trick is to avoid the touristy village and shops and go straight on up to the dramatic, desolate and ancient fiefdom, perched on a high mesa so spectacular that your imagination runs wild. The one village detour in Les Baux I would suggest would be to the restaurant L'Oustau de Baumanière. By the way *bauxite* (aluminium) comes from Baux but is no longer mined there. WARRIORS ALL

– VASSALS NEVER was the powerful cry of the lords of Baux in the Middle Ages. Too bad they finally succumbed because they invented the most smashing war machines – giant catapults and *trébuchets* (bird traps) that could chuck 100kg stones 200 metres, breaking thick walls and sending the inhabitants flying. Weighing seven tons it was entirely dismantled, taken to the battlefield and reconstructed, taking 60 big macho warriors to handle it. The *bélier* (battering ram) was able to whack down heavy doors and ramparts of besieged fortresses with flaming projectiles. It consisted of a long beam of wood tipped with an iron head, suspended in equilibrium horizontally by chains. These mediaeval birds of prey the size of apartment buildings were sitting in the middle of the ruins with a sign that said IT IS STRICTLY FORBIDDEN TO CLIMB UP ONTO THE MACHINES. The site itself is 900 metres long with vertical ravines on either side and is white like the Alpilles. From the eerie, empty fortress and ramparts there is a spectacular view of the invading enemy. It was from here that Raymond de Turenne was driven to tears of joy as he chucked anyone who crossed him over the walls. There is another gruesome story of thwarted love associated with this castle; I've heard it elsewhere but this is how it's told at Baux.

In this legend the *châtelaine* of the castle fell in love with the hero, a member of her husband's retinue – an event she bitterly regretted and which ruined her tastebuds forever. Her husband, the lord of the castle, found out about the wooing, moaning and general subterfuge going on behind his back and, as anyone would do in such circumstances, sent the hero off to the front line where he belonged. Of course the hero was mortally wounded by a poisoned arrow and as he lay dying, wrote one last passionate love letter to his châtelaine. He gave it to his lackey, instructing him to deliver the letter to his lady love along with his heart and a lock of his hair. I couldn't stop thinking about the lackey opening up his chest wall, going in behind the sternum and removing the still warm muscle. Anyway the lackey was intercepted by the lord's men, who delivered the barbaric little present right into the hands of their master. He had his chef cook the heart up with spices and herbs and served it to his unsuspecting wife for dinner. Don't run away, because the ending is superb. Upon finding out what she had just eaten she was overcome with euphoria and, looking her husband straight in the eye said: *This is the most noble, tasty meal I have ever eaten and I need never eat again.* And she didn't.

Nevertheless, Les Baux had its gentle, intellectual side too, for it was a 13th-century court of love to which troubadours came from all over to write passionate but platonic poems to ladies they esteemed. To belong to this club of ladies you had to be of noble birth, well read and desperately beautiful – which doesn't seem too difficult – and all you had to do to reward the cleverest and most adoring verse writer was give him a kiss. In the company of this élite court questions of chivalry and gallantry were argued and clarified, *n'est-ce pas*, and everyone wore pointy-toed slippers and gorgeous frocks embroidered in gold. The troubadours spoke in Provençal, the language that survives to this day amongst amateurs of southern culture.

Before leaving for Marseilles, I finally talked our non-gourmet group of travelers into a decent meal in a recommended restaurant at Tholonet near Aix. Chez Thomé was a very pretty country-style house with a big garden outside and a warm, family feel inside. The village is an old *bastide*, and men were playing *boules* outside in the warm evening when we arrived. The tables were all laid with Provençal tablecloths and the food was typical southern fare, as were the staff, who were friendly, good-looking and young and seemed to have just invited you into their home for dinner. I ate a perfectly acceptable salad of roasted peppers, courgette flan, eggplant purée and charred tuna followed by the classic lamb with gratin potatoes and the ever-ready roasted tomato. It wasn't ground-breaking but it wasn't German hemlock either and we had so much fun it was worth every lettuce leaf.

Next morning I somehow squeezed my belongings back into my suitcase and went up to say goodbye to chaos city at Le Petit Prignon. Amanda and Piers had to move out of their flat that day and they were frantically trying to pack up three times what they had come with while others cleaned up and emptied the kitchen for them. In spite of the fact I had regularly pointed at Bunbuns then at the big jar of Dijon mustard and the oven as a form of discipline, he had eaten through the email line so there was no access to messages. I went to the big house to farewell the gentle Josette and retrieve my book I had loaned her. She and Pierre were in their dressing gowns as it was the crack of dawn at 10.30 in the morning, but they did stumble out to say goodbye. In my copy of *Fêtes Gourmandes* (the title of the French version of *Fête Accomplie*) she had written, *Je me suis régalée, je l'ai dévoré.* (It was a real treat, I devoured it.); and they refused to let me pay for my paradise garden shed.

The train station at Aix was more or less deserted in the heat and, as is completely normal, the snack shop was closed between 12.30 and 2 p.m., the exact time a traveller would need lunch. Marseilles, on the shores of the Mediterranean, is only 20 minutes from Aix but this was a milk train and took an hour, stopping at every ugly, graffiti-emblazoned stop on the way. As I chugged past tragic and sinister apartment blocks in the *zones* (slum belt) and grey industrial areas I figured I could just as easily write a book on the sordid side of France. The taxi driver at Marseilles station was very nice, took me past the Vieux Port and straight to Michèle's place on the Corniche Président J.F. Kennedy with no 'touristic' detours and helped me with my bag. Michèle considered this staggeringly admirable as even Marseillais get ripped off, plundered and abused by taxi drivers. Michèle, whom I stayed with in Paris, spends the winter there and the summer in her home in Marseilles.

The minute you hit this city you know you're in the wild west. It is sizzlingly different from the rest of France and to my mind there's no city like it. When you tell people you're going to Marseilles they squiggle their Froggie noses and say '*beuk*' (yuck). It's known to be tough, rough, dangerous, a sailor's port town, full of Arabs and goodness knows what exotica. All this only serves to give it flavour in my eyes. I like a city with guts, independence, sex appeal and a strong personality. Marseilles hits you between the eyes and is as addictive to me now as Paris was all those years ago. If Paris was like the man of my dreams then, Marseilles would be the man of my dreams now – and one accepts it, for better or for worse.

It's almost unbelievable to think that calm, refined, bourgeois Aix is only up the road – two cities more different you couldn't find if you tried. Aix is the man you should have married and Marseille is the man who sets your loins on fire. The Marseillais consider Aix to be beautiful but boring. Marseille is the oldest city in France and not a city for tourists because it's not good-looking, if you're interested in skin-deep beauty – plus you really have to speak the lingo there. You want to hear an accent? Marseille does a very good one – it's as thick as the soup and they have a very ribald sense of humour. It is a city for travellers who love history, love going in behind the façades, love straight-talking people. It also helps if you like fish. There are areas of chicness and good shopping around rue Rome, rue du Paradis and rue St-Fierriol off the main street, the Canebière, but the real heart of Marseilles is deeply proletariat and full of southern craftiness.

Michèle was working on a translation, so I dumped my bags and jumped on the bus outside her house that took me around the water-front into town. In Marseilles the bus tickets reek of sunshine and are called *réseau liberté* (freedom network) which describes the inhabitants well – a network of free spirits. The tickets have blue waves, a flying gull and yellow sunshine printed on them. When the driver hands it over, you have the feeling you are going on a happy adventure. No sooner had I alighted at the port, which is so crowded with blue and white boats and yachts you can barely see a bit of water, than I went mad and bought a Paloma Picasso lipstick. I hadn't had one of these very expensive but great quality lipsticks since I lived in Paris. In a brilliant marketing stance, Paloma Picasso only makes one colour – blood red. Red or dead – pink is for wimps. It stays on for ages, doesn't bleed and always looks good. Now I was dressed I could continue on to Le Panier – the old town – to see what would happen to me. What happened was *impensable*. In Marseille in July, which is supposed to be 30 degrees with a pastis, it rained and went down to 20 degrees. Coming from a country which thinks it's a rainforest, I always carry an umbrella – a perversion I have often been ridiculed for. Now I was strolling comfortably around smiling benevolently at everyone else getting drenched. And if there's one thing a girl needs apart from lipstick and a jolly good brolly when it's raining, it's a café to sit in and a cheering cup of coffee.

The Vieux Port was full of tourist restaurants serving bad *bouillabaisse*, that famous Marseillais fish soup, *louche* bars and fishing shops. Men stare at women openly, cars toot ferociously and young men race around on scooters. Once upon a time it was crawling with pimps, prostitutes, foreign legionnaires, thieves, resistance fighters and of course sailors, and it was all terribly exciting and grubby. During the Second World War the Germans moved the 40,000 residents out and bombed it to smithereens for 'health reasons', but mainly to interrupt the good health of the Resistance. Most of the Panier was also blown up by the Germans, and reconstructed after the Liberation. It still undergoes fixing-ups in an attempt to ruin the flavour but the flavour sticks with its sky-high washing lines, multinational inhabitants, repainted tall facades, criss-crossing narrow streets, mysterious flights of steps, intoxicating cooking smells and little kids running underfoot. I walked up the steep streets to the Panier, built on the Moulins hill on the site of ancient Massalia, where I discovered one of the best chocolate shops in the universe.

Chocolate – that heart of darkness, that dangerously addictive drug, that corrupter of cocoa virgins. Few foods inspire passion and loyalty on the scale that chocolate does. Like most people I have eaten chocolate all my life and it has always been associated with 'special treat'. We were chocolate and lolly-rationed as children, our parents wanting neither high dentist bills nor hyperglycemic werewolves instead of children. This we strangely accepted, which created a culture for us around chocolate – sweet-toothed Dad bringing plain dark chocolate home for us on Friday nights after work, our wealthy and doting grandparents bringing expensive chocolates in boxes with beautiful ladies on the cover at Christmas time ... even a chocolate ice cream was a special occasion. But it wasn't until I went to live in France that I became a genuine chocophile, seduced by the blatantly pornographic displays in those precious glass-plated shops called *chocolatiers* in Paris. At Angelina's tearooms on rue de Rivoli, I tasted for the first time a chocolate drink made with real chocolate and cream that you could almost stand a spoon up in. It took me a while to get used to quality chocolate with its high cocoa content and to appreciate its slight bitterness, because I had been educated to sugar- and milk-polluted confectionery, clearly the work of the Devil.

For almost a century the Spaniards kept the secret of the 'food of the gods' to themselves, Christopher Columbus having discovered xocolatl in Mexico a century earlier in 1502. According to Aztec legend the god Quetzalcoatl gifted the cocoa tree to man. It gradually crept over the Spanish border into France, to St-Jean-de-Luz, Biarritz and Bayonne, and this is still where some of the best chocolatiers are to be found. In 1615 when Anne of Austria married Louis XIII of France she popularised chocolate amongst the French aristocracy, then it sailed over the Channel to the House of Queen Anne. Princess Eugenia of Spain, who married Napoleon III, made sure the French kept eating it, and by the end of the 17th century there were many small factories producing fine chocolate from the raw materials. After that van Houten opened shop in Amsterdam, Suchard in Switzerland and Cadbury in England, but it was not until 1893 that filled chocolates were invented in Switzerland. The best chocolate in the world today is the French Valrhona. Quaker families often established chocolate factories in the past as an alternative to alcohol – Cadburys of Bournville in Birmingham is a prime example.

There is a shop in Le Touquet called Le Chat Bleu which sells chocolate containing 99 percent cocoa solids, which is practically inedible but very good for cooking. The secret to choosing good chocolate, like choosing a good bottle of balsamic vinegar or a good wine, is in carefully reading the information on the label. Ideally chocolate should contain nothing more than cocoa paste, cane sugar, cocoa butter, maybe a little cream and natural vanilla. With a cocoa content of 60–70 percent, which is a very good quality chocolate, there is little room for other ingredients such as sugar. Too much sugar and a low cocoa content means that any chocolate flavour will be masked by sweetness. There are three types of cocoa – Criollo, Forastero and Trinitario, which is a hybrid of the first two. Criollo, grown mostly in Central and Latin America is the most expensive because it is rare, producing only three percent of the world's crop. There was a big drama in 1996 when the EU ruled that chocolate producers could supplement the butter with up to five percent vegetable oil and the Swiss followed suit. This ruling set chocolate-makers on the slippery slope to hell, as it lowered the image of high-class chocolate.

If you have ever tasted a 'grand cru' chocolate, you will know it is like tasting a grand cru wine. Good chocolate can be recognised by its uniform dark, glossy surface, silky smooth to the touch, making a clean break in your fingers. In your mouth it will break with a crisp snap. As you eat the chocolate it will melt in your mouth and you will be aware of its silky, uncloying texture, smooth but not fatty, and its intense, deep, rich flavour with a pleasant bitterness and a lingering, fruity finish. Are you still sitting up or have you been asked to leave the room? Chocolate contains small amounts of caffeine and theobromine, which are stimulating uppers, and also causes or increases the release of endorphins, natural opiates in the brain that reduce pain – the same chemicals that are released during exercise and create the runner's high. It has also been found to contain trace levels of anandamide, a substance that mildly mimics the effects of marijuana by acting on the same receptors in the brain and increases levels of seratonin, which alleviates depression. Chocolate also contains significant amounts of phenol, a chemical found in wine, which reduces the risk of heart disease by preventing the formation of plaque in coronary arteries. One and a half ounces of good chocolate contains as much phenol as a five-ounce glass of red wine. As you can see from this impressive research, you would be ruining your health by not eating chocolate.

All phenol addicts eventually find their way to the tiny shop on the Place des Treize Cantons in the Panier – and so did I, completely by chance. It is so small and unassuming with no apparent name, I almost missed it. The rusty old roller door frontage was three quarters rolled up, the door appeared to be half open and the interior was dim. It was only because I saw other people going in that I suspected my nose needed to be stuck in there. Inside were cramped half a dozen well-heeled customers who were not there by chance. A messy desk covered in cellophane and ribbons was just inside the door, dusty dried flowers hung on the walls and the room was overcrowded with tables laden down with big handmade chocolates. *Bar Marseillaise* (Marseilles Bar), rose- and lavender-flavoured white chocolate, fruit and almond chocolate, pistachio, lime, onion(!), rum and raisin in big balls, *pralines feuilletées, les incontournables noirs* (indispensable blacks) – pure cocoa at 70 or 80 percent.

This entirely rustic operation had no business cards, no machines, the far from pristine kitchen was down a few steps at the back, and the mother, Rose, served. She took her time, smilingly giving constant tastings to everybody, slicing bits off chocolate balls to reveal layers of flavourings topped with chocolate paste and dipped in chocolate covering. Everything costs 15€ a kilo, you pay by the weight and it is wrapped in cellophane and ribbons. Customers come there for certain favourite chocolates, and there's no point in making faces if they're not there. You can't reserve or give orders. Like all noble rustics, the chocolate-maker Michèle Leray makes what she feels like making when she feels like making it. No chocolate is the same – they are all made by artistic inspiration. I bought some orange and almond, and apricot and walnut balls, introduced myself to Michèle and went outside to have a *panaché* at the old bar across the tiny square.

Bar des Treize Coins had tables and chairs outside and the owner kindly wiped the rain off one for me to sit down. The odour of chocolate floated in the air and I could hear Arab music wafting around with it. Place des Treize Coins is the old and incorrect name for Place des Treize Cantons. The square was previously owned by a Swiss *hôtelier* who had an auberge on the site which was of such renown that even Casanova is reputed to have stayed there. The hôtelier named his auberge after the 13 *cantons* or districts in Switzerland, but the Provençaux couldn't pronounce or spell it, and

Cantons became Coins (corners). It has only recently been changed back to the real name, but the bar keeps the old one. It had stopped raining, some men were inside playing cards and after a while Michèle came out to chat with me in a white T-shirt covered with chocolate. In between sucks on her cigarette she told me the story of the Marseilles Bar.

The original Marseilles Bar was a heavy, thick chocolate bar made at home because it was cheaper, more rustic and could be shared in the consideration and love of other people. Its size varied according to the family and it was made for parties, cousins or even whole streets. Michèle's father made it, as did his father, as did his father. Now it's her turn to carry on, and her daughter Marine will follow. Her father made it for family and neighbours and it's been a commercial proposition for about 20 years. In the naïve tradition, Michèle has great talent and sincerity. 'I am not influenced by fashion,' she says. 'I am constantly searching my memory for childhood tastes.' Temperature is all in the chocolate business and at this time of year Michèle can work for only two hours in the morning when it's cool, so she's decided to expand into next door and invest in an air-conditioner. Her chocolate paste is a mixture of cocoa paste with the cocoa butter that she primarily buys from Central America, maintained in a liquid state by heat. To these she adds fine sugar, vanilla and various flavourings. There are no preservatives, butter or cream sneaked in. Michèle has been fêted by all the best magazines for years and people come from all over France to bliss out on her intoxicating delicacies.

An unusual and frightfully good thing to do with chocolate is to hand-make chocolate pasta (see page 178).

In the southwest there is a peasant stew of mixed meats, called simply La Sauce, which contains chocolate. The chocolate influence probably comes from Spain, where it is often used in hare dishes – and of course, Bayonne is huge chocolate country. In this dish the meat is cooked for so long,

Chocolate Pasta

1⅓ cups white or semolina flour
3 tbsp cocoa
2 large eggs
½ tsp salt
2 tsp olive oil
1–5 tsp water, if needed

To make dough by hand: Sift flour and cocoa together and mound on a work surface or in a large bowl. Make a well in centre and put eggs, salt and oil in. Gradually draw flour from inner edge into centre, using your fingertips, until all flour is incorporated. The dough will be very stiff and dry but will soften during kneading as moisture becomes more evenly distributed. Clean your hands and knead dough on a clean work surface for about five minutes or until fairly smooth and pliable, flouring only if dough is sticky. Wrap dough in plastic wrap and stand for an hour.

To make dough in food processor: Combine flour, cocoa, eggs, salt and oil in food processor fitted with metal blade. Process until ingredients are well blended and dough holds together in sticky crumbs that can be easily pressed together (about 10 seconds). Press dough into a ball and knead for a few seconds. Wrap in plastic wrap and stand for 30 minutes.

Proceed to roll and cut dough into tagliolini (thin noodles) following the instructions on your pasta-making machine, or hand-cut into pappardelle (wide ribbons). If you can be bothered, fresh, handmade pasta tastes much better than bought.

Chocolate pasta is not only good with rich stews, it is very good as a dessert eaten with ice cream and chocolate sauce enriched with Grand Marnier.

it literally becomes a thick sauce. You brown shallots, carrots, rabbit pieces, stewing beef, hare pieces and lumps of pork in pork fat, then add garlic and a bouquet garni and stir in a little flour. Pour over a bottle of red wine, enough water to cover and stir in 1tsp sugar, a square of dark chocolate and salt and pepper. Cover and simmer gently for about five hours. The peasants used lots of thick bread to soak this 'sauce' up, and if it was good enough for them then it's good enough for you.

I desperately wanted to eat a bouillabaisse but Michèle said if you could buy it for 15€ it would be disgusting, if you could buy it for 30€ it might be all right but if you want the real, fresh thing you would have to pay at least 60€ and reserve at least twenty-four hours in advance.

'For bouillabaisse? The dish of poor fishermen?'

'*Oui*. This poor fisherman's dish is *la haute cuisine* now, *ma chère*. There is even an official chart stating what has to be in a real bouillabaisse.'

For the record this is how a bouillabaisse (from the Provençal *bouiabaisso* meaning when the soup boils *boui*, you must lower *abaisso* the flame) goes according to the *Charte de la Bouillabaisse Marseillaise*. First of all you can't make this soup outside Marseille and call it a bouillabaisse, so you can forget any pretensions on that level – it has to be made with the ugly, unmentionable little fish that no one in their right mind would eat except a starving fisherman. Only creatures like *rascasse* (spiny, red hogfish), *vive araignée* (weaver fish), *grondin* (red gurnard), *scorpène* (scorpion), *baudroie* (anglerfish), *congre* (eel) and *St-Pierre* (John Dory) can be used – and preferably so fresh they think your hand is the rock they were just sitting under. If you could see these prehistoric throwbacks you would eat tomatoes for the rest of your life; but they, especially the strange rascasse, absolutely give the unique flavour to the soup. Optional additions are *cigales* (flat little lobsters) and *langouste* (crayfish). The other essential ingredients by law are tomatoes, fennel, potatoes, onions and garlic, olive oil, parsley and saffron, salt and pepper. You need a good stock made from rockfish and a tangy *rouille* – aïoli with saffron and chilli in it. The fish is served separately from the soup, brought to the table and removed from its bones before your very eyes. The soup is served with garlic toasts and rouille. It takes time and talent to cook a bouillabaisse and even if the ingredients are perfect, it can only ever be as good as the cook.

So I wasn't to get a bouillabaisse, but Michèle suggested we eat at her friend's restaurant, Ce Cher Arwell at 96 Cours Julien. Cher Arwell (pronounced Arvell) really is a dear man and that really is his name. He comes from Brittany and cooks self-taught Périgourdin cuisine in Marseilles – *étrange* but true – and he has many faithful clients. He cooks what he wants, is only open in the evening, refuses clients when it gets too full and goes sailing for the whole of August and September. How come I couldn't pull that lifestyle off when I had my restaurant? He works alone in the kitchen – entrées, mains, desserts and dishes – and has one waitress, usually an actress. The one we had was adorable. The restaurant had stone walls covered in paintings, antique bistrot furniture and a little wooden cabinet behind us hid tiny glasses and an array of *digestifs*. Our first course was a copious foie gras de canard with warm baguette slices and sprigs of red currants. Michèle had a melting pork stew with cream and fresh sage, cooked just the way she likes it – for hours, garnished with sautéed potatoes made to order. I had duck breast cooked in a sea salt crust and served with baked fresh figs. It was all simple but refined and well thought through. Afterwards Arwell joined us for the digestifs. He got us to taste a marvelous tarragon wine a friend had given him and another secret digestif that I'm not allowed to talk about.

Michèle always drove as if her passenger's waters had just broken and dilation was already at 8cm for quintuplets; she drove as if she was playing chicken; she drove as if she'd seen too many gangster movies; she tooted as if it was part of a gear change. Most of the time it worked out but there were also lots of bumps and scrapes. Marseillais ignore red lights and the right-hand rule so one always drives with this in mind. Michèle drove at night as if alone on the road and flashed her lights when turning blind corners (without slowing down) to warn others that she also was Marseillaise and not to mess with her, mumbling things like, 'They congenitally lack the part of the brain concerned with driving.' The Corniche is a great place for speeders and people regularly drive right over the edge at night and into the sea. She took me up hill and down dale in the little car, pointing out all her favourite bits, and as the days went by I realised how much she loved this town, her birthplace. I had never seen her passionate about Paris but she wanted to share every little loved corner of Marseilles with me.

If Michèle's house in Paris was serious and dark, her house in Marseille was the antithesis. Right on the street, it was built into rock and went straight up four storeys overlooking the sea. Originally designed by an American architect for himself, it had a tower on the right side housing winding stairs with little windows in the walls like a medieval castle. Facing the entrance was a small cave where Michèle kept her wine, then one went up a few steps to a studio on the first floor, with mezzanine bed, toilet and washing and drying machines. The best part of this room was three shelves of her husband's shoes, boots and riding boots, all of the same beige/ochre/tan colours, all perfectly lined up. I felt sure if I changed the place of one pair, Jean-Louis would notice. It was a fabulous vision of the most beautiful, expensive shoes I had ever seen – mostly lace-ups, mostly fitted with old-fashioned wooden shoe shapes, all shining and all well looked after. There were no rundown heels, no scuffs and no looseness of character showing anywhere in these shoes. The Imelda Marcos of Marseille. You never know what is behind a quiet exterior and a pair of glasses.

One continued up the winding stairs which, like a castle, were just wide enough so one could still wear one's armour, to a bedroom and bathroom on the second floor with narrow slits for windows to keep heat out and privacy in. Up the stairs which opened out on to the bright, luminous dining/

living room/kitchen on the third floor. The whole house was painted pale eggshell, all the floors were white tiles and the rooms full of antique and modern furniture, books, large ornate gold-framed mirrors and Jean-Louis' cool, mysterious paintings. There were brochures and photos from his latest exhibition on the table. The windows in one large room were tall and opened inwards with profuse plants climbing everywhere, surely thinking they lived in paradise. On the right side there was a terrace full of plants, table and chairs and a barbecue. This room had a very high ceiling permitting the stairs to continue up to the fourth-floor mezzanine bedroom and second bathroom, with Persian rugs hanging over the balcony. There was a rooftop balcony to view the stars that you got to by crossing a little perspex bridge, mounting a few steps and climbing through a window. With the press of a button, automatic curtains descended to block out the strong morning sun. There was only one thing wrong with this house – because it was on a main road, it was very noisy.

In the morning I knew not to even consider talking to Michèle before her first coffee. With the second coffee she became human and even sometimes smiled. It was Sunday so she took me to the fishing village of L'Estaque dotted with factories where all the Impressionists had painted, just along the bay from Marseilles. I had just missed by one day La Sardinade, the annual sardine festival comprising *bal musette*, sardine dinner with exchange of recipes and a play called *The Sardine Affair*. All this happened on the Quai des Pescadous outside the bars and restaurants with sunny names like Bar de la Plage, Bar des Pêcheurs and Bar du Soleil. The delicatessens were full of Marseillais specialities like cured ham, *coppa*, *panisse*, paella, stuffed vegetables, nose salad, sardine fritters, taboulé, stuffed vine leaves, *brandade de morue*, fresh ravioli and olives. *Panisse* is a Marseille dish made from chickpea flour. A bit like polenta in consistency, it is sold in a thick roll and one cuts rounds off and deep fries them to go with a salad. We went on one of Michèle's famous 'walks' that last for hours and always include hills, stairs, alleyways and great speed. She has no concept of the word stroll and, in spite of being the size of a toothpick, a heavy smoker and no spring chicken, she never sweats, puffs or gets tired. We went up and down little *ruelles*, steps and passages and visited Paul Cézanne's house with pale green shutters, where he painted many pictures of L'Estaque. He described L'Estaque as being just like a playing card – red roofs on a blue sea. This village was made famous by him and other avant-garde painters. Afterwards I was allowed to have a coffee and a warm *chichi*.

On the way home we stopped the car on the Corniche near No 120, just before the viaduct, to go for another 'short walk'. Marseilles is really a secret city – all its beauty and interest is hidden behind façades, doors, alleyways and up steep hills. We descended the little winding streets up and down to the water to explore boat-shaped terraces out over the sea, Moorish architecture, mixed-up oriental Arab architecture, little palaces out on peninsulas and tiny fishing bays with their boats and little cabins. People were sunbathing on the rocks everywhere. This was a magic land I knew I would be drawn back to. In the afternoon we went to the beach across the road from Michèle's house, one of the few patches of sand on this rocky coast, then it was whisky, Michèle Leray's chocolates, reading Provençal cookbooks and watching the constantly changing light of the sun setting on the terrace. I was wearing the black skirt with yellow and green flowers Michèle had given me, yellow earrings found at the flea-market in Aix and my skin was growing more and more like the Provençaux. I felt glowing and happy and comfortable. Michèle was wearing her customary white pants, white tennis shoes and white cigarette.

She has always been an incredibly good host and even if you asked for and expected nothing, the service was

Terrine Provençal

The beauty of using goat's milk cheese in cooking is its softness, sweet pungent flavour and pure whiteness. Unlike cow's milk which is tinged yellow by carotene, goat's milk is beautifully snowy. It's expensive but not terribly fattening and in this recipe, I've cut it with quark which is a fresh curd cheese made from skimmed milk.

Serves 8

250g green and yellow courgettes
extra virgin olive oil in a spray pump
sea salt and freshly ground pepper
3 different coloured peppers
100g quark
100g soft chêvre cheese
a few tbsps of milk
2 tbsp tapenade
½ cup fresh basil leaves, chopped
extra virgin olive oil for drizzling
small ceramic or glass terrine

1. Chop stems off courgettes, wash and cut in thick slices, lengthwise. Spray with oil, sprinkle with salt and pepper and grill or fry until golden on both sides.

2. Heat oven to the hottest it will go. Cut peppers in half, core and seed. Brush an oven tray with oil, throw peppers in and roast until blackened – about 10 mins. Place peppers immediately in a plastic bag to sweat for 10 minutes. Peel blackened skin off.

3. Mix quark, chêvre and milk together with a fork.

4. Spray terrine dish with oil, layer half the courgettes and spread 1 tbsp of tapenade over them. Lay half the peppers on top then spread with half of the chêvre mixture. Sprinkle a layer of basil then drizzle with a little oil. Repeat this layering again, using up all the ingredients. Press down well, cover and refrigerate overnight.

always laid on. This southern night she presented me with aubergine caviar sprinkled with chopped spring onions. I waited patiently for the rest of the meal. She raised her eyes heavenward: 'You're not going to be Anglo-Saxon and mix

flavours for heavens sake; eat this first.' Oh right, of course.
We poured our Cornille olive oil over everything. Michèle,
who, in spite of my 20-year interest in gastronomy, still considers me a bit of a peasant, was impressed that I actually
had the best olive oil in France in my bag. We waxed lyrical
over the oil, dribbling out words like hazelnuts, yesterday's
grass clippings and freshly ground pepper. While we ate it
we talked recipes and she told me about a *Terrine Provençal*
(see page 184) her friend makes.

I tried this idea later when I was at Frédéric and Kathy's
house in Auxerre, substituting *brandade de morue* for the
cheese and adding grilled courgettes. It was very good, but
the next time I would leave out the brandade and maybe
put just morue. Michèle also gave me another invention of
hers – *Terrine de Morue* – layers of morue, very thinly sliced
potatoes, garlic and olive oil which one cooks in a terrine in
the oven until melted.

Next came the beautiful Parma ham we'd bought in
L'Estaque, with fresh figs and *fougasse* (one of the oldest of
French breads – a sweet Provençal flat bread with big cuts
slashed right through it, sometimes sweetened with orange-
flower water but often made with bacon, onion or anchovies
in the dough and sprinkled with fennel seeds), followed by
English cheddar and a Corsican liqueur. Michèle turned her
nose up at my precious giant chocolate balls but I had one.
The bottom layer was green pistachio, the next layer was fig
confit and the rest was chocolate paste with walnuts in it. To
say it was celestial would make the angels blush in shame,
so I'll just say it tasted of moonbeams.

In the morning I visited the fish market at the port. There
were about a dozen little stalls of fishermen and women
selling what they had caught that morning – rock fish and
rock octopus that literally looked like rocks, something called
lasagne, *daurade* (sea bream) in a little pool looking sorry
for themselves, crabs and baby lobsters that really shouldn't

have been there. Housewives were buying for their soups and it was late, so things were going cheap. If the *mistral* is blowing, you get nothing at all. Out in the harbour I could see the Château d'If where the fictional Count of Monte Cristo was imprisoned. I wandered up to the Cours Julien, passing a beauty shop where you could get your eyelashes permed. Didn't even bear thinking about. I visited lots of kitchen shops and dress shops on the way then had lunch at Le Jardin d'à Côte, ordering rabbit with mustard sauce in memory of the many laughs had over that dish when I served it up to Americans on the barge. When you order house wine in the south, they ask you if it's rosé or red – there doesn't seem to be any question of white, and water is an aberration. After the bunny I ordered *crème caramel* (caramel custard) and coffee at the same time please, a waste of breath. Waiters don't even hear such nonsensical orders. Cours Julien is a large square in a very old quartier full of pools, fountains and trees. It's decrepit, relaxed, fixed up and very original in flavour. The woman sitting next to me was dressed in a typically French look which I personally find extremely tragic – bottle-blonde hair, kilos of gold earrings and bracelets, striped T-shirt with gold embroidery, navy jacket with lots of gold buttons, white pants and blue stilettos. I can find no possible excuse for this behaviour. Why can't they leave vulgarity to the lower classes who do it so much better?

That evening we ate at Chez Aldo, the pizza and fish restaurant of Michèle's friend Gérard in the 8th arrondisse-ment, rue Audemar-Tibido. One could never come across this large place at the end of a nondescript street by chance, but once there one never wants to leave. The restaurant itself had unremarkable décor but the location was sensational, right on the water, with the best sunsets in Marseilles. In the near distance a lone fisherman had his line out and families were starting to arrive. Gérard was a nice-looking man with oval glasses, a gentle smile and a great southern accent. I ordered a Bandol rosé which Michèle forced herself to drink, saying Marseillais never touch rosé because it's shit. We were sent tiny pizzas as *amuse-gueules* (appetisers) then had a small pizza to start – a good, thin crust topped with mozzarella, brousse and chèvre. The fresh fish was brought to us on a platter to choose which ones we wanted. We chose two very Marseillais fish, the *pageot* and *rouget* (red mullet), which were grilled on a wood fire and sprinkled with fennel-infused olive oil. They were of course infested with tiny bones.

'This drives me crazy,' I said to Michèle, 'I could be here all night taking the bones out of this fish.'

'But that's the pleasure of eating fish,' she replied, 'its only *ploucs* who have a problem with bones.'

'Oh, right. And aristocrats have no problem with them whatsoever.'

'No.'

'I'm going to choke.'

'Grow up.'

This area, called the Pointe Rouge, is a mixed area of fishermen, bourgeois and working class. After dinner we had a walk around the fishing village with all the boats pulled up, then drove to the southern-most point where Michèle had her romantic rendezvous as a young heartbreaker. At night the beach was isolated and beautiful with a few restaurants at the very end. Okay, so we'd had a few drinks and Michèle absolutely wanted to find the water notice. In Marseilles all the beaches have a water notice posted where you can check the state of the water that day. By and large the water is good for swimming but after a storm there's lots of wood and seaweed to wade through. We got out of the car, stumbled in the blackness along the beach to find this notice, found it, couldn't read it, went back to the car to get our glasses, returned to read: NO SWIMMING – POLLUTION; in other words, swim here and you die. We spoke to a salty dog on the way back who said the notice was put up 10 years ago and he's been swimming there twice a day ever since.

Upon our return home Michèle decided it was time for a proper walk. I was beginning to wonder if she had some sort of substance abuse problem.

'It's midnight, for God's sake,' I said.

'Yes, yes, but just a little walk. I have to show you behind and above the house.'

It was like a magical fairy world in the soft blue night light with steep steps and paths lined with trees, leading to sumptuous homes and sublime gardens. I wondered how people got their groceries up and down so many steps.

'Well,' said Michèle, 'the old ones die, the young ones have strong thighs and the rich ones have lifts that go from their garages down on the street, through the solid rock and up to their homes.'

'No.'

'Yes they do. They really have rock lifts.'

Before bed we had the *digestif maison* – tasty bicarbonate of soda. Yum.

In the morning we drove up to visit the Notre-Dame-de-la-Garde basilica perched on top of a limestone spike. It was built by Espérandieu in the 19th century in Romano-Byzantine style and dedicated to La Bonne Mère (Our Lady). To this end it has a huge gilded statue of the Virgin on top of the belfry which can be seen for kilometres. Inside, things get very ornate with mosaics, murals, multi-coloured marble and naïve paintings of accidents and ships lost at sea, pleading with Our Lady to find their loved ones. Model ships and boats hang from the high ceilings, the history of Marseilles can be seen in the names on the thank-you plaques around the walls and there is still a pilgrimage there every year on the 15th of August.

The oldest and most extraordinary basilica in Marseilles, the Basilique St-Victor, was our next stop. Originally built in the fifth century in honour of St Victor, the patron saint of sailors and millers (how he got those two together I don't know but I think it had to do with the fact he was martyred by being slowly ground between two millstones. In my opinion, millers don't deserve him), it was rebuilt in 1040. The interesting bit is, the old church was submerged underneath the new one and became the crypt containing catacombs with ancient pagan and Christian sarcophagi and remains of martyrs and even supposedly Mary Magdalene, Martha and St Lazarus. Every year on the 2nd of February the Marseillais, led by their fishmongers, go in procession to St-Victor to commemorate the legendary arrival of these saints on Provençal soil. The oldest bakery in Marseille on the Place St-Victor, the Four des Navettes, makes special little cakes for this occasion called *navettes* in the shape of hollowed-out boats.

We rewarded ourselves with a stroll, a coffee and a view of the boats on the Quai Rive Neuve, precisely at the Bar de la Marine where they serve a good aïoli on Fridays. Aïoli was always eaten on a Friday because Catholics couldn't eat meat, and the tradition has remained. Along the quai we looked in at Brasserie 27, full of artists, theatre people and writers. Michèle knew she could always find her friends there – but of course it was July and everyone was away for the summer. She was dressed in her simple but stylish bourgeois/artist look of little white lace-up shoes, fitting white pants, white T-shirt and blue Chinese linen jacket with the collar up. The alternative might be a black sweater with a scarf around the waist or at the neck and dark red lipstick. I always feel as though I got dressed in a circus tent where I just took a bit of everyone's costumes, when I'm with Michèle. We got home just in time for 'that time of the day', 6 p.m. – whisky and olives. Tomato halves were draining upside down on the chopping board and the garlic and shallots lay chopped, emitting their addictive perfume. Sea breezes blew in the large windows and intense light illuminated my reading of Simone de Beauvoir's *A Very Easy Death* about the demise of her mother. Michèle was reading John Le Carré's *Our Game*. She loves English literature and reads it voraciously. She and other people keep telling me secrets about famous French people that they make me promise not to repeat. This is the terrible conundrum of the writer – do you tell the truth and write well or do you censor yourself, therefore diluting and self-editing to please your friends and family? The truth is so much more stirring and urgent.

Michèle began preparing dinner in her usual brisk and efficient way. Fish (the tender white pageot) emptied and sprinkled with salt, pepper, olive oil, basil, parsley, fennel, garlic, shallots and bay leaf. Drained tomatoes also sprinkled with above. She decided to do a barbecue which always makes me nervous because the French, frankly, haven't a clue. They either burn the house down or steam the food. Nice if you want a cup of duck breast tea but tragic if you want to make contact between lower and upper molars. All this in spite of the fact that 'barbeque' derives from the French *babracot* or the Spanish *barbacoa*, both adaptions of Caribbean words, which mean a framework of sticks set upon posts for supporting meat over a fire. She got the carbon going then threw perfumy *sarments de vigne* (grapevine twigs) on top. Only, the twigs were wet and everything went kaput so out came the starter fluid. I recognised a crisis and ran down two flights of stairs to refill the wine jug from the basement supply. Starter fluid lasted for a while then twigs went out, more supplies from basement, more starter fluid, placement of fish on grill, extinguishing of flames, more crisis treatment. This continued in a series of farcical layers. Michèle thought it was funny and I didn't care because what the hell when you're happy, but France needs Australian immigrants, the world's best barbequers, desperately. Desperately.

Another wonderful place in Marseilles is the market at

Place du Marché des Capucins opposite the Noailles métro stop. It's there every day and is a typical combination of Marseille rudeness, hilarity, *joie de vivre*, colour and southern salesmanship: bursting with Arab groceries full of preserved lemons, melting baklava, juicy Agen prunes, jet black olives, couscous, red rice and spices; African hairdressers with fantastic wigs I was dying to try on; African stalls with opened melons, weird fruit, exotic vegetables and dried fish; the usual colourful Provençal fruit piled up high; anchovies, capers, herbs; the smell of roasting coffee; people laughing and yelling at you to buy their wares; fish shops with dozens of kinds of fish and shops selling Provençal fabrics. I bought a few metres of pistachio green fabric with black olives, dark green leaves and yellow flowers printed on it to bring Marseilles to my home.

Camargue red rice is a product introduced to me by my sister Keriann and there it was at the market. If Marseille is the wild west, the Camargue around the coast a bit further, swaddling the Rhône delta, is real cowboy country with real cowboys and girls. Camargue means black bulls bred for bull fighting, salt lakes, horses and flamingos in that swampy, desolate but passionate, wild land. It's desperately hard to grow crops in salt-ridden, water-logged soil, so someone came up with the clever idea of growing rice. The land is flooded with water from the Rhône which pushes the salt down, the rice seeds are sown on top of the earth at the end of April, the land undergoes controlled flooding and the crop is harvested in September. No one knows where the red rice came from – it just appeared one day in amongst normal long grain rice and was cultivated. It looks like brown rice until two weeks before harvesting then suddenly blushes a deep garnet red. It tastes slightly salty, slightly nutty and remains firm and pretty when cooked, which is most simply achieved by boiling it in salted water for 30 minutes, removing the pot from the flame and leaving the rice to steam for another 20 minutes.

The night before I left Marseille we again went up into the neighbourhood behind the house to visit Michèle's friends Isabelle and François in their lovely old home with large garden and stunning view of Marseilles and the neighbours. Out came the whisky and olives, some of which were fake and to François' frustration I inadvertently avoided them. Isabelle, in her flowery skirt and bare feet, was an intelligent, smiling woman and sophisticated conversationalist, while François, a retired sea captain with silver hair and a dapper way of dressing in beige trousers, pale linen jacket and boat shoes, regaled us with his amusing and whimsical talk. He was the very charming sort of man who gives older men a good name. Like Michèle they were both voracious readers of literature and our conversation quickly turned to books and religion, with François and me vying for more damaging Catholic/Protestant childhood stories. Michèle said she didn't believe any of it and insisted we were exaggerating. 'At least you weren't beaten as I was – the school teachers always wanted to know why I had broken fingers.' I was due to leave Marseilles the next day but François insisted on lending me a small book called *Silk* by Alessandro Baricco to read overnight before I debarked. As we walked out of the garden he gave me a flower to mark the page I got to. Of course I only got through a dozen pages before falling asleep, but was captivated by the simple story and bought a copy at the railway station. Even the bookseller had read it and smiled enigmatically when I asked what it was about.

I settled into my seat on the train and watched the Provençal country slip away. This land that didn't provoke love at first sight, but grew on me, resulting in an unshakable attachment. I sighed and kicked my shoes off. Keeping in mind the literary dictum: outside of a dog, a man's best friend is a book; inside of a dog, it's too dark to read, I got my copy of *Silk* out.

Thon Mi-cuit au Sel Fumé, Salade du Sud
Half-cooked Tuna in Smoked Salt with Southern Salad

Serves 6

For the salad:
100g dry coco beans
1 bay leaf
1 sprig of thyme
½ tsp salt
1 capsicum, any colour you like
200g cherry tomatoes
50g pine nuts
100g black olives
½ preserved lemon
½ cup chopped flat-leaf parsley

3 medium courgettes, finely sliced lengthways
avocado oil

For the vinaigrette:
⅓ cup lemon juice
½ tsp Dijon mustard
½ tsp sea salt
freshly ground black pepper
⅔ cup avocado oil
2 tbsp finely chopped chives

For the tuna:
6 x 180g tuna steaks cut 2½cm thick
smoked salt

1. Soak the beans in plenty of water overnight then boil in fresh water with the bay leaf and thyme for 30 minutes. Add salt at the last minute. Drain.

2. Make up the vinaigrette by whisking together the first 4 ingredients (lemon juice, mustard, sea salt, pepper) then gradually add the oil. Stir in the chives.

3. Blacken capsicum, remove skin, core and dice finely.

cont.

4. Halve or quarter tomatoes, depending on how big they are.

5. Fry the pine nuts in a little oil until golden.

6. Stone and chop olives.

7. Discard flesh from preserved lemon and chop skin finely.

8. Toss all the salad ingredients together.

9. Heat a little oil in a frying pan and quickly sauté the courgettes on a high heat.

10. Remove fish from refrigerator 30 minutes before cooking.

11. Heat a heavy-based frying pan to very hot, sprinkle with smoked salt and place tuna on top.

12. Cook for exactly 6 minutes on one side and remove from the pan.

To serve:

Place some courgettes on a plate, top with some salad and drench with a few tablespoonfuls of the vinaigrette. Place tuna on top.

Tarte Fine aux Tomates
Tomato Tart

Serves 6

350g puff pastry
1.5kg acid-free or Italian tomatoes
150g fromage blanc
50g parmesan cheese
4 stalks of fresh basil, leaves chopped
sea salt
freshly ground black pepper
extra virgin olive oil

1. Roll pastry out into a 30cm-diameter circle. Roll it onto a baking tray and place in the refrigerator.

2. Slice tomatoes.

cont.

3. Mix the fromage blanc, parmesan and basil together with salt and pepper. Spread it in the middle of the pastry circle, leaving at least 10cm at the edges, as it will melt when heated.

4. Preheat oven to 200°C. Lay the tomato slices on top in overlapping, concentric circles until they are all used up and cover the pastry completely. Sprinkle with salt and pepper and lightly drizzle with olive oil.

5. Bake the tart for 30 minutes then lower the heat to 150°C and continue for 45 minutes. This seems like a long time but you need the tomatoes to completely reduce and caramelise.

The Sor

hwest

IN CERTAIN VILLAGES in the Pyrénées the pig slaughterer, knife in hand, would intone *La prière du cochon* (The pig's prayer) in front of the firmly restrained pig:

'*Pardonne-nous, cochon, de te tuer aujourd'hui. Nous t'avons nourri avec amour et engraissé à l'envie, mais tu vas assurer dès à présent la subsistence de toute une famille. Nous te privons de ta vie pour la donner aux habitants de cette vallée et nous te remercions, cochon, pour tous les bienfaits que tu vas nous apporter.* (Pardon us, pig, for killing you today. We lovingly fed and fattened you to your fill, but now you are going to ensure that a whole family can live. We take your life to give it to the inhabitants of this valley and we thank you, pig, for all the benefits you will bring to us.)'

Then the throat is slit.

At the crack of dawn, Jessica and I arose for our rendezvous with the train taking me to Cordes-sur-Ciel to visit my brother-in-law Jacques and his wife Aline. Very little sleep, but I was conscious enough to be aware of the 60 kilos of luggage (two suitcases plus red basket plus laptop) I now had to drag around on my own. I had already sent home a carton of stuff at great expense to try to lighten my load but it didn't seem evident to the naked eye or the naked arm. On top of that I had to change twice to get to Albi near Cordes, where Jacques worked. Now I was traveling south to the region of the Languedoc and I could feel it – I was sweating sitting still, all the curtains on the sunny side of the carriage were drawn, the windows were open and the women had their fans fluttering. Opposite me sat a cross-eyed gypsy wearing a head scarf, long skirt and orange platform trainers, a look guaranteed to confuse anyone, and a man with a grey beard smoking a pipe (non-smoking carriage, obviously). I sat with my feet on the seat, my eyes closed, sweat pouring off me at 10 in the morning, wondering what my poor husband's brother would be like. When my husband Alexy died of AIDS in 1995 after a long illness, Jacques had written a very kind letter to me, inviting me to visit them if I ever came back to France. I was moved by this letter from a person I didn't know, who had no reason to communicate with me because after all, Alexy had been a husband of convenience, not a real one: he was a gay man who had married me so I could legally stay in France. His family never knew, as his parents ostracised him for being homosexual. They found out about me just before Alexy died.

On the phone Jacques' voice was very deep, gruff and not particularly warm. I wasn't encouraged but was determined to see the meeting through even if it turned out to be awful. Alexy had become family to me and I had to know what his family was like, I had to close a chapter in my life, and, who could tell, maybe commence another.

I called Jacques when I got to the station and the brusque voice said he had taken the afternoon off to show me around Albi. I waited outside the café near the station in my blue Provençal shirt with my red basket on my knee. After a while a car drew up, a man got out and walked towards me. This can't be him, I thought, he doesn't look anything like the voice on the phone. I expected someone big with horn-rimmed glasses and a serious demeanour. The trim man in jeans, pale shirt and sandals took off his sunglasses and stood in front of me.

'C'est vous? Je ne vous ai pas demandé comment vous étiez.

(It never occurred to me to ask what you look like.)'

He smiled. '*Moi non plus*. (I just assumed I would know you.)'

I stood staring at this man who looked so much like Alexy, if I had seen him in the street I would have asked him if he was related. He looked as Alexy would have looked had he lived to the same age. Handsome, tanned and slim, a young-looking late forties, Jacques had an aquiline nose, square jaw and high cheekbones. They had different mouths and Jacques was a bigger man, but as the days went by I noticed manners of speech, facial expressions and even a style of moving with that charming bit of shyness that was Alexy.

We drove to the *commissariat de police* where he worked, left my bags there and set off on a tour of Albi. First I had to get over the shock of how relaxed and unlike his voice he was, then I had to get over his being a major in the police. I made a mental note never to mention my criminal past, no matter how nice he was to me. Albi is a small and very charming pink (because of the red bricks) town full of snobs, so they say, because it's wealthy and has this absolutely stunning cathedral of unmitigated severity. There is a modern part to the town but I always ignore those sections, preferring to loiter around the beautiful Renaissance mansions. Albi is famous for two things – in the 15th and 16th centuries they made dyer's woad or the colour indigo. This blue dye, extracted from the *Isatis tinctoria* plant, made them rich – turned their place into a land of milk and honey, because they were the only ones who knew how to do it and certain colours like red and blue were considered luxurious. The other thing Albi is famous for is being the seat of Catharism (from the Greek *Kathari* or pure ones) in the 12th century. When Jacques said he loved cathedrals and classical church music I suspected we would get along just fine. When he said he was thirsty and we should start the tour with a stop at the first café, I knew I could relax.

Henri de Toulouse-Lautrec was born in Albi in 1864 and there is a museum dedicated to his works. Toulouse-Lautrec had a bone disease, and broke both his legs as a child, which stopped their growth. Unable to lead the normal life of an aristocrat he took to painting, then decided to brighten up his life by moving to Montmartre in Paris and immersing himself in the marginal world of artists, writers, prostitutes and cabarets. In spite of being a debauched alcoholic he was a brilliant and original painter and lithographer. He finally died in a terrible state of collapse in 1901 at the family château at Mairomé in the Gironde.

The huge cathedral-cum-fortress dominates the town with its harsh, macho, red brick exterior, built after the Crusade to get rid of the Cathars. It was built like a fortress because, as everyone knows, the faithful can be swayed – especially if they're starving – and a bit of physical force never goes astray. However when you get inside it is exactly the opposite – flamboyantly, excessively, overwhelmingly feminine. There are two sections to it, in the sense that there is a church within a church. In the Middle Ages the faithful never saw the priests performing the Mass, they only heard them; hence the expression often used even today by Catholics, 'I'm going off to hear Mass' rather than 'see' Mass. Inside this extravagantly flamboyant inner church with its lace-like stonework the powerful priests reigned and said Mass and the faithful outside heard it, thanking God they were alive. In those days the church was also used as a meeting place, there were no seats, no hushed whispering and once a week there was even a chicken and vegetable market in there. The walls were covered from floor to ceiling with paintings, *trompe l'oeil* and what looked like art deco, painted onto the walls, but in fact it was all original medieval artwork. There wasn't one inch that wasn't painted or engraved or embossed in the whole huge place. We stayed for an organ concert that was stunning not only because of the talent of the organist but also the breathtaking sound of the gigantic organ. Silent for a long time, the organ had been dismantled pipe by pipe and sent away to be repaired at enormous expense in 1981.

After our tour of Albi we drove to Jacques' home in the fields. He and Aline live at the foot of Cordes in an old, two-storeyed farmhouse made of white stones and blue shutters. As is usual in the south all the shutters are kept closed during the day because of the heat and it's cooler inside than it is outside in the shade. There were flowers outside the house and a garden full of vegetables. Their back yard was literally the fields of the farm, with a clear view of Cordes floating on the clouds. Aline is a secretary in a bank in Toulouse where they used to live and drives there and back every day, an hour each way. I was upstairs in my room once again arranging my perfumes, lipsticks and hair combs on someone else's table when I heard her car drive in. I grabbed the present I had carefully packed and unpacked I don't know how many times since I'd left home two months ago and went down to meet her. I had no idea what to expect. What I saw was a tiny creature wrapped around one of the cats, covering it with a long curtain of black hair. She was the size of a clothes peg and fine-boned with large brown eyes in a very pretty face, and a cute gap in her front teeth revealed itself when she smiled, which she did often. The copious waist-length hair was parted down the middle and she was dressed in leggings, a flowing red top and little gold shoes. I thought she must surely have been a doll, even when she opened her mouth to let out the bird-like voice.

Aline and Jacques bent over backwards to be hospitable from the moment I walked into their lives until the moment I walked out four days later. They opened their home, their hearts, their pain and their joy to me in a way that was deeply engaging. It was to be a stay of gourmandising, drinking good wines, dancing and much talking about Alexy and the family. Like a lot of French people they were very open and self-disclosing, talking about relatively private things like politics, relationships and personal philosophies right from the start. The French are not superficial people. They talk about the meaning of life and history and food the way we talk about cricket or sailing. They lost Alexy in 1995 and Jacques lost his only son in a motorbike accident in 1996. Bizarrely, there was to be another family death during my stay. They decided to work through their pain by never wasting a moment of their lives, by living the good times to the full and by being a lot more open with family and friends. Aline's main interests are wine appreciation, her home and shopping, and her one dream in life is to be able to stop work and be at home making things beautiful. She is a collector of household goods and has whole rooms and cupboards full of valuable plates, kitchenware, cutlery and glassware. She buys a lot of clothes and has turned one room into a wardrobe. Jacques is a voracious reader of philosophy, history and religions, his special area being the Cathars, and one room of the house is consecrated to his books. He calls her *choupette* and she calls him *chou*.

I was fascinated by Catharism. This 'heresy' hit the Languedoc in the 12th century with great force even though it was a minority religion, and was closely tied up with commerce. The Catholic church was as rotten as a case of old bananas and the clergy led the life of Riley in contrast to the Cathars, whose 'Perfect Ones' (leaders) led an austere life of poverty, chastity, patience and humility. The basic thesis of the Cathars was the obsessive separation of 'good' from 'evil'. Good was the spiritual world ruled by God and evil was the material world ruled by the Devil; the idea was to lift yourself out of material concerns and enter into the world of light. It was a religion that mostly hit the elite, powerful and well educated and was progressive in its use of birth control, economic practices and equality of women.

They spoke the *langue d'Oc* (the language of Oc), which was the language of the troubadours and the south, were not authoritarian and practised what they preached, whereas the Catholic Church spoke French, which nobody in the area could understand, and was corrupt. Needless to say the Catholic Church just couldn't stand it and began eliminating the Cathars in the traditional way by sending in the troops in a Crusade to pillage and slaughter. The Languedoc was placed under the French monarch, but 20 years later there were still a few Cathars crawling around in the blood and grief so the Inquisition organised a big massacre at nearby Montségur, burning them at the stake in Albi (a dozen of them were saved by the townspeople) and throwing the rest in prison forever.

This is an example of what the Occitan language looks like from a song about the Crusades written in 1209:

> Lo vescomes de Beziers s'es la noit ben gaitetz,
> A l'alba pareichant s'es al mati levetz.
> E li baro de Fransa, can seforon disnetz.
> Se son per tota l'ost cominalment armetz.
> E eels de Carcassona se son aparelhetz.
> Lo jorn i ac mans colps eferitz e donetz
> E, d'una part de'autra, mortz e essanglentetz.

We had dinner in Cordes in the clouds and I ordered the region's most famous dish – the *cassoulet* – haricot beans with pork, goose, duck confit, mutton and Toulouse sausage. It's really a sumptuous winter dish. Aline looked at me askance but I had to have it for research's sake, didn't I?

I used to make cassoulet when I lived in Paris. There's no point in making it for less than a dozen friends because it's time-consuming and it has to be made properly – but it's really worth it on a cold night when you need something to stick to the ribs.

With the cassoulet, we drank a red Gaillac from vineyards

Cassoulet

1 kilo white kidney beans
1 x duck or 1 x goose or 6 confit duck and/or goose legs
½ kilo garlic sausage
goose fat
½ kilo baby onions
½ kilo bacon cut into *lardons* or match-sticks
1 kilo lamb cut into big chunks
1 kilo pork cut into big chunks
½ kilo Toulouse sausage, cut into thick slices
1 kilo peeled, chopped tomatoes
200 ml white wine
1½ litres meat stock
1 big bouquet garni
lots of chopped garlic
2 tbsp tomato paste
freshly ground black pepper
100g dried breadcrumbs

1. Soak kidney beans for at least 2 hours, then place in a huge saucepan and simmer covered in salted water for almost 1 hour or until they are just soft.

2. Meanwhile, roast or fry the duck/goose.

3. Poach the garlic sausage for 30 minutes then slice it into big chunks and put aside.

4. Heat goose fat in a large, heavy-based frying pan and brown baby onions and bacon.

5. Remove onions and bacon and place in a big ovenproof dish, then brown the lamb in the goose fat. Add lamb to the dish, then brown the pork and throw it into the dish as well.

6. Brown Toulouse sausage and put aside.

7. Add to the dish: tomatoes, wine, meat stock, bouquet garni, garlic, tomato paste and freshly ground black pepper. Bring all this to the boil, cover and bake in the oven at 200°C for 1 hour.

8. At the end of the hour melt the fat off the duck or goose meat and chop into quite large pieces. Add these, the Toulouse sausage and garlic sausage to the saucepan. Cover and continue cooking for another 30 minutes.

cont.

9. Drain the beans and add them to the casserole. Gently stir everything in, check for seasoning, discard the bouquet garni and add more water or stock if necessary to keep the cassoulet moist.

10. Sprinkle the top with breadcrumbs and bake for 30 minutes or more until there is a golden brown crust. Now you can serve it. The beans should be soft and melting and so should you. This is baked beans in its original majestic form.

near Albi. Gaillac wine was highly valued in the 16th century then went into decline. Most of the vines were destroyed by phylloxera then replanted in their old varieties, some of which are the oldest in France. Producing reds, whites, rosés and sparklings, Gaillac has an *appellation d'origine contrôlée* and has refound its originality, a taste that is unique in France.

I rose early and rode into Toulouse with Aline to spend the day there. We parked at the métro, got the underground into town and walked to the market near her bank on Boulevard de Strasbourg, arranging to meet at the end of the day at a café in the arcades of Place de Capitole. The market reeked of fruit and I found the irregular, flat, little *pêches de vigne* that I had tasted at Jessica's. The usual rôtisseries were there, with chickens and pork roasts lined up on spits dripping onto sausages, potatoes and brochettes on the rack below. Toulouse is famous for its sausage and saucisson and fat, handmade *boudins* (black puddings) hung on every charcuterie stall. We are still in the southwest here, so it's confit and foie gras country. There were watermelons split open to reveal their blood-red flesh with its black seeds, mountains of limes, fresh almonds, tiny avocados, pineapples from the Ivory Coast and purple figs. There were what we call brown mushrooms, which the French call *gros blonds* (fat blond ones) being sold by a fat blonde with thick black eyebrows.

I walked up rue Alsace-Lorraine to the covered market at Place des Carmes, where I reccied the cheese shops then settled on the best one, Chez Betty, which turned out to be Alines' favourite. This area's most famous cheeses are Roquefort and Brebis des Pyrénées. They had every cheese imaginable, but specialised in goat's cheese – chèvre wrapped in vine leaves, chèvre in pyramids, heart-shaped chèvre, peppered chèvre, herbed chèvre, fresh, half-dry and dry chèvre. There was even a necklace of Gers chèvre in little hard balls called *collier de St Martin*, which I bought and munched on for the rest of the day. I walked past the bar where people were drinking already at 9 a.m. and wriggled into a position at the stand-up café Catherine further along the market. At one end of the bar three merchants were having their lunch, having had breakfast at 5 a.m. At 9.30 a.m. they were happily and noisily slurping up foie gras and Sauternes as a first course. I ordered a crème and a croissant and asked them if that was their breakfast. Hearing my accent and assuming I was one step from Neanderthal, the one with the big moustache and stomach sneered condescendingly,

'*Ce n'est pas le petit déjeuner, Madame, c'esi du pâté de campagne et du coca.* (It's not breakfast, Madame, it's country pâté and coke.)'

'*Eh bien, regardez-moi ça, et moi qui ne savais pas qu'un pâté de campagne puisse être si moelleux.* (Well, fancy that – I didn't know country pâté could be so smooth.),' I said, straight-faced. He turned and looked at me more closely.

'*Vous venez d'où, par exemple?* (Where are you from then?)'

'*De l'autre côté du monde. Mais dîtes, ça sert à quoi vos ustensiles-là?* (I'm from the other side of the world. But tell me, what are these utensils for?),' I asked, pointing to their knives and forks.

'*C'est pour manger, bien sûr, Madame.* (They're for eating, of course.)'

I put a look of wonder on my face. '*Ah-h-h. Vous savez, chez moi on n'a pas ça. On mange par terre avec les mains.* (Where I come from we eat on the ground with our hands.)'

Silence. Staring uncomfortably.

'*La malpolitesse. Monsieur, n'est pas une rue sens unique. Bon appétit.* (Rudeness, Sir, is not a one-way street, it can go both ways.)'

It really aided digestion to have the butcher enthusiastically karateing his meat in front of the café, workers walking past with carcasses over their shoulders and a man at the other end of the bar eating herrings in tomato sauce out of a tin (with a glass of wine of course). The young couple who ran the café were very nice and I got to talking with them. They open at 5 a.m. and close at 1 p.m. with the arrival and departure of their clients. Against the back wall of the tiny café were two gas burners for cooking steaks and eggs. One frying pan had shallots quietly simmering away in preparation for the second course of the fat man's lunch, the other was heating up for the steaks to be thrown in. They were whipped out just as quickly and smacked down bloody on their plates, there being nothing so pathetic and wimpish as vegetables or lettuce leaves in this real man's meal. Slapping my coins down on the counter I moved on to the fish department sparkling with *petits gris* snails and little crabs crawling all over each other. There was the subtle and tender *flétan* (halibut), fresh sardines, mackerel, eel, *bar* (bass or sea perch), tiny *crevettes grises* (the crunchy shrimps that you eat whole), *cigales* (cicada-shaped prawns), *violets* (purple cockles), *bigorneaux* (winkles) and the delicious bright green seaweed called *salicorne*.

Stylish and beautiful Toulouse is another one of the luminous pink cities bathed in Mediterranean light. It is made out of the thin, red bricks typical of the alluvial plain of the Garonne and as I walked through the day, the pinks of the buildings changed with the light from smoky pink to soft salmon to red/purple. Toulouse is famous for its aeronautical construction industry, has a first-rate university and lots of museums, art galleries, theatres and music. The town hall at Place de la Capitole is a splendid 140-metre-long harmony of colourful red brick, stone and gold. One can walk inside and up the majestic stone and marble stairs to the Salle des Illustres, rooms extravagantly covered from floor to ceiling with paintings of famous Toulouseans, chandeliers, trompe l'oeil ceilings, pillars and statues of women with perfect breasts. Outside, inlaid into the large square, is an enormous bronze Occitan cross surrounded by the signs of the zodiac. I saw a Bonnard exhibition at the Bemberg Foundation in the Hôtel d'Assézat and a wonderful Henri Rousseau exhibition of paintings and sketches of Arab horses and hawkers at the Musée des Augustins. There are typical southern French Gothic-style double cloisters inside the museum; and within the cloisters is a flower, vegetable and herb garden.

On the way home Aline and I treated ourselves to a tasting at Plageole, a third-generation vineyard and one of her favourites. When we got home loaded down with boxes of wine to keep us going, we found Jacques busy in the kitchen whipping up a feast. The Laguiole table set came out, a different glass for each wine was lined up, the toaster was placed on the table and the Sauternes decanted into a crystal jug. Gosh, I thought, all this for a Tuesday night – they'll be lucky if I ever leave. We started with champagne and pistachios and the dragging out of family photos. I saw the severe father and the seven sons who in fact all looked very different – Jacques and Alexy were the only two who resembled each other. Alexy wrote a lot of poems in the years he was ill and Jacques put them all together into a book. With tears of ink Alexy accuses and condemns his inflexible father and the insidious society that won't tolerate difference. I read the sad, joyous, painful poems and was surprised to find a fantasy love poem to me called '*Chevelure de Feu*' (Flaming

Hair). I knew my husband liked me, but I didn't know he had been in love with me. The poem spoke of his desire for us to be a proper man and wife, and of how good that would have been, in another world. These bitter/sweet revelations came as a total shock to me.

The bread was popped into the toaster and out came the homemade foie gras.

'Mmm I lo-o-ve fois gras. What a treat,' I purred happily.

'I read the passage in your first book where you say you ate foie gras for breakfast every day for a week,' smiled Jacques. That made me suspect you liked it. This foie gras is special because it was made in 1985 by Aline's mother.'

There was no such thing as a quick or boring meal chez Jacques and Aline. They even set the table and sat down for breakfast, something I haven't done since I left home, an excited 17-year-old nurse. Every meal was an opportunity to talk, discuss and regulate the world's problems; every morsel a way of giving of themselves. Following the foie gras we had a salad with lots of things in it, including blue borage flowers. The St-Emilion red came out for the roast lamb which was *à point* – absolutely perfect – and we finished it off with Roquefort from down the road and my chèvre necklace. Dessert was cherries preserved by Jacques and a glass of plum eau-de-vie made by the plumber.

Aline took the next day off to drive me past hills of sunflowers to the market at Carmaux and of course buy yet more dresses. She bought *ail rosé de Lautrec*, which she describes as the best garlic in the region, and led me to the *échaudés*, which she hadn't stopped talking about all morning. I thought it was going to be some revolting tripe omelette or something but when we found the stall it was surrounded three-deep by people desperate to get at these hard little biscuits. They were all the same shape but of differing sizes – bread dough rolled out and folded into triangles, some with anis seeds in them. The French love dunking them in their coffee for breakfast or dipping them in wine and sugar so they swell up. We also tasted a *fouace de l'Aveyron*, a turnover stuffed with prunes. 'Of course it's good,' said Aline, 'it comes from my home, the Aveyron valley – everything they make is good. *Tout est bon en Ayeyron.*'

Lunch was chèvre and cured ham from the market with cold lamb, tomatoes from the garden, leftover foie gras and homemade saucisson from its jar full of oil served with a different tablecloth, different plates and different cutlery. This was followed by coffee in Royal Albert cups (English tableware is Aline's favourite), sugared violets from Toulouse, Valrhona chocolate and Thuries chocolate. Thuries is a very well known chef who has a three-star restaurant in Cordes, one of the best cooking magazines in France and now naughty chocolate shops all over the place. All meals were always accompanied by discourse on food and wine.

Jacques brought out his Laguiole pocket knife, showed me how to open and close it without committing unnecessary surgery, explained that you never wash it, only wipe it and said, 'Now its yours'. I was very touched because I had wanted a Laguiole knife for years, and now I had one that meant more to me than a bought one could ever mean. In France the country people always carry their own knife and whip it out for every meal. The bull engraved on the blade and the bee at the hilt of the handle guarantee its authenticity. The town of Laguiole, pronounced 'Layole' by the locals, is famous for its Fourme cheese, its cattle, its knives and one of the best restaurants in France, Michel Bras' Lou Mazuc. In 1829 a craftsman called Pierre Calmels started making the elegant and easy to use Laguiole knives with their distinctive horn and aluminium handles. Some of them have corkscrews and a long pointed implement for getting stones out of horses' hooves. They have become a kind of cult now – even Parisians pretentiously take out their Laguiole in restaurants.

After visiting Najac with its ruined fortress which sits on

a conical peak in the Aveyron, we drove to a farm-auberge called Les Chênes for a farm dinner. Jacques and I share a fault: we have absolutely no sense of direction, so he drove us around in circles for a few hours through the Grésigne forest, past deer, until we finally got to Les Abrioles, then Peyre Blanque and a farmhouse sparkling in the night.

'Oh, look at the beautiful animals,' exclaimed Aline.

'Yes. Look at the venison with red wine and croutons,' exclaimed Jacques and I.

'You are both horrible,' exclaimed she, 'and I forbid you to eat wild animals.'

'But if it's already dead, then it is my duty to eat it,' said Jacques.

'How could any woman sleep with a hunter?'

'Maybe we really are what we eat,' I ventured.

'No, we are what we think,' said Jacques.

Exhausted from arguing about wild animals and directions, we fell into the arms of the very nice farmer's wife and her big, handsome son Serge. The restaurant was attached to the farmhouse by the large kitchen, the wine was already open on the table and everyone else in the restaurant fell over laughing at how long it had taken us to get there.

Serge in his big boots and check shirt brought out a salad with *friands* (little meat pasties), duck meat and duck liver terrine and *rillettes de canard* (potted duck), all made by himself. You have to call in advance to eat at Les Chênes, they tell you what they've cooked that day and you make your choice. Aline and I chose *canette farcie au foie* (liver-stuffed female duckling) and of course Jacques chose *civet de sanglier* (wild boar stew). It came with potatoes sautéd in duck fat. This was real, hearty country food from their farm that they killed, dressed and cooked themselves, the food they had eaten all their lives. Unfortunately it was warm rather than hot, but maybe that's how farmers eat. By the time we got to the chèvre we were seriously flagging, but perked up

Terrine de Foie Gras
Fattened Duck Liver Pâté

1 kg fattened fat duck liver
2 tbsp port
2 tbsp cognac
½ tsp sea salt
6 good twists of the pepper mill (white pepper corns)
1 small black truffle (optional), sliced finely

1. Gently separate the lobes of the liver. Never cut them. Gently remove the veins, pulling them through the soft liver with the back of a vegetable knife. Avoid damaging the liver as much as possible.

2. Put liver pieces in a bowl and pour over the marinade of port and cognac. If you're using truffles they may be inserted into the liver now. Cover and marinate overnight in the fridge.

3. Preheat the oven to 90°C. Place the liver in an earthenware terrine, pour over any remaining marinade and press down so there are no spaces. Cover with tin foil or the lid of the terrine.

4. Cook for an hour then remove and allow to cool in the terrine. Refrigerate overnight.

Alternatively, you can cook foie gras *a la torchon* (wrapped in a tea towel with the ends tied) and poach it gently in water on top of the stove.

To serve:
Cut into centimetre-thick slices and eat with toasted brioche bread and a glass of Monbazillac.

with the very melting pear tart. They also made such rustic classics as stuffed chicken, coq au vin, country soups and confit de canard. Although it is very isolated, people come from as far as Toulouse to eat there and if you're too tired to go home you can stay the night in one of their rooms. Our hosts loved talking and cooking and we were there until well after midnight gossiping over the inevitable cognac, in spite of the fact that they had a farm to run and had to get up at the crack of dawn seven days a week.

The next morning Aline and I were up and off to the market at Cordes with her disco tapes blaring, leaving Jacques at home with Beethoven's 9th. At the market I stood rooted to the ground watching a plump pretty woman selling fresh trout. When someone bought one, she scooped it out of the tank, grabbed the tail with a teatowel wrapped around her hand, whacked it on the head a few times with her truncheon, emptied it and handed it all ready and quivering to the customer. I thought, if business ever fell off, she could get a job with the police force. All the butchers and charcuteries in the region only stock meat from local farms that they personally know – nothing is brought in from anywhere else and you can ask them exactly what farm it came from. The best thing we bought that day makes my mouth water just thinking about it. A lady farmer was there selling her vegetables and at the end of her stall were three white cardboard boxes with many bees hovering over them. In these boxes were slithers of heaven, flakes of molten goodness, layers of ecstasy that she called *la crostade*. Aline said it looked like a *pastis de Gers* – an apple tart made with flaky pastry that sticks up like golden wings on top. It's really hard to describe, even harder to make and extremely easy to eat.

We ran home with our treasure. By now the 5th symphony was on and it was sunny, so we set the table outside in the sunshine and of course used different tablecloth, cutlery, glasses and plates. In a moment of madness Aline got out a majestic and full-bodied Châteauneuf-du-Pape in a deformed bottle she had been hoarding. It was perfect with the liver saucisson, garden tomatoes dripped with balsamic vinegar, crunchy country bread and jambon du pays. All this, however, was just to pass the time until we got to the heated crostade which melted and crunched with layer upon layer of caramelised apples, rum and sugar and was helped down with Sauternes. It was the best tart I ate that whole summer.

Pastis de Gers
Flaky Apple Tart

Orange blossom water is produced by the distillation of the flowers of the Seville orange. It originated in the Middle East and is used in sweets, salads and tagines and sometimes to flavour coffee. You can even sprinkle it over your bed linen. In the southwest of France where this magical recipe comes from, bitter orange was cultivated for the production of orange blossom water, primarily as a perfume then as a flavouring. Traditionally this tart is made with goose fat but I have found olive oil to produce a light and delicious pastry. Lemon or mandarin infused oil would be even better.

6 tart cooking apples
6 tbsp armagnac or other cognac
6 tbsp orange blossom water
12 sheets filo pastry
extra virgin olive oil in spray pump
runny honey

1. Peel, core and slice apples and marinate in armagnac and orange blossom water for at least a couple of hours.

2. Preheat oven to 180°C.

3. Spray a fairly deep tart tin with olive oil. Keeping the rest of the filo pastry protected with a semi-damp cloth, lay one sheet on the bench and spray with oil, lay another sheet on top the other way and repeat this process until you have four sheets on top of each other. Place in the tart tin, scrunching up the overlapping edges into delicate, high folds.

4. Drain apples well (drink the delicious marinade) and lay most of them in the bottom.

5. Spray last sheets of filo with olive oil and gently scrunch into interior of tart tin. Now hide the remaining sliced apples in amongst the folds and drizzle with lots of honey.

6. Bake for half an hour or until golden and crunchy but not brown. Cover the top with tin foil if necessary while baking.

The pastis version is apparently made with calvados and flamed at the table. The hospitality stretched to the doing of dishes also. Every time they found me bashing around at the kitchen sink they said OUT, we don't make guests do the dishes here.

In the late afternoon we got dressed up and set off for the beautiful Aveyron valley on an adventure. When we crossed the bridge into the Aveyron Aline was elated to be *chez elle* again. We followed the Viour River to her sister Andrée's house in the village of St-Just, where they were both brought up. This was really *la France profonde*, deepest darkest France, and suddenly in the valley things didn't look southern anymore; they were lush and green and damp and smelled of wild mint and heather and grass. We all went for a walk in the dappled evening light along the river with Andrée's (Dédé for short) deaf dog, winding back to the house to get ready for the adventure. Aline emerged in the little gold shoes, silver bracelets and silver nailpolish, Jacques was very chic in white linen shirt and pressed khaki slacks and Dédé was transformed by a pretty blue dress, crystal necklace and bright red lipstick. Aline spoke with a typical southwest accent wherein she sort of sang her sentences, ending them all with '*eh*'. Instead of saying *mon Dieu* she said *mo-o-on Dieu*, dragging it out, and all words ending in *ain* became *aing*. Dédé spoke with the same accent but more pronounced and when we got to her friend's house to pick her up she spoke with an even stronger accent. We all sat around their kitchen table drinking Pernod with pappy (grandpa) with his beret and glass of wine. In the country they seem to talk at the tops of their voices and with the thick accents, I lost a lot of the conversation. We piled into two cars and after a while arrived at the village of Tayac for our adventure – the famous annual Fête de l'Aligot.

Aligot is a dish that combines two of my favourite things – potatoes and fresh Tomme cheese all whipped up together. The aligot festival has three parts to it; first there's an aligot eating competition, then there's a dinner, followed by a bal of old-time dancing with an accordion band. Country people from the village and miles around hung around outside the *salle des fêtes* (party hall) in the warm evening drinking *des jaunes* (Pernod), catching up with old friends. The plain, unadorned women, mostly of the stocky, no-nonsense variety, had cardies over their shoulders, and the weatherbeaten men had caps on their heads or unnaturally well-combed hair. One woman stood out like a lit match in a blackout and I couldn't even begin to imagine where exactly she thought she was – of 'a certain age' with bright orange cockatoo-style hair, nail varnish to match, bright blue eyeliner not distracting from the hooked nose, tight top, fitting yellow skirt and plastic high heels. I liked the colour of her hair but the rest was a horror. A long table was set up, numbers from one to 10 written on the paper tablecloth and plates and utensils set down, along with water and wine.

'Mo-o-on Dieu,' said the woman next to me, 'they shouldn't put water on the table. You never drink water with an aligot otherwise you'll blow up.'

I thought it might have been wise for me to stand back. People were gathering around the table, the mayor made a speech about the time-honoured contest of stuffing as much aligot down your throat as you could in the shortest possible time and asked for volunteers.

After a bit of shuffling around the contestants, one of whom was a brave woman, settled themselves at the table, what looked like white cowpats were weighed, slapped onto their plates, the timer was set and the bell rang. The crowd ooed and aahed. The contestants blanched with fear and made jokes in patois. Due to certain past excesses resulting in prostration, the mayor decided that the contestants weren't allowed to eat more than a kilo of aligot. There were 500 people all yelling and encouraging the contestants. As a potato eater of Irish extraction of some repute, I thought they were eating very slowly. The farmer in front of me was the favourite, shovelling the gloopy mixture down with a huge smile on his face. He screamed back at the crowd, who were laughing to the point of tears, with food hanging out of his mouth, drank gallons of wine and paused every so often to eat some from the woman's plate, to help her. Everyone was encouraging her and yelling, '*Tu ne vas pas faire des petits ce soir, ma poule.* (You won't be making any babies tonight, chicken.)' When he won, the crowd went mad.

We filed slowly into the hall and took our places for dinner. Red wine was on the long tables and the first course was (and always is every year) melon with Muscat wine in the hollow followed by *jambon du pays* with *pain de campagne.* All the farmers near me whipped out their Laguioles. I quietly took mine out and began eating. They noticed, so we compared knives – they showed me theirs and I showed them mine and I felt at one with the universe, a real woman with a real knife at last. Jacques was saying how much he loved snails in vinaigrette for breakfast and the peasants around us were discussing the best way to cook foie gras. The *pièce de résistance* arrived with great fanfare as a gigantic pot was carried by the chefs to the front of the room. One of them jumped up on the table and stirred it with a huge wooden spoon the size of a broom, lifting the aligot up as high as it would go without breaking or sticking to the sides to prove to the crowd that it had been properly made. There is no short cut. An aligot has to have the strips of cheese stirred into the mashed potatoes by hand all in the same direction and it takes about three quarters of an hour.

The aligot was scooped out of the pot with small bowls into big bowls and placed on the tables for people to help themselves. There's an art to getting the aligot onto your plate because it has the consistency of play-dough. The woman next to me was really good at rolling it with her fork, scooping it up and plopping the delicious, pale mixture onto plates. And boy was it worth it – smooth, subtle and filling.

Wood-grilled sausages covered in herbs came around next to go with the aligot. When I asked what they were called I was told, '*Ça s'appelle des saucisses de Tayac*. (Tayac sausages.)'

'Why? What's special about Tayac sausages?' I had to ask.

'*Parce que ce sont des saucisses d'ici, pas d'ailleurs.* (Because they're made here, not elsewhere.)'

Aline watched me talking to the peasants and said, 'You know, I couldn't wait to get out of my village when I was young and I was embarrassed by these people and their unsophisticated ways. Now I find that I appreciate their honesty and straightness. Unlike city people, they are your friends for life and will always stick by you when you are in trouble. It takes longer to get close but the relationships are much more genuine.'

Some of the older people near me were speaking in patois. Here's an example of what it looks like, taken from an old poem about wheat growing:

> *La sason buta las erbas totas.*
> *Pren coratge pagés, tos blats an bona cara.*
> *Deja de la seguiol l'espiga se desclara;*
> *Mas, se l'i pensa pas, un orre mescladis*
> *Amb un aire insolent sus tos camps s'espandis.*
> *Jos la planta estrangiera, ailas! lieja estofada*
> *La filha de l'ostal d'aliments es privada.*

The cheese course was followed by chocolate and coffee eclairs followed by a knees-up to beat all knees-ups. The *bal musette* band was composed of three accordionists, one a young girl with fat legs, dimpled knees and miniskirt, a guitar, keyboards and a *cabrette* – a sort of bagpipe. They sang a patriotic Occitan song in patois then struck up the *bourrée*, a folk dance where you sort of turn in fast circles, clap your hands and do a jig. Everyone poured onto the dance floor. Jacques, who I was told rarely dances, was the first of our group up and at it. Being very *javaneuse* (liking dancing) myself, I danced with all the ploucs, with Jacques, with the farmers, with anyone who asked me and every dance was different. Some of them you did in rows holding people's hands at your shoulders, some you danced in a circle round the floor, some you changed partners, some you stamped and jumped and some strange ones you did on your own. A lot of them reminded me of the jigs and reels I did at the Irish club as a gel. There were also the more classic dances like waltzes, foxtrots, paso dobles and tangos. We didn't get to bed until five and were up again a few hours later, bug-eyed, for the market at Saint-Antonin-Noble-Val.

The pretty town of St-Antonin is on the right side of the Aveyron valley on a very beautiful site and the big Sunday market winds up and down streets, seeming to take over half the town. There is live music, most of it Spanish or *gitane* (gypsy), lots of local produce and so many people you can't move. There were *grillons*, those moreish bits of fried duck confit leftovers, *oreillettes* (deep fried sheets of orange-flavoured pastry covered in sugar, see facing page), and *rasquil* (a round loaf of brioche covered in sugar). I went mad and bought a kilo of fresh cèpes for dinner and Jacques bought some *magrets* (duck breasts) to go with them. There were the inevitable children and toddlers with dummies stuffed in their mouths. French parents have the most revolting custom of keeping dummies in their kids' mouths right up to the age of two, three and even four. Maybe it is for this reason the French are such gastronomes – they are educated from birth to always have something in their mouths, be it food, wine, a cigarette or a kiss. It was sunny, we were in a good mood and I got caught up with watching an extraordinary band. Under the trees seven swarthy men in black suits, black shirts, black ties, black hats and black moustaches played heart-stopping gypsy music and sang. The instruments included a *cymbalum*, or gypsy piano, which was open and played on the strings with two soft batons, an accordion, two

Oriellettes
Deep-fried Pastries

Makes 20–30

2½ cups (300g) flour
½ tsp salt
3 small eggs, beaten
30g soft butter
grated rind of one orange and one lemon
1 tsp orange flower water
2 litres peanut or vegetable oil
frying thermometer
caster sugar

1. Sift the flour and salt onto the bench and make a well in the centre. Into this put the eggs, butter, grated rinds and orange flower water.

2. Using fingers, gradually work in the flour until all is incorporated and you have a smooth, soft ball that comes away from your fingers. Wrap in plastic and refrigerate for at least 4 hours.

3. Divide pastry in four and roll out very thinly. With a pastry cutter, cut into 8 x 4cm rectangles.

4. Heat the oil in a deep fryer to 190°C and drop in pastry rectangles in batches. Fry until they are just golden then remove to a cake rack to drain onto paper towels. Sprinkle with lots of caster sugar and eat immediately.

violins, a double bass, cymbals, an auto harp and other things I couldn't identify. When I asked them where they came from they replied, 'Gitania' – Gypsyland.

Jacques cooked my farewell dinner and here is the menu:

Le Festin de Jacques

Apéritif: Ondenc from Plageole's vineyard with grillons and liver saucisson

Entrée: Green salad with grillons
Main: Duck breasts marinated in garlic, salt and pepper
and barbecued, sautéd cèpes with pale salmon-coloured
Listel gris, the best rosé I've ever tasted
Cheeses

We sat outside in the warm evening and everything was served on English plates with plants and butterflies on them. We drank out of crystal glasses and ate cheese off crystal plates. They said it was heresy to drink rosé with duck but after our excesses we really did need something light. But something was wrong and I couldn't put my finger on it; Jacques seemed sombre and reflective and I assumed he was tired. The next morning we said our fond goodbyes and Aline drove me to the train station at Toulouse. On the way she told me Jacques' father had died yesterday afternoon. He got the news as he was preparing our dinner and he continued without saying anything. The father who in life had alienated his son, not even seeing him before he died, wished to be buried next to him. What you can't achieve in life you try to achieve in death.

Burgundy

THE WEALTH OF ALL Burgundian towns and cities comes from wine and up to the start of the 19th century, the land surrounding Auxerre was covered with vines. On the square where the Palais de Justice is, farmers and winegrowers lived and worked. There was a medieval 'curtain' wall surrounding the town that was demolished in the 18th century to be replaced by the boulevards circling Auxerre. The moats were filled in, walks were created on the old mounds and the bourgeois moved in and built magnificent, gracious houses, most of which are still standing. Before they allowed the bourgeois into town, Auxerre was a very aristocratic place, inhabited only by noblemen and clergy. The new civilian era was celebrated by the construction of the dazzling clocktower on one of the gates to the old castle which doesn't exist anymore, now the centre of town. The street names of Auxerre tell its story – for example, rue des Boucheries was a street full of butcher shops, rue des Lombards was inhabited by Italian bankers called Lombardi, below it rue des Sous Murs was constructed under the walls of the houses on rue des Lombards.

When I arrived in Burgundy I was in a state of complete exhaustion. The trip from Toulouse to Auxerre was a day-long nightmare with the train from Toulouse leaving 20 minutes late, giving me 30 seconds to make all my connections. At Montpellier I leapt across the platform from one train to the other as it was leaving the station. I got on at the end of the train and of course my seat was at the beginning, only it was the longest train in the history of the universe. Absolutely no question of dragging two heavy suitcases, a laptop and the red basket through a mile of backpackers, children, dogs, travelers and mail, so I left the cases there. Twenty minutes of tripping over people later I fell into my seat, dripping in the heat, and frankly wouldn't have cared if the cases had fallen off the side, except for the J-P Gaultier shoes and the French nightie.

When we arrived at Dijon I jumped off and ran down the platform to the other end of the train to get my suitcases, and just as I got there the train started leaving, which is when I started screaming. Someone threw the cases off and out of nowhere the stationmaster picked them up and said calmly and suavely, '*Suivez-moi, Madame.*' I was so out of breath and roasting hot I couldn't talk so mutely held up my ticket. We crossed the lines and he put me on the train on the other side which was just leaving, smiled and said *bon voyage.* I slumped into my place, sweat pouring off me in buckets, running through my lipstick and literally sticking me to the seat. I asked myself honestly if I really needed these adventures. At Laroche-Migennes I again had 30 seconds to transfer so when I got off the train at Auxerre my first friendly words to Frédéric and Kathy were I AM NOT TOUCHING THESE BLOODY BOLLOCKING BAGS.

Frédéric put his hands up at my exclamation but obeyed, as is his wont, Kathy smiled sympathetically as is her lovely wont, and I slouched like a beaten dog to the stationwagon, my hair plastered to my face.

Kathy was looking radiant, slim and pretty, and Frédéric was tanned, expansive, relaxed and funny. He's a master of the 'all-over-kiss' wherein every part of your body gets covered by every part of his body in the space of one kiss. All the men in his family are just like him – tall, big and intense. They had brought back all sorts of things from the south of France – wine, saucissons, cheeses, garlic, rosemary. Kathy was braiding the garlic to hang it up and planting the rosemary while Frédéric told stories and unloaded the wine.

After a long cold shower and a long cold beer and freshly ironed clothes I was ready for dinner. By now I was stringing proper sentences together and feeling borderline human. We picked up the gorgeous Jean-Luc from down the road and went off to have dinner at the Piscine restaurant on the river Yonne. In the complicity that only comes with old friends who are pleased to be together again, we all ordered the same thing. First up was a big plate of *friture* (deep-fried whitebait), then steak and chips with rosé, followed by ice cream. It was a great pleasure to be back in Auxerre again – always so elegant and well-heeled and feeling just like home. Frédéric and Kathy's large first-floor apartment looked out over the Place de Maréchal Leclerc and the view from the five French windows was of the library, the stunning Tour de l'Horloge (the 15th-century clocktower), and the pretty backs of the 17th-century houses on the other side. The next day I wrote all day without leaving the room and in the evening made dinner for my sterling hosts plus Jean-Luc and another friend, Jeremy.

Jean-Luc is rather good-looking in a French/Italian, dark sort of way, is a very warm, charming person and owns a chain of hairdressing salons. Jeremy is a tall, blond Lawrence of Arabia-type character who has four luxury touring barges. He also drives a gigantic BMW bike and flies his own small plane and a few years ago crashed it, suffering severe burns all over his body and long hospitalisation. When I saw him last year he was in a protective body suit under his clothes and visibly very scarred – almost unrecognisable. Like the phoenix he rose up and went back to work, got on his bike and climbed back into the cockpit. Now he has no body suit and his face is almost flawless, although he has scarring on other parts of the body. He kindly contributed a Condrieu Château du Roznay which impressed everybody, and let us touch his new toy, a cellphone that vibrated rather than rang so as not to disturb other people. There were many helpful suggestions as to what parts of the body could profit from this phone. The second favourite topic of conversation for the French after food and wine is sex and of course we got to the inevitable, old-fashioned party trick of telling our first sexual experience. I said I didn't know what they were talking about, and Jeremy's story was best, hands down. As 15-year-old schoolboys, he and his friend had been seduced by a wealthy older woman whom they met on a train. She took them home and got out the black stockings and suspender belt and everything. Afterwards they rode around in her convertible Rover with their hands under her skirt. Frédéric added lots of titivations to the story as it went along. Kathy and I thought it was too good to be true, and Jean-Luc said there was no question of his being able to sleep that night.

It doesn't matter where you are, French men always make a fuss of you, and lunch at a great Lyonnaise bouchon in Auxerre called Le Bistro du Palais provided the usual outrageous compliments and smart remarks.

'Oh là là, il y a que des belles ici,' exclaimed Joseph Carino the patron, no matter what the women's physical attributes or lack thereof.

Le Bouchon is a bistrot specialising in the cuisine of Lyon. Most people think it's called a *bouchon* after the cork of a wine bottle, but the true story is that when the wine sellers came to eat, they used to *bouchonner* or rub down their horses with straw wisps. Frédéric, Kathy and I were joined by Emmanuel and Abdallah, friends of theirs. Abdallah had inherited his unusual dark looks from Lebanese and Algerian parents. Unlike Algerians he was very tall and slim but like them he loved eating and cooking. In the crowded bistrot, we were all squeezed into a stall for four people, all yelling our heads off like the rest of the customers. It was a typical outfit with red checked tablecloths covered in white paper, old photos and posters on the walls and photos in the window of famous people who had eaten there.

The restaurant was in fact two little restaurants accessed through adjoining doors. Both were impossibly small, impossibly hectic and apparently, always full, with the chef thanklessly slaving out the back in a tiny kitchen. Joseph serves both rooms on his own and at the end the chef comes out if things get desperate. A good Brouilly red was plonked on the table and I ate a confit de canard followed by Joseph's speciality, a Saint-Marcellin cheese, so ripe it was almost running out of the room. According to Frédéric, a Saint-Marcellin should always taste of the cow's teat, and according to Joseph, politics should always smell of *andouillette* – a little bit like shit. I noticed with pleasure that I was not the only 'princess' at the Bistrot du Palais and wondered if this was what *liberté, égalité, fraternité* meant. We princesses were all given pink roses as we left and it was with a warm heart I made my way home watching the sunset tinting the church spires pink in the balmy evening.

When I went back to Le Bistrot du Palais with Emmanuel on another day, Joseph welcomed me like a long-lost friend as he does everyone and immediately placed two glasses of a 1995 *Bordeaux moelleux* in front of us. This creamy, slightly sweet wine is made from Sauvignon, Sémillon and Muscat grapes. I chose *os à la moelle* (beef marrow) served with toast and sea salt and Emmanuel ordered crumbed, fried pig's ears which were tender and delicious. Following that we had pig's trotter and *tablier de sapeur*, which literally translated means fireman's apron – but what it really is, is some ghastly bit somewhere around the intestines, a great Lyonnais delicacy. French patrons always look after and cultivate their regular customers so the meal was followed by the customary gift to faithful customers – the little glass of plum eau-de-vie from the Perrier bottle. Joseph also gave me one of his black aprons embroidered with Le Bistrot du Palais and two of his *pots lyonnais*, pale green 50cl bottles with 5cm bases, used for serving chilled Beaujolais. Some people won't eat chez Joseph because he *tu toies* everyone but I'm not a snob and I don't find his familiarity rude; it brightens up my day.

On a subsequent visit Joseph proudly showed me a large box full of plump, fresh, meaty cèpes, just picked. This heralded the beginning of autumn and everyone in the bistrot was ordering them, so of course I did too. They were served in the customary way, simply and quickly fried with butter, parsley and garlic – heady, earthy and nutty with that unmistakable fungusy smell. From then on cèpes were on sale all over the place and I bought them almost every day. Men in suits were tucking serviettes into their collars and rubbing their hands together and everybody seemed to know each other. Relishing my Lyonnais sausage and steamed potatoes I reflected that there were few things as perfect as eating alone at lunchtime with a glass of wine and the literary review from an English newspaper.

An article that interested me, because I get on the bandwagon about it whenever I can, was on the proposed raw milk ban. The International Dairy Federation were considering a proposal that would spell disaster for all the small craft cheesemakers in the world – i.e. the people who make the best cheese – by banning trade in cheese made from unpasteurised milk. This is wickedness on the part of bureaucracies shamelessly manipulated by powerful lobbies (scientists, industrial cheese makers and supermarkets, none of whom you would invite to your home for dinner) furthering their own agendas. The anti-unpasteurised lobby almost persuaded a United Nations Food Safety committee to ban raw milk in the food handbook of the World Trade Organisation. As any cheese-lover knows, beneficial microbes in raw milk are not only crucial in giving top-class cheeses their unique quality and flavour, but also make them safer by preventing the growth of harmful organisms. The ability of live raw milk to allow the cheese to grow and develop depth marks the cheeses out from the tasteless, homogenised stuff one finds in supermarkets. It is true that lait cru cheese can make you sick but it is very rare – 100,000 tons of it are consumed each year in France and almost no-body falls ill. Healthy animals, hygenic milking and sanitary production ensure the absence of unhealthy bacteria. If you've ever eaten a raw milk cheese, it's hard to go back to pasteurised. Most New World cheeses are made from pasteurised milk by law and they can be very good, but you can never make great cheeses with these restrictions, in my opinion. There is a place and a market for industrial cheeses, but why punish the artists who care about quality and sublime taste above everything else? The old ways of doing things must not be lost and I for one pledge to be vigilant. It would be very *dur fromage* if I couldn't eat real Roquefort.

Sometimes I went to the swimming pool in Auxerre, which is very flash with all sorts of secret codes and regulations. You cannot get anywhere near the pool without first having taken your clothes and shoes off, locked your things in a coded locker and showered. Once there, horrible little boys splash you, get in your way and jump on your head; and as is the custom in France even in a family setting, a lot of the women are topless. Quite often I ran into friends whose one abiding fault was to criticise moi for not swimming: 'Peta, you're supposed to get wet at a swimming pool.'

'How ridiculous. I've been to hundreds of swimming pools all over the world and have rarely come across a stretch of water.'

Swimming pools are for lying about, drinking gallons of mineral water, looking around and privately thanking God that even though you look pretty bloody bad, at least you don't look that bad. One trick to make yourself look good at a swimming pool is to go with a handsome younger man. Sometimes Jean-Luc, whose family were on holiday, filled this function for me. Periodically I did slide quietly into the pool to prevent heat explosion, and it was at these times I would hear '*Papite! Papite!*' and darling little Jules would be madly paddling towards me, supported by water-wings and surrounded by enough energy to supply a hydroelectric dam.

One evening we went to the home of Jules' parents Emmanuel and Catherine for dinner. Jules can't say Peta, so now they all call me Papite; and on top of that they had a new little creature called Louis who just smiled and said goo-gaa all the time. Catherine is an attractive, talkative woman; and Emmanuel, a man with a generous belly from a love of the good life, has the dark looks and sharp wit of his Jewish heritage. They had just come back from holidays in the south of France and were full of southern stories of markets, the corrida (bullfights) and rugby. I contributed a tomato, potato, egg and mayonnaise salad that I learned years ago in Paris. It's simple enough but has to be made with summer or autumn potatoes and tomatoes. In France I use little rattes, and in other countries, any waxy potato.

Chop the tomatoes in large chunks, cut the hardboiled eggs in quarters and cut the potatoes in half if necessary. Toss gently with salt, freshly ground pepper, chopped parsley and fresh mayonnaise. To eat this salad cold would show a lack of tenderness in your character – it is best at room temperature. Because I can't help myself I usually put garlic in also.

We sat in their flower-filled garden, drank rosé in deference to the south and talked wine.

'It's impossible to judge a wine anyway – it's just like a woman,' said Emmanuel. 'It's a question of taste, experience, knowledge and memories. What is good for one person is not good for another, *n'est-ce pas.*'

After the salad had been wolfed down, Emmanuel brought

out fried calamari and saffron rice followed by a goat's cheese called Bûchon de Vonnas that they had brought back from Béziers. It was dry and hard enough to chop wood on and tasted slightly of parmesan. We thought it would be very good grated onto pasta; in fact a common way to eat extremely strong cheese in France is to grate it onto your bread rather than eating it in chunks.

'I like cheeses that smell strong,' said Emmanuel, stretching out and rubbing his belly, 'because if you can smell like this and still attract women, it means they are beyond beauty and odour – they want you for your brains. By the way, you don't feel like touching me on my thigh just here?' Catherine, who is no slouch and is possessed of an explosive temperament, just raised her eyes heavenward and kept smoking.

Another happy evening she made me a Camembert tart. This was fast food *à la française* to die for. You put the baby to bed, having almost suffocated it with kisses, bribe the older one with a scary video, open a bottle of good white wine, roll out a packet of flaky pastry from the supermarket, spread it with a Camembert sprinkled with pepper and nutmeg and stick it in a rather hot oven for about 15 minutes. Eat immediately.

Catherine didn't advise using a good Camembert, just an industrial one. The result is a warm, creamy, slightly salty taste going down your throat, twinned with the crunchiness and featheriness of the pastry. This is where your really dry white wine is essential – anything else would instill fear and the baby would wake up. They told me of a winter dish made with Mont d'Or (Vacherin du Haut-Doubs) cheese from the Jura mountains. This heavenly cheese has been made in the Franche-Comté on the Swiss border for two centuries. It is a round cow's milk cheese of about 12–30cm in diameter and 5cm high, sold and presented in a spruce box, the scent of which permeates the cheese. It is cured on a board of spruce wood and turned and rubbed with a cloth soaked in brine so by the time you get your hands on it, it is pale yellow, creamy, smells distinctly of spruce and is quite runny. If you're just eating it *au naturel*, you eat it out of the box, often with a teaspoon or just spread it on bread. If you're at Catherine and Emmanuel's they will reinforce the wooden box with thick tinfoil, dig a hole in the middle of the cheese and fill it with Marc de Bourgogne then bake it in a hot oven until melting. It is eaten with bread or potatoes. Mont d'Or is only made in the winter but can be eaten in the spring and autumn.

Our second course took a lot of guts. That morning I had been to the market with Jane and bought a tube of *andouillette* (tripe sausage) and some grey shallots. I asked the *charcutière* where the andouillette was from and she said, 'Chablis, of course.' I asked who made it and she said, 'M. Soulier, of course.' She had passed the quality test. I knew no English friends would eat this so I brought it with me to Catherine's dinner and Emmanuel slid it in the oven with sliced shallots and white (in principle Chablis) wine. He left it in for quite a long time until the liquid had soaked up into the andouillette, the shallots were melted and the sausage was crispy on the outside. It was absolutely delicious, of course, because everything Emmanuel cooks is delicious, of course.

On a hot, muggy Saturday evening we decided to try out a restaurant in the village of Beauvoir that had been recommended to Frédéric. It was a dozen kilometres west of Auxerre in an entirely charming building of stone with shutters and lace curtains. We were joined by his brother Nicolas, sister-in-law Sophie, their daughter Laurianne, his mother Mimi and her friend Rena. We had no idea what to expect but it turned out we couldn't find one thing wrong with Le Bellovidere. It's another of those classic small restaurants run by a young hard-working husband and wife team, in this case Claire and Régis Tatraux. The dining room was chic and comfortable with a calming view of the countryside and as it had been a workers' bistrot in a previous life, it still had the bar with a few tables in another room. The child, who was pretty and strong-willed, spent the evening at the bar talking to the customers. The two most beautiful and interesting women at the table were without a doubt Mimi and Rena. Mimi is a painter, ceramicist and devoted grandmother. She has long brown hair piled up on her head, a full mouth, piercing blue eyes, and dresses in artistic clothes with long necklaces. Her friend Rena is a Greek etcher with a marvellous accent and an intelligent, worldly face full of mischief and humour. Her long brown hair was parted in the centre and attached at the back of her head with big pins and her fingers and wrists were adorned with large rings and silver bracelets.

While we perused the menu we snacked on little *gougeres*. Gougères, or cheese puffs, are a Burgundian specialty. They come in different sizes with different stuffings. These ones were the same as I make them – small choux pastries with tiny cubes of Gruyère cheese stirred into them. They're best eaten warm: the tiny cubes of cheese explode in taste sensations in the mouth.

The Bellovidere had set menus and also served à la carte. Everything was perfectly fresh, prepared with a light hand and seemed rather southern in its influence, for example there was *morue à la provençale*, duck confit with *sarladaise* potatoes, aubergine caviar and rabbit with rosemary and thyme, which took me straight back to the Alpilles. The home-smoked salmon was very succulent and the *minutes de saumon* on a bed of aubergine caviar was heavenly in its complex flavours, garnished with fragrant olive oil and lemon juice – a perfect summer dish. Nicolas told me there used to be salmon in the Yonne river and when the Revolution came, the people of Auxerre demanded as one of the changes they wanted, not to have to eat salmon any more. We've had it up to here with salmon they cried, give us more beef. The table

Gougères

185ml water
½ tsp salt
75g butter
100g sifted flour
3–4 eggs
100g Gruyère cheese
pinch freshly ground nutmeg
pinch cayenne pepper

1. Heat the water in a saucepan with the salt and butter.

2. When the water boils and the butter melts, remove the saucepan from the heat, throw in sifted flour and stir like mad with a wooden spoon.

3. Put the saucepan back on a very low heat and continue stirring for a few minutes until the dough is dry and pulls away easily from the sides.

4. Remove from the heat and carefully beat in eggs, one at a time. (The pastry should be shining and firm enough to barely drop from the spoon. If it's too wet the gougères won't rise – they'll splat.)

5. Next, dice Gruyère and stir it into the pastry along with nutmeg and cayenne pepper.

6. Crank oven up to 225°C and spoon little rocks of the mixture onto a greased baking tray. We're not talking smooth here – AKA pastry bag. You want a rugged look.

7. Bake them for about 20 minutes or until they're golden, then open the oven, turn it off and let the little darlings dry out for 5 minutes.

Note: In the north they put little shrimps in instead of cheese. I think they'd also be good with grated lemon or lime rind or finely chopped sundried tomatoes, or add sugar to the mixture and stir in candied orange peel.

had a big discussion on how best to reheat a duck confit. Frédéric gently heats the duck in its fat in a bain-marie then puts it in the oven to crisp the skin; that way the flesh doesn't dry out. He and Nicolas occupied themselves with the wine, choosing a Brocard Chablis to start and a Côtes de

Beaune to continue. The *assiette de sorbets et fruits de saison* was like a Van Gogh painting, bursting with delicate flavours and colours. As seems to be the custom now, tiny cakes and biscuits were served with coffee. Before we went to bed Mimi served us verbena and camomile *tisane* from bowls on her terrace overlooking the lit-up St-Pierre church.

I had stayed in Mimi's home on a previous visit to Burgundy. This time she was away and I would have the house to myself. Wandering around her home opened a treasure trove of memories for me. Everything was in its place – the stone wall on the street covered in honeysuckle, the large wooden outside door that opens with the huge key, the front garden with the tall cherry tree, and up the steps to the front door. I opened it to find the same citrus-green cupboard doors greeting me and the staircase with a paisley shawl and bangles hanging on the balustrade. Dragging my suitcase inside, I went into the little kitchen with its walls covered from head to foot in kitchenware and antique ornaments. On the table was a tray of homemade jams, cherries in eau-de-vie, stewed prunes and, unusually for France, a kettle – most people boil water in a pot. The homemade vinegar in a crock with its mother floating darkly in it permeated the room, and drying herbs hung over the cupboards.

The large dining room with its long table lit by a flamboyant old chandelier with green candles in it and round table covered in books was exactly the same, overflowing with antiques and paintings, dried flowers, lamps and things picked up from the fleamarkets. Keys with lilac ribbons attached to them opened the big dressers full of wine, eaux-de-vie and kitchenware and a large box of antique silver cutlery sat on a velvet footstool. The television was hidden in a green cabinet that, when opened, revealed old puppets hanging on the insides of the doors. The outside was painted with flowers and fruit by Mimi and across the top she had written *L'Amour m'est Tout* – Love is Everything to Me. The huge fireplace where we had all sat around the fire playing Trivial Pursuit on winter nights was full of wood just waiting for a chilly evening and some marshmallows. This house is actually two houses put together so there are lots of levels and labyrinthine turns. Going up four steps I came into the living room which looked out onto the three-level garden and terrace. Again this room was full of paintings, a large carved mirror, old furniture with beautiful shawls draped on them, tables piled up with books, objects like an antique lace-maker, lovely boxes, photos of the family, lamps. To the left of this room was Mimi's private apartment, always locked when she wasn't there.

Up the narrow, mirror-lined stairs where I poked my head into the light-infused painting studio, then up three more steps to four bedrooms and a bathroom. Everywhere in this crooked house the walls were lined with ornate false doors stuck onto the walls; little tables supported lamps, sculptures and statues hid in corners, antique chairs sat in nooks and the floors were very old, cold, crooked stone. On this floor, the top one, little high windows looked up to the sky and the bedrooms, with their occupants long gone, now sported baby cots and grandchildren's toys.

Every evening I sat and wrote on the terrace with fresh lemonade and listened to the church bells and birds serenading me in a sort of harmony. With its peeling white shutters covered in yellow roses and wisteria, the terrace overlooked the rooftops of Auxerre, providing a perfect place to watch the sunset surrounded by hollyhocks, pot plants, bonzais, white garden furniture and a chaise longue covered in cushions. I opened the rusty white gate and went down the steps lined with lilacs to the next level of garden full of tiny wild strawberries, where there was a white table and stone sculptures. More steps led down to another garden resplendent with old-fashioned pink roses, raspberry bushes and red and blackcurrant bushes. This is big *cassis* (black-currant), raspberry and cherry country, so Mimi's garden was like a mini Burgundy for me. Every evening when I watered the garden, I rewarded myself with treats from these bushes.

One of the best products made from cassis is *crème de cassis*, which is mostly used to make *kir*, that heavenly Burgundian cocktail of cassis and Aligoté white wine. Blackcurrants with their inky juices and sultry perfume make one think of dusky woods and summer evenings. Kir was invented by Canon Kir, a former Resistance hero and mayor of Dijon. For 300 years blackcurrants were essentially used for treating ailments like fevers, sore throats and coughs. Packed with vitamin C at over 200mg per 100g, six blackcurrants contain more ascorbic acid than a whole lemon. Red currants are sweeter and both are natives of northern Europe, but blackcurrants are in fact more closely related to gooseberries. Sharply astringent, they are pea-sized, irredeemably, deliciously purple and clustered on frail, thread-like stalks. Aside from flavouring cassis and being eaten raw, blackcurrants make divine sorbet and ice cream, are good with apples and pears, in summer puddings, folded into fools and in sauces for duck and game. In Burgundy they also make a *pâte de cassis* or blackcurrant paste like the quince one in the south. Put one kilo of blackcurrants in a pan, cover and simmer until the berries are soft and squishy. Push them through a sieve, return to the pan, add 500g of sugar, gently bring to the boil and boil for half an hour, stirring constantly with a wooden spoon. The mixture should thicken and pull away from the sides. Allow to cool and pour into a shallow, oiled container. Let the paste lie around for a few days away from the heat then cut into cubes and roll in sugar or not, as you wish.

Frédéric and Kathy went away on holiday again, leaving me *toute seule*, so my days in Auxerre were quiet and filled with writing or touring the region, sampling the local cuisine. Sometimes Jean-Luc would invite me to a drongo-adolescent-outer-space movie, sometimes I had dinner at his place with friends, sometimes I bought the *Sunday Times* which kept me going all day, and sometimes I went to magnificent organ concerts in the cathedral. I also called Jean-Marie, whom I belittled for not having bought my book yet. He didn't see why he should pay for something he figured so prominently in.

'Because there are other interesting things in the book besides you, *mon cher*!

'Are there recipes?'

'Yes, of course.'

'What am I supposed to do with a recipe book?

'Read between the lines and look at the pictures.'

'Okay, okay, I'll buy it. The things I have to do.'

I invited him for dinner to catch up and cooked a beautiful meal for which he declined to show. '*Mal élevé*,' snapped one friend. '*Goujat*,' sighed the hairdresser. As I sat at the empty table watching the sun go down I reflected on all the wonderful meals I had shared. When you cook a meal for someone, you are not just feeding them, you are giving of yourself; in some way you are giving love. If you cook in a bad mood the food will taste bitter and if you cook with happiness, this is transmitted. If your guests reject your food they are rejecting you in a way that is much more direct than a spoken insult. Jean-Luc cooked some friends and me deep frozen chop suey, chicken breasts and raspberry mousse served out of the mixer bowl on the table. I had this meal on a Saturday night and again on a Thursday night but it was delicious simply because he made an effort, gave of himself and was just so unaffectedly thrilled to have us there. I once had a man 'cook' me a meal that was utter perfection – soft lights, beautiful music, candles, flowers, lace tablecloth, slavering service etc. and . . . a frozen dinner from the supermarket.

He even fried onions in the kitchen so the smell would trick me into thinking he had cooked the meal himself.

I had much more pleasant memories of the last time Jean-Marie and I met. We hadn't seen each other for six years but, as with all my friends in Burgundy, it was as if I'd only been away six months. I walked down the street and looked up to see him leaning out of an upstairs room. We stood staring at each other silently then finally we smiled and he ran down to open the door. Initially he seemed unchanged – handsome, talkative and natural as ever – but as the hours went by I realised he had become more worldly, more battered by life and slightly less carefree. At 27 he was still a boy but at 34 he was a man. He gave me some *pâté de campagne*, some Cantal cheese from his little trapdoor cheese box, a glass of his father's Chablis and we talked and walked and laughed all day. For dinner we indulged in a game of 'no-win' with the Spanish owner of the only restaurant in the village:

Moi: 'I'll have the cèpes please.'

Mme Espagnole: 'Is that all?'

Moi: 'Yes thank you.'

Mme Espagnole: (*exploding*) 'You can't do that! They take 20 minutes to cook.'

This should have warned me. Cèpes take five minutes to cook.

Moi: 'Okay, I'll have some rillettes first.'

Mme Espagnole: 'Do you want garlic with the cèpes or not?'

Moi: 'Yes please.'

Mme Espagnole: (gasping) 'Are you serious? Garlic will ruin the subtle taste of the cèpes.'

Moi: 'Okay, so I won't have garlic.'

The cèpes were frozen and gluey, the ham had three centimetres of fat on it and the rillettes were dry and tasteless. I won't even TELL you what happened when Jean-Marie mentioned that the *jambon Chablisienne*, which was drowned in dried herbs that had no business whatsoever being there, didn't taste as good as his mothers.

Real jambon Chablisienne (see page 244) is made by first cooking the rice until fluffy and nutty, then keeping it warm. Then you sauté lots and lots of chopped shallots, add some Chablis, some cream, salt and pepper and chopped tomatoes or a little tomato purée. Reduce a little till thickened at which point you may or may not strain the sauce – depending on what your mother says. The sliced ham off the bone is now gently and barely heated through in the sauce and served up with the rice on the side to someone who deserves to marry you.

After dinner we walked along the river and through the country lanes arm in arm, catching up on six years of news. We sat on a bench in the fading light listening to the birds and yawning. There was no more need to talk – as Jean-Marie said, 'If you feel comfortable with silence with a friend, its a good sign.'

But as he had declined to show up, I set about exploring Burgundy again on my own. I visited the Chablis market, which was in full swing when I arrived, bursting with fat white asparagus, different coloured cherries, red currants looking like boxes of rubies and apricot coloured Charentes melons. What I was really after was goat's cheese and I found lots of them on a little stall – tiny, hard, knobbly, black Crottins de Chavignol. You have to be a real diehard to eat this cheese. It goes from weighing 140g when fresh to 40g four months later when it's ready to eat, blowing your tastebuds with its strong, meaty, robust flavour. There were rows of larger moist fresh chèvres and little ones rolled in ashes. I was also introduced to a local creamy cow's milk cheese called Soumaintrain, which I instantly fell in love with. This is a bit like the famous Burgundian cheese Époisses, in that it is eaten young and washed with brine for six to

Jambon Chablisienne
Ham Chablis-style

Serves 4

1 tbsp butter
100g shallots, finely chopped
½ cup Chablis white wine
½ cup crème fraîche
1 tbsp chopped fresh tarragon
1 tbsp chopped parsley
freshly ground black pepper
sea salt
4 thick slices of cooked ham

1. Sauté the shallots in the butter until golden – about 5 mins.
2. Add the wine, crème fraîche, herbs and pepper. Reduce over a bubbling heat until the sauce thickens – about 5 mins. Add salt to taste.
3. Very gently heat through the ham in the sauce. Serve with rice.

eight weeks during the *affinage*. On my way out I fell upon the best charcutier in my two weeks of travels in Burgundy. The queue was very long and I soon figured out why. This serious, slow man sold hams, sausages, boudin, merguez and saucissons he had made himself in the traditional Burgundian method and sliced respectfully with a huge, flat, black knife. The people in the queue waited patiently. He cut me thick slices of his unimaginably succulent ham on the bone, explaining that the correct way to cut such meat was by hand – never by machine. I would happily go back to my beloved Burgundy uniquely for this man's ham. He also sold me a Corsican pig liver saucisson called *figatelle* and a *rosette artisanale* or dried pork sausage.

There was a stall with nothing but garlic. From the Loire south, garlic is used extensively in French cooking and the further south you go, the more you find it. White garlic is quite mild, purple garlic is medium in strength and red garlic will knock your espadrilles off. The fresher the bulb, the milder the taste. Eating garlic for pleasure is actually fairly recent, as in the past it was mostly used for medicinal purposes. It was used as a preventative against the plague in 1722 and doctors made soup of it as an antibiotic. Even in the sixth century the peasants were eating it because they eat everything and thank God they're alive but at court they refrained as it wasn't considered cricket to reek of garlic. In fact in the 6th century the first ever French cookbook was written in Latin by Anthimus which the French say proves they were doing very sophisticated stuff long before anyone else in Europe. Anthimus was a Greek doctor sent by the emperor in Constantinople as ambassador to the King of the Franks in Ravena, northeastern Gaul, where he wrote the cookbook. Called *De Observatione Ciborum* (On the Observance of Foods), the cookbook shows the use of rich peppery and spicy sauces, oodles of cream, butter, milk and salt, peacock stew and rice boiled in goat's milk. A thoroughly sterling foodie called Mark Grant, who is also a classics teacher, has recently translated this book into English.

For lunch I popped into a bistrot called La Vraie Chablisienne which specialised in *andouillette*, snails and *salade bourguignonne*, a salad composed of *oeufs en meurette* (eggs poached in red wine), snails, *jambon persillé* (parsleyed ham), and andouillette. I ordered Jean-Marie's famous jambon Chablisienne to make a comparison with Mme Espagnole's, and this one was completely different and more like the recipe above. The only thing I had against this place was the toilets – bisexual. Bisexual, for God's sake! I'm prepared to share a lot with strange men but not the bloody toilets. I can't stand it – first in Paris and now in Chablis. I know it's now the latest thing to show people in movies on the toilet having a good old dump, I know we can't even have our babies without husbands homing in on the act, I know rock stars have sex with power poles but there's got to be a limit. The privacy of the toilet is the only thing left. I do not want to go into a toilet in a restaurant and be faced with a man's willy quickly and nervously disappearing behind a startled back. I just don't.

Smoothing my feathers down and leaving Chablis I went to Vézelay. I walked up the hill to the sumptuous cathedral with the dazzling white interior. There was a wedding going on with a high mass, a bride in an enormous white gown, ladies in floppy hats and men in tails. Then I visited Marc Meneau's three-star restaurant, L'Espérance, down the road in the village of Saint-Père-sous-Vézelay. Marc Meneau is the chef who taught the chef I worked with and ran away from in Auxerre all those years ago, how to throw tantrums and plates full of food. But I didn't hold that against him because he turns out some of the best food in Burgundy. They have their own herb and vegetable garden, milk products come from the cousin's farm across the street, they make their own bread and now their own wine. The restaurant is a dream of elegance, brightness and comfort, with a greenhouse dining room leading out onto a park with streams, little rose-lined bridges and flowered walkways. They serve such delicacies as foie gras with caramel and pepper, potato galettes with caviar, lobster with almond milk, pigeon stew, and are famous for their drop-dead desserts. Across the road is their other restaurant, Le Pré des Marguerites, serving simpler and more traditional cuisine (and a lot cheaper). The food is no less stunning and the location charming. I walked along the narrow leafy lane that runs by the Pré des Marguerites and came across three maids in starchy white aprons all in a row, as if they had just fallen out of the clouds.

Another day I tripped over to the famous wine town of Beaune along tree-lined roads and through neat vineyards separated by ancient, low stone walls and protected by ornate iron gates. Upon arrival I wandered into a routier and asked if I could just try the main course without all the other things that always go with these cheap menus in France. The owner looked at me as if I'd asked him to hand over the till, and the filthy truckers at the bar gaped at me askance. I ended up at Chez Félix eating *duo de foie gras*, which was a slice of cooked and a slice of raw foie gras sprinkled with sea salt. This turned out not to be as terrifying as I expected, in fact raw goose liver is a tastier, more intense version of the cooked. I washed it down with Meursault, a clear Beaune wine that seems almost to be ageless. The waiter was vile and every time I asked for something, said, 'Make yourself at home.' The owner had obviously been told I was behaving strangely (writing notes, asking questions) and without doubt stealing all their ideas to open up a restaurant next door, so he came over to ask me what my business was. I smiled sweetly and explained. The woman at the table next to me was massaging her partner's knee and he was calling her *ma petite fleur*. Why did I have to be sitting there on my own doing research for a book? Who was going to look after my knees?

The sparkling, polished town of Beaune is wine, wine, wine. The place is bursting with cellars carrying their prestigious wines and crème de cassis, kitchenware supply shops, antique shops, restaurants and art galleries. I had to jump out of the way as two huge trucks escorted by flashing lights and policemen on motorbikes passed slowly through town carrying gigantic, wooden wine presses that extended almost onto the footpaths. At this precise moment the battery fell out of my camera. Such is the life of a simple cook who fancies herself as a researcher. Beaune also has one of the best mustard-making outfits in Burgundy called Fallot et Compagnie, a fantastic market on Saturday at the Place de la Halle, a wine museum with a 14th-century fermentation cellar and historical buildings like the Hotel Dieu.

Basing myself in a hotel there with a hired car for a few days, I fearlessly set out to conquer the most valuable arc of hills in the world, the Côte d'Or (golden slopes). Being in the Côte d'Or is really like being in a golden land, as the 'wine road' is bursting with glorious vineyards, châteaux, Cistercian abbeys and lush countryside. Here one finds such great names as Nuits-St-Georges, my favourite Gevrey Chambertin, Meursault, Pommard and Beaune. The climate here is ideal and the soil varied and rich, producing red wines of outstanding depth and quality with very good aging properties. I got lost approximately 36 times but it was a pleasure as I revelled in chance discoveries like the Abbaye des Citeaux in the village of St-Nicolas-les-Citeaux. There, in perfect simplicity and quiet, the Cistercian monks make their creamy cow's milk cheese the same way they've been making it since 1900 and the only place you can buy it is right there in the little shop at the abbey.

Deciding to drive along the vallée de l'Ouche, to my mind one of the most beautiful parts of Burgundy, I followed the canal, passing through gorgeous villages and locks covered in flowers and vines. I couldn't help myself and got out of the car at every village to drink in the breathtaking beauty and lean over the little bridges to watch the barges float by. Eventually I came to Pont sur Ouche and the Hôtel de l'Ecluse, owned by acquaintances, where I stopped for a morning coffee. The other ruddy *campagnards* at the bar were drinking wine already and indulging in gentle abuse of the nice-looking young wine merchant at the other end of the bar. They told me the way to tell a real Burgundian was by the way he rolls his Rs, but the best piece of information they gave me was where to have my lunch.

On my way to this restaurant at Vandenesse-en-Auxois I visited the mountaintop village of Châteauneuf perched in the clouds and pretty as a picture, then descended the mad, skinny cliff-face they call a road to one of the best meals I ate in Burgundy. Lucotte is run by Madame Lucotte, a plump woman in flowery dress and apron, who does the cooking and the bills. In France, the patronne never lets anyone else near the till. The service was done by a marvellous, no-nonsense creature called Josette who kept the workers in order with a few swiftly placed adjectives. Every time she told them off they all yelled, 'JE T'AIME JOSETTE.' Flowery wallpaper, paper tablecloths, artificial flowers, stone floor, no-choice menu. My happiness was complete when Josette placed two sturdy white dinner plates, one on top of the other, in front of me. You keep your knife and fork for the whole meal. Josette tried to put me away in a side room and when I burst into tears (only kidding) and said I would be lonely, she said tenderly, '*Mais, ma petite madame, la grande salle est pour les ouvriers.* (The large room is for the workers.) They have to get in and out fast. Well, okay, I'll put you in this corner here.'

'*Merci, Josette.*'

'*Ici c'est le coin des écrivains.* (This is the writer's corner.)' Last year an American film maker sat here all summer and wrote a screenplay.

Now I could watch the show unfold before me. A bottle of red Côte d'Or table wine with the characteristic stars around the top was placed on my table and I took as much as I wanted and paid only for what I had drunk. The workers (I'm always amazed at how filthy French *ouvriers* are – they look like they've emerged from a coal mine) had water glasses for their wine but I was given a wine glass and my first course – a generous plate of fresh regional charcuterie, comprising the famous Burgundian parsleyed ham, slices of saucisson, jambon du pays, chicken *galantine*, little pickles and a thick slab of butter. This is the real core of French cooking – simplicity, freshness and good quality.

Loud Dutch tourists arrived and got put in the back room where they belonged (why do the Dutch always shout?). The workers took priority and the tourists waited – as was only correct. The main course arrived in the form of two thick, rosy slices of roast lamb and a bowl of snowy, light mashed potatoes. I was in heaven. People who visit France and never eat in places like this are completely missing the heart and soul of French cooking. When food critics complain about the standards of cooking in France, they are obviously not talking about honest, real food like Madame Lucotte's. She would no more throw a lettuce leaf on a plate as garnish than fly to the moon.

Next, Josette placed a huge cheese platter on my table and told me to take as much as I liked. There was a subtle sweet Morbier with its horizontal black furrow through the middle. The story of Morbier is quite quaint. In the old days, soot was sprinkled on the fresh curd to prevent a rind from forming and to sidetrack insects. It was left lying around all night and in the morning more stray bits of cheese were put on top and that's how it got the dark line through the middle. These days they get the line by painting on a vegetable dye, I'm afraid, but lots of people think it's ashes. Amour Nuits-St-Georges, Bleu de Bresse, goat's cheeses, Cantal nice and dark around the edges, and something I had never seen before – *fromage fort*. This is a blended mixture of leftovers with *marc* (like cognac) and garlic added and you spread it on your bread like a paste. This is a Burgundian specialty originally made at home from leftover cheese fermented in whey, milk or vegetable broth. Oil or eau-de-vie was added to stabilise it and herbs, spices, salt and wine were stirred in, then it was ignored for months in an old stoneware pot. When someone finally took the lid off and the smell made the cows fall over, it was ready.

My coffee arrived in a little cup, no saucer, spoon in cup. The price was very cheap. The famous, rushed ouvriers were still there when I left. I drove back on the *route nationale* to the multi-leveled doll's house in Auxerre in the fading evening light, behind smelly trucks and bizarre-looking agricultural machines crawling along like giant prehistoric birds.

Burgundy is the best wine, mustard and beef country in France and has always been famous for the high standard and abundance of its food. The original Morvan cow which had a red pelt has now been replaced by the huge white Charolais steer, often called beef factories. Charles VI's wife, Isabeau of Bavaria, invented the written menu which was called the *escriteau*; but until she came along, you took what you got and thanked God you were alive. That erudite gastronome Brillat-Savarin, who said that a meal without cheese was like a beautiful woman with only one eye, was a Burgundian. The most refined Burgundian cooking never gets far from its soil – it's honest, hearty and nourishing and Burgundians have famously good teeth which they attribute to the wine. It has been said that you will dig your grave with your teeth much faster on rich haute cuisine than you will on the natural cooking of this blessed land. The snail trail begins in Burgundy also and goes right back to the Romans, their black escargots being the best in France, snacking on grape leaves until they become plump and degenerately luscious. The *petit gris* snails from the south are also popular and much more numerous. The Romans, those little epicureans, figured out how to fatten snails and the necessity of fasting them for a few days just before the farewell dip in the boiling pot to rid them of toxins because they eat plants that are poisonous. In fact, purists say snails are like oysters – they have a season and it is in the autumn. Snails should be eaten only during the time when they close their shells for winter hibernation.

One starry night there was a big reunion dinner party held at a friend's lodge, Le Moulinot, in Vermenton. It seemed as though everyone I had ever met in Burgundy was there, sitting around the long table by the river in the moonlight. Even though I hadn't seen them for years they looked the same to me – and they had the grace to say I looked the same to them. Such is the power of love. Jean-Marie, who has missed a career in stand-up comedy, was there providing non-stop entertainment and doing imitations of Jacques Cousteau talking under water with Mark, one of the balloonists. They insisted you could watch the fish from the windows in Eurostar, and gave demonstrations. Agnes screamed her head off about my first book *Fête Accomplie*, how outraged she was by my incorrect portrait of her and how I didn't know her at all. By the end of the night she was proudly reading extracts of it over the phone to absent friends and DEMANDING I send her a signed copy. No question of her paying for it. When they weren't abusing me for either not putting them in the book or putting them in the book, they were saying, 'I never said that, I never did that and that's not me in that photo anyway.'

The conversation mostly centred on wine that evening. Two of my friends have now become winemakers, someone had brought a couple of bottles of Marc Meneau's red which everyone agreed was pleasant but not to fall over about, and there was the Chablis from Jean-Marie's father's vineyard, which is always well received. I provided a bottle of premier cru from Nuits-St-Georges that Gael, our hostess, deemed far too good for the likes of them and hid in the kitchen. And I gave a late night wine-fuelled reading from the book.

I decided to include the walled town of Sancerre on its abrupt hilltop in my private gastronomic tour of Burgundy, even though it is strictly in the Cher department on the Upper Loire. They make the best Sauvignon Blanc in the world and very good goat cheese, the two of which are a marriage made in heaven when taken together. Being a trail-blazer by temperament, I avoid at all cost the direct and simple approach. Anyone can follow a sign, but then they wouldn't discover dead villages, dead ends and deadpan policemen who try to tell you you're actually on the way to

Italy. I took a complicated, *campagnarde*, rain-soaked route to Sancerre and arrived to a suddenly blue and sunny sky, which I thought was very public-spirited of their chamber of commerce. The finest Sancerre is reportedly in the village of Bué from the Clos du Chene-Marchand vineyard, but I had lunch at the Auberge de Joseph Mellot and loved their Sancerre, so decided to stick with them.

This old-fashioned restaurant on the main square had wooden tables and chairs, old plates and photos on the walls and the counter was lined up with their wines and jam made from their grapes. An elderly woman shouted at me from the depths of the room, 'You don't have to slam the door, Madame.' I obediently sat down where I was told. It came as no surprise that this was another one of those no-choice deals where you get what you're given. On putting the wine to my lips, a sensation exploded in my mouth that I hadn't experienced for a long time – there is nothing to compare with the unusual dry and sweet taste of flinty, spicy Sancerre. Their other passion in a good year is the pale Sancerre rouge made from Pinot Noir. You get your terrine, which came with *beurre au sel de mer* (rock-salt infested butter), which I drank with their rosé (Sauvignon/Pinot Noir); then your omelette with smoked ham which I drank with the generous, refined white (pure Sauvignon). One look at the omelette told me it was perfect – succulent and creamy. A chef in Vancouver taught me how to make a good omelette. You must have a heated, non-stick pan and the eggs must only be lightly stirred, not beaten, with no cream or milk added. As the omelette heats up you tip the pan towards you, gently pushing back the egg mixture with a wooden spoon as it cooks. The result is not only tender but looks like waves when served. I asked the cook in the kitchen what her secret was and she said, a very hot pan.

Finally you get your Crottin de Chavignol goat's cheese; and as it was midday, I felt I'd had enough to drink.

'Mais, Madame, on ne peut pas manger le crottin sec comme ça. Je vous donne un centimètre. (You can't eat a Crottin dry like that. I'll give you one centimetre of wine.)'

'But I have to drive.'

'Un centimètre. Voyons.'

The Crottin was indeed dry to the point where on first impact you get a flush in the glands and your eyes practically water, then a sip of heavenly Sancerre and it's all evened out. As is often the case when you eat alone in restaurants in France, the other customers just can't bear it and have to find out who you are. The people at the neighbouring table turned out to be the family who owned the restaurant and vineyard, so I accepted an invitation to join them for some coffee and lichou, a sort of almond pound cake, and croquet, which is something like biscotti. Catherine Corbeau runs the company office and kindly offered me a glass of what they were drinking – La Grande Châtelaine, made from grapes with the skins left on. If I hadn't instructed my friends to shoot me if I ever opened another restaurant I'd do something just like this – terrine, omelette and goat's cheese with a different wine for each and special dishes ordered in advance occasionally.

Mme Corbeau had advised me to drive to Gien, my next stop, via the Briar Canal, a much prettier route than the route nationale. By now it was raining again (it's not always fair weather in Burgundy) as I drove up there in my trusty Renault, passing through the lovely canal town of Briar, full of barges and boats, big and small. I stopped to have a sentimental look at the Pont Canal that I had waltzed across when I cooked on the barges. In a stunning feat of engineering by Eiffel, the man who built the tower, the Briar canal actually GOES OVER the Loire River on a bridge of water. The barge usually approached the Pont Canal around sunset, all the lights would be turned off, the Strauss waltzes put on and everyone would get off the barge and literally waltz across the bridge. The Gien porcelain factory was astounding in that the 'seconds' shop was like a supermarket with trolleys and everything. I found my favourite set with the fruit and stripes on it, determined that one day I would buy the whole set then kill myself if one piece broke.

I had forgotten how beautiful and full of life Dijon was, and how wealthy. This little city is basically a living, sparkling, touchable open-air museum bursting with architectural heritage, art galleries, restored 15th-century buildings, a huge market place and lots of great restaurants. Friends who live there say it's bourgeois and boring, but it's a wonderful place to visit. The Burgundians were a Scandinavian people who crashed into the Roman Empire as mercenaries, later establishing a powerful kingdom along the Rhine. In 430AD the Huns destroyed this kingdom and almost entirely wiped the Burgundians out. The few that escaped plunder hid along the Soane where they reproduced like mad and rebuilt their numbers till, by 1477 the powerful dukes of Burgundy controlled land from Mâcon to the North Sea, rivalling their overlord the king of France in both power and wealth. Their capital was Dijon which became a centre of culture and learning – one of the best places to visit is the Ducal Palace. I sat in the Gothic Notre Dame church full of colour, tapestries, flowers and candles and immediately the organ began playing. I couldn't move, waiting for the angels to appear.

Gastronomically speaking, there's a lot to do in Dijon – visit Grey-Poupon, the mustard people, buy lots of crème de cassis, check out the market especially on Friday when the farmers come in with their chickens and vegetables, eat the famous spiced bread and gloat over the cheese shops. Once I had photographed almost everyone in the covered market, I threw myself into a seat right next to the kitchen, where I could smell and hear everything, of the fashionable Le Bistrot des Halles looking out over the market. This restaurant is a baby of one of the best Burgundian chefs, Jean-Pierre Billoux, who has a fabulous starred flagship at Place Darcy opposite the Art Museum. Black and white tiled floor, the underside of buttercup coloured walls, huge wine glasses, huge utensils and pink check tablecloths – everything one needs to feel one is in good hands. I started with a *gâteau de chèvre frais*, having no idea what that might be, so I was pleased when my two favourite things arrived together – goat's cheese melted on a ring of waxy potatoes. The mains included dishes like roast lamb with gratin potatoes, oxtail with chestnuts, Charolais steaks, homemade pâtès in pastry and pork belly with cabbage.

On the way back up to Auxerre, I stopped in at Ecutigny to visit my sculptor friend Declan and his wife Ginny and they told me of La Grange (The Barn), in the village of Flavigny. Every weekend the farmers' wives bring in their local produce and cook up a storm. Anyone who wants to eat sits around a big table, pays a bit of money and eats home-cooked food in the big barn. Monks also make aniseed there. One is always going somewhere ... one never has enough time to visit all the places one wants ...

I spent one sweltering afternoon at Mimi's house getting dressed up in her costumes and posing for photographs. She had me putting on many different hats, lying on couches in my swimsuit like a latter-day odalisque, sitting in the garden in an antique black lace dress holding a bunch of grapes, standing next to a dart board with the darts in my teeth, swathed in a Miró print electric blue shawl and sitting next to a white plaster nude torso holding an armful of fruit. With these photographs as inspiration after my return to New Zealand, Mimi was going to paint some portraits. There was a very beautiful painting of her in the dining room done by her husband, where she is sitting holding a basket of fruit, resplendently and voluptuously pregnant with her sixth child. Later when I saw the photographs I screamed, ran for the toilet bowl and resolved never to eat again in my life.

'My God,' asked Kathy when she returned home, 'how did she get you to pose in a swimsuit? I would never do that.'

'I'm going to kill myself,' I wailed. When I looked at the lovely Mimi she was smiling contentedly.

'*Je suis très très contente, C'est exactement ce que je voulais. Vous êtes Vénus dans les années trente. Je vais appeller mes oeuvres "Comment garder un corps de Vénus tout en mangeant bien". En plus j'ai envie de les envoyer à des magazines de mode pour dire – voilà une vraie femme en pleine bonne santé.* (I am very happy. This is exactly what I wanted. You are Venus in the thirties. I will call my works 'How to Keep the Body of a Venus and Still Eat Well'. On top of that I feel like sending these photos to fashion magazines to say – this is a real woman in blooming health.)'

Artists find beauty in places where others wouldn't think of looking.

Another desiccated, baked day I spent the afternoon at the writer Colette's museum in the castle at St-Sauveur-en-Puisaye. This place was a real revelation because, in spite of the fact that there's not actually much there aside from photos and a wonderful collection of her friend Jean Cocteau's sketches, it was a magical place full of warmth, light and beauty, impregnated with the impressions, sounds and feelings of Colette's life. The drive there through the beautiful countryside and woods she loved so much is a pleasure in itself. As you wander through the museum you hear Colette's recorded voice reading her own words with the rolling Burgundian accent she never lost, in spite of the fact she spent little time in St-Sauveur after she left the village. If you looked up you could see the tops of Burgundian trees projected onto the ceiling accompanied by birds singing and the walls were covered with her blue handwriting. Colette loved the colour pale blue, painted her walls blue, wrote on blue paper and even had pale blue ink in her fountain pen. The steps going up to the first floor had the titles of her books written on them and cabinets were full of her collection of glass objects, crystal balls and paperweights. These paperweights were *millefiori* (thousands of flowers) which Colette called her little frozen gardens. According to her daughter, when Colette looked through these balls for hours on end she saw the ponds and springs of her natal province, but it is said the reason she was so entranced was due more to being stoned on opium, a habit she shared with Cocteau. On the second landing was a slowly changing giant projection of Colette's extraordinary cat-like eyes from childhood to the end of her life.

Colette was born in 1873 and paid for her deliriously happy childhood by marrying the dreadful Willy at the age of twenty. He locked her in her room and forced her to write novels which he published under his name. Finally giving him the push she took to the stage where she did all sorts of risqué things and got into her seriously bohemian lifestyle. Colette married another abusive man but her third husband was a good one and she stayed with him until her death in 1954. She was badly crippled with arthritis but never stopped writing, plastering lots of kohl on her eyes and holding court to all her admirers from the bed. When she died France went into deep mourning at a massive state funeral. She rests in Père-Lachaise cemetery, where I and my friends often laid flowers in our little pilgrimages. A short walk through the village and you find the house she was born and brought up in with the little garden full of fruit trees and flowers across the road where she sat. The house is privately owned so you can't visit it but if you close your eyes you can hear her voice and imagine her beloved mother Sido in the garden out the back, surrounded by cats, dogs and children. Colette wrote in the most extraordinarily poetic way with a dry, spicy style, quite unique and amongst the most beautiful prose in French literature. Describing her mother, she wrote:

D'un geste, d'un regard elle reprenait tout. Quelle promptitude de main! Elle coupait des bolducs roses, déchâinait des comestibles coloniaux, repliait avec soin les pariers noirs goudronnés qui sentaient le calfatage. Elle parlait, appelait la chatte, observait à la dérobée mon père amaigri, touchait et flairait mes longues tresses pour s'assurer que j'avais brossé mes cheveux ...

Colette was also a very good cook and specialised in *cuisine bourgeoise* (middle class cooking) – hearty, honest and lusty in the pot-au-feu, blanquette de veau, *potée* tradition. Years ago I found one of her recipes for a *daube* or stew, similar to the famous *Boeuf Bourguignon* but called *Daube de Boeuf Provençale* (see page 260) because of the addition of olive oil, orange peel and tomato juice. (By the way, a fabulous thing you can do with Beef Bourguignon is to leave the beef in very large pieces and stick bits of bacon or lardons in slits cut in it and cook it that way). Right, so first marinate the beef in these wonderful things. Using olive oil is not Burgundian (as they're butter people) but the oil gives the stew a great succulence. While this is marinating you should read *Sido*, Colette's book about her mother, drink a few kirs then drain the marinade, retaining the liquid. Surrounded by birds and flowers you then bend down and retrieve the big black casserole dish from your cupboard and proceed to create your daube. Sit down with a cup of rosehip tea and read Colette's *Chéri*, occasionally checking that the daube is just simmering and no more. In Burgundy this dish is normally eaten with potatoes or pasta.

Colette's Daube de Boeuf

Serves 8

1.5kg stewing beef chopped into large chunks
2 cups red Burgundian wine
⅓ cup Marc de Bourgogne or other cognac
¼ cup olive oil
1 onion (about 150g), finely sliced
1 carrot (about 150g), finely sliced
1 stalk of celery (about 150g), finely sliced
4 large cloves of garlic, chopped
1 tsp salt
freshly ground black pepper
1 bouquet garni
½ tsp allspice
2 bay leaves
3 strips orange peel
Marinate the above for at least an hour. (I'm not a fan of long marinating – I don't think it adds anything).

Flour
9 slices of bacon
200g sliced mushrooms
3 tbsp red wine vinegar
2 tsp sugar
1 tbsp tomato paste
1 cup beef stock
chopped parsley for garnish

1. Drain marinade from beef and vegetables and reserve. Preheat oven to 150°C.

2. Piece by piece, roll the beef in flour, shaking off excess.

3. Line the bottom of a casserole dish with 3 slices of bacon, place a handful of marinated vegetables and mushrooms on top, followed by a layer of beef. Place another three strips of bacon over and continue this layering until all is finished.

4. Pour over the marinade, vinegar, sugar, tomato paste and beef stock and bring the stew to a boil on top of the stove. Cover and cook in the oven for four hours.

The Car

ls

I HAD BEEN ASKED to cook for a week on the barge I had worked on nine years ago, to relieve a chef who wanted a holiday. My immediate reaction was 'No, never, out of the question!'

'Think about it,' they said, 'it might be quite amusing for you to do it. We're desperate and we'll pay you well.'

'I want my own cabin.'

'You've got it.'

'I'm only doing it for one week.'

'We wouldn't dream of asking for more.'

A few days later, the lot of the impoverished writer and the realities of my market spending led me to look at the barging offer more leniently, so after a day of obligatory depression and complete submersion in black clouds, I called the barging people back.

'Oh,' said they, 'in that case we have two more weeks for you if you want them.'

'I'll do it,' I said, not at all looking forward to hard work when I was used to sitting down in front of a laptop all day. I had no cookbooks, no chef's whites and no knives.

The reassuring and charming thing was that nothing in the barging world had changed. The menus the chef was to have sent me didn't arrive, no one was at the train station to pick me up as arranged and everyone was complaining as usual about how badly organised everything was. I waited at the station for an hour, then called the barge manager, who acted as if he'd never heard of me, so he made me wait another hour in the stifling heat for good measure. My 45 minute journey in the car was a non-stop tirade from this man against the company and the crew, which I found quite astounding. When I left all those years ago the word was, there were going to be big changes – no more wild parties, much stricter running of staff on board, fabulous service and a higher standard of cooking. To my mind, the standard of cooking on all the barges had always been very high – in fact, the one thing worth taking the trip for; the service had always been perfectly good, and the crew had always got on well with each other.

Even though it was years since I had set a red-toenailed foot on a barge, it was like stepping back in time. I thought it would be strange, but I slipped back into my old life as if I had never been away.

The barge was sitting at her port on the canal in a nondescript village near Dijon, with cleaning tools lying around, paint touch-ups being done by the *matelot*, and hostesses (affectionately known as scrubbers) sitting outside on the grass reading. I slipped into the same staff shirts, wrapped the same big white apron around me and sharpened the knives I had been loaned. A chef never lets anyone else use their knives, and even in big kitchens chefs have their own set, so I was grateful for the loan. I looked in the mirror: my hair, which had gone through many styles, was back to the one I wore when I was cooking on the barges years ago. I could easily have forgotten I had a life and career on the other side of the world except for the fact the staff were reading my books and screaming with laughter all day. I arrived on the Friday and the passengers were due at 4 p.m. the next afternoon. The place looked like a bomb site, as it always did on 'turnaround', and the kitchen was piled up with crates of vegetables and fruit to be put away.

In the evening we all went to the local dive for drinks and dinner. It was the sort of place you would eat at only if (a) you didn't know any better, (b) there was nowhere else or (c) you worked on a luxury barge and were sick to death of boring old salmon, eye fillet steak and the best wine in the world. 'Order the salad and the omelette,' they warned me, 'everything else is inedible.' The Café du Commerce had a large terrace with plastic chairs and a tendency for orange and brown in the décor department. Strangely enough, they did very good chips. It was a beautiful evening and we got to talking about the first single we had ever bought. One was AC/DC, another was Sister Sledge, Kylie Minogue, Culture Club. Mine was The Beatles' *A Hard Day's Night*. They all looked at me admiringly. Imagine having someone at your table who had bought the Beatles' original music and danced to it in their parents' basement – and were still alive! This was a very young crew, all in their early twenties, and they were talking about the The White Stripes – can they sing or can't they? Which sibling gets on their nerves and which one doesn't?

After dinner the little ones amused themselves by riding their bikes into the canal and I went for a walk to find out where the saxophone music was coming from. I crossed the bridge to the other side of the canal and found a garden party in full swing, but didn't really feel I could gatecrash it. I went to bed to write and the others turned the volume up and boogied to some salsa music until the wee hours. They were up again early, cleaning and readying the barge for the new passengers. By early afternoon the place was transformed – everything shone, crisp linen was on the beds, flowers were everywhere and the bar was stocked.

The most famous barman of all the canals was Steve, whom I had the pleasure of working with nine years ago. Whereas Steve was very knowledgeable about wine but rarely lowered himself to revealing this to the passengers, the barman on this trip, Huw, was deeply unknowledgeable and was happy to recount any bullshit that came into his head. Over the years barmen on the barges were known to have absolutely zero interest in wine, other than tipping it down their throats, but they were all very passenger-friendly, which in a way is more important. Huw was what you would call a lovable rogue – short, nice-looking, very confident and funny, naughty (like most male staff on barges), loved by the passengers, indulged by the girls and loathed by the manager. The ostensible reason for this loathing was his not doing his job properly, but in my opinion it was jealousy. Huw was loved in a way the manager couldn't hope for and it drove him crazy. Huw didn't have the outrageous entertainment value of Steve, but he was not a bad understudy. You always need one big personality on a crew, otherwise it's deathly boring drudgery because you're repeating the same work day after day. Huw was having a romance with one of the girls, who had an impenetrable Scottish accent. She was extremely good-natured about my imitations of her voice, and every time someone made a joke about her being sweet on the barman, she blushed like a *langoustine* landing in the frying pan.

The story of the canals is quite an interesting one. There are three in Burgundy – the Canal du Centre, the Nivernais and the Canal de Bourgogne which is 242km long and has 190 locks. They were begun in 1775 to transport grain, animal feed, sand, gravel and wine and eight years later they began to be used. Construction was slow, and was interrupted by the Napoleonic wars and the Revolution, but finally a through route was achieved between Paris and Dijon in 1832. The canals were now fully in action, with *péniches* (barges) pulled by people and horses, all wearing harnesses with rope attached. As usual the women and children did most of the work, while the men sat on the barge smoking and steering. It took an hour and a half to travel a mile. This method of moving the barge continued until well after the Second World War. In 1873 mechanical bank haulage was introduced and in the 1960s motors were installed, mostly with diesel engines. The barges are now almost entirely, but not exclusively, used for pleasure cruises or private homes. Many romantic and evocative stories have been written about canal life. I remember a classic old film set on a péniche, starring Jean Gabin.

Cooking on barges was always dreadfully hard work in the heat, but I had forgotten just how hard. After the first day I thought I was going to die – my feet and legs were aching and swollen, I sweated kilos of water and drank even more. Having had a 'desk' job for two years, I was totally unaccustomed to physical work and the stress of producing lots of perfect meals all at once. But as I adjusted, once again the charm, quiet and beauty of canal and country life overtook me. The lifestyle I had so loved still existed – the lock keepers still led their simple existence with gardens full of flowers and vegetables, I went for a fast walk most mornings along the towpath and through whatever village we were moored at, and the *matelot* still cycled off early to get the passengers croissants and pain au chocolat for breakfast. The canal was full of all sorts of other boats, some rented, some privately owned, some a permanent way of life, some luxury barges that even had little swimming pools. And everybody looked blissfully happy and relaxed, especially couples who were doing it for a few weeks of their holiday. They wore striped T-shirts, old wrinkled shorts and waved and smiled at everybody.

Call me old-fashioned, but to me there is something sexual about the way the locks open and let the barges in, taking them deeper and deeper into the heart of Burgundy with each embrace. Fishermen were dotted at intervals along the canal, all decked out and fully equipped should a fish chance along. Huge trees shadowed the canal as we slid along quietly and slowly past little country cafés, families having picnics, the Côte d'Or in the distance and church spires in the foreground. It was a jolly group of passengers that week, with people very interested in and appreciative of the food. The star passengers were a delightful English couple who told me all sorts of things about food shows in England.

'You know, Peta,' smiled the lovely lady, 'Delia Smith was offered a peerage for her services to the world of cooking, but refused it, saying she was just a simple cook and didn't wish to be involved in politics.'

'Really,' I said, stiffening. 'I often feel I am verging on royalty myself and would be quite happy to receive any peerages left lying around. It wouldn't be too boring, would it?'

'No, its not boring at all.'

'Well, you should know.'

'You're not supposed to know that. We haven't told anybody.'

'I read that you were Lord and Lady W on the passenger list. You can no longer hide.'

'We didn't inherit it. My husband worked very hard for it – he's a High Court judge.'

Oh God, I thought, another one I have to hide my criminal past from. After dinner one night, Lady W rose from her chair, fearlessly broached the sacred barrier between the kitchen and the dining room and embraced me for the meal.

On the first night I cooked them salmon with leeks, cherry tomatoes and oyster mushrooms, followed by an apple and saffron tart (see page 270) which was simple, but on the second night I cooked a complicated meal that was a nightmare to serve and dirtied every pot and pan in the kitchen. It was duck breast grilled and sliced with Xeres vinegar sauce, grilled vegetables and fresh pasta. By the

Tarte au Saffran et aux Pommes
Apple and Saffron Tart

For the pastry:
250g flour
¼ tsp salt
1 tbsp sugar
1 egg yolk
120g butter, cubed
icy cold water

For the filling:
1 cup hot milk
2 good pinches of saffron
3 eggs
3 tbsp sugar
⅓ cup currants
5 tart apples, peeled, cored and sliced finely

1. To make the pastry, pile the flour onto work surface and make a well in the centre. Into this put the salt, sugar, egg yolk and butter. With your fingertips gradually work in the flour to the ingredients in the centre, bringing it in until a soft dough is formed. You may need to add a little water as you go. Work quickly and methodically. Form a ball, cover in plastic wrap and rest in the fridge for half an hour.

2. Preheat oven to 150°C. Drop the saffron into the hot milk and allow to infuse.

3. Roll the pastry out and gently fit it into a 25cm flan dish. Sprinkle the currants over the base then arrange the apple slices in an incredibly artistic way over the top.

4. Beat together the eggs and sugar, beat in the milk and saffron infusion and pour over the apples.

5. Bake for about 45 mins or until just set and golden on top.

end of getting it all out and still warm, I was drenched and exhausted. 'How did I do this for eight months?' I thought. I had no holiday and no break for that period and was never offered one. One thing that has changed is that the staff now get holidays, and they get them at prime time – which was why I was there in the middle of August.

The staff accepted me as if I had always been there, and went out of their way to make me feel welcome. Periodically Huw would come into the kitchen with a glass of wine for me on a silver platter with a little cocktail serviette; sometimes the matelot would take my garbage out; sometimes the Dutch pilot scrubbed my kitchen floor; if a passenger ordered a cooked breakfast the lovely housekeeper Louise never woke me up and the girls regularly turned the air-conditioning on in my room if I forgot to do it. One of the directors of the company turned up unannounced to have dinner with the passengers and kissed my hand at the end of the meal. Little perks like that kept me sweet and good-humoured so that when the management called on the cellphone to see if I was throwing knives around the kitchen yet, the Scottish lass said, 'Ooh noo, she's no lake tha.' In the afternoon while they played loud Abba, Disco Hits and Tina Turner in the kitchen, I read Colette and André Malraux in my air-conditioned paradise downstairs. Not that I wish to sound posh . . .

The one thing that was a drag was that all the food had been ordered in advance so I had to work with what was there. I was deeply uninterested in cabbage of any colour, or 3000 celery roots. Two celery roots make a great traditional French salad, but you can only serve it once. Normally it's grated raw and mixed with mayonnaise, but I took Louise's chef boyfriend's advice and did it with lemon juice, olive oil and freshly ground black pepper. They're not as mad on freshly ground pepper in France as they should be and to my mind the taste of powdered pepper is completely different – there's just nothing so zingy and racy as those little grounds still emitting their aromatic nicotine of the spice world. While I'm on my horse I'd also like to mention that pre-ground nutmeg should be banned. There is nothing so delicious as the smell and flavour of freshly ground nutmeg. Locked inside that hard little nut is an essential oil that is as good in sweet dishes as in savoury. You can grate it with an ordinary grater or even with a kitchen knife. I always grate it into béchamel sauce, fruit and rice dishes and a mixture of nutmeg, pepper, fresh ginger, ground cloves and mace is divine wrapped around beef or venison just before cooking. As I am very southern in my cooking preferences, I noticed a lamentable lack of capsicums, aubergines, courgettes and vine tomatoes. Also there were no olives, anchovies or capers, which almost sent me into low-salt coma, so I jumped off at the nearest village and bought piles of the aforementioned plus lots of fruits rouges like strawberries, raspberries, blackberries and red currants. Very quickly I reduced my dishes to the stunning but simple variety. The French overcook all vegetables, the idea of bright green, crunchy green beans and broccoli being completely foreign to them.

The second night we moored at Chagny, which is a dump save for the extraordinary three-star restaurant and hotel, Lameloise. I noticed they had a fixed menu and made a mental note to go there next time I was in the area. On the Monday night we moored for the night at Chalon, a polished, sparkling city whose wealth comes from wine as does almost every other big town in Burgundy. The bridges and quays were very grand, with majestic white steps leading from the moorings up to the wide street bordering the river. We all scrubbed the sweat off and went onshore at 10.30 p.m. after the service to have a drink in the crew's favourite bar. In the moonlit night we strolled through the beautiful little city, past chic clothing stores and along cobblestoned streets to arrive at Cathedral Square, lined with up-market cafés, bars and restaurants. It was full of very Parisian-style, hip young people and the little ones set to drinking seriously, as they do. I got up as early as I could the next morning to go for a daylight walk in Chalon, but unfortunately the barge left at 9.30 a.m. so I didn't see much. I did, however, see lots of specialty food shops, huge glistening fish shops, quaint little cafés in the morning sun with people taking their crème and *tartine*, half-timbered houses and winding pedestrian streets.

The Chalonnaise wine slopes, in between the Mâconnais and Beaune, have their own appellation *côntrolé* with large amounts of good land, a few famous wines like Mercury, Rully, Givry, Montagny and Bouzeron and, of course, Bourgogne Côte-Châlonnaise, but there doesn't seem to be any real spark. The problem appears to be that, in the marketplace, the Chalonnaise wines are overwhelmed by their well-known neighbours on top of and underneath them. They need to be recognisable not just as Burgundies but as Chalonnaise, allowing the buyer to identify the origins and the seller to get a fairer price. They make a lot of simple small wines, and when they're good, they're good – the reds give out an aroma of great delicacy, very berry, spicy and almost tasting of cherries, while the whites are often opulent, fruity and very buttery.

The barge then left Chalon, floated from the Central canal into the river Saône and stopped for the night at St-Jean-de-Losne, the smallest city in France, remarkable mostly for its beautiful little cathedral and pretty port where all the boats get repaired. I walked around the town, which took approximately five minutes, and couldn't drag myself away from the baroque, florid, flamboyant décor of the old church. There was a large antique model ship hanging in one corner with a side altar of thanks for prayers answered, a fantastic 18th-century organ and an ornate altar like a stage set. The roof was steeply sloped in the traditional coloured tiles of Burgundy and the whole building looked like a beautiful dolls' house. One of Jeremy's barges, the *Fleur de Lys*, was moored right next to us so I sat outside on the grass and had a natter with his chef, Lucinda. I must say, one nice thing about barging is the chatting and exchanging of recipes with chef friends passing in the night, as it were. Everyone from the old days whom I came across was astounded to see me. When you go back home, you are effectively removing yourself from the face of the earth and when you come back to France, it's as if you've come from another planet.

We floated along a bit more. I made multicoloured salads, cooked artichokes, roasted butterflied lamb, baked lemon tarts for lunch, and the sun beat down. The passengers lounged around drinking cocktails, going for walks and discussing important issues like how to dry their silk knickers and what to do with a wife who's suffering from vaporous gasification due to excesses of lentil salad. We hardly ever saw the manager as he spent his time doing tours with the passengers or retiring to his home, but the moment he came on board, the atmosphere went downhill as he didn't seem to be on speaking terms with anybody but moi. Louise calmly and efficiently went about her work and was easy to get along with, and Huw revealed himself to be quite an acceptable court jester/barman in the classic tradition. The passengers wanted to adopt him, with his round, angelic face; and on the other side of the dining-room wall we became quite fond of each other as the days went by. He was a natural peacemaker, intelligent and very funny, and became my chief plater-upper when it came to serving time. He would put on my lipstick and apron to be like me and dish up little works of art.

'Oh my God!' he would yell, throwing himself into the kitchen. 'The cork's come out of this bottle of champagne. I can feel a mimosa coming on darling.' As everyone knows, a mimosa (champagne and orange juice) is practically the only way to start the day. He had taken his degree in sports psychology and we had many discussions about the meaning of life, his future, my past, his women, my men and his love of France and the French.

On the afternoon of the fourth day the passengers went for a tour of the Château de Longecourt in the village of Longecourt-en-Plaine taken by the Countess de Saint-Seine herself. I wanted to go, but I had caught a cold thanks to overheating in the kitchen then lying in an air-conditioned bedroom. I felt close to death's door but had agreed to prepare a barbecue which the Countess had kindly said we could have chez elle. I made up plastic boxes full of vine tomatoes, aubergines, merguez, all sorts of meats and sauces and peaches for grilling, then lay down until I got my marching orders. Huw and the matelot said they wanted to be the chief cooks.

We piled everything onto the bus that always travelled with the barge for visits and set off for the château – tables, chairs, chilly bins full of wine and water, plates, cutlery, barbecues, cheeses and the illusion that it would all be easy and *vite fait*. We drove into the village – the entrance to the château was on the Place Hôtel de Ville. Across the moat we motored into a fairytale castle that I instantly regretted not having visited with the passengers. A lovely-looking woman with soft brown hair, sparkling dark eyes and a relaxed but dignified manner came toward us down the grand, double steps with a handsome, slim man in his late forties wearing jeans, and a bouncy young boy dancing around them both. She was introduced to me as the Countess, the man Roland as her son and the boy Jonathan as her grandchild by her daughter. We set up our outdoor kitchen. Of course the two barbecues were tiny, and it took the designated cooks ages to drag them out of their new packets and assemble them. The passengers were already there, had done their tour and were looking parched for some champagne, the poor darlings. We immediately plied them with bar snacks and alcohol and set to cooking the merguez and setting up tables on the bridge that led from the main entrance to the steps leading down over the moat.

Lady W, someone who naturally cared about other people, saw I had an 'I can't stand this' look and immediately took my arm and led me up the grand winding steps saying 'I'm taking you on a tour of the château, you absolutely have to see it and they don't need you to cook a barbecue.' This château, perfect on the inside and crumbling a bit on the outside – which only added to its charm – had survived through many glorious years of French history. Built in 1200 as a *maison forte* (fortified house), it elegantly married its round pointed towers of the 16th-century manor house style with the neoclassical Italian embellishments of the 18th century. Bordered by the Canal de Bourgogne, it was very close to the Côte d'Or wine slopes – in fact, Beaune was just a glass of Gevrey-Chambertin away. We went on a lamentably quick tour of a place in which I would normally have spent an hour in each room, then came back down to see how badly the meat had been massacred. It looked like a nightmare, with Huw and the matelot bravely fanning the coals and getting approximately nowhere and time marching on and passengers drinking more and more. Finally Huw leapt into a karate stance and screamed, 'For God's SAKE, girl, there must be a quicker way to cook a sausage than to sweat on it. While you're pratting around with the aristocrats, the peasants are starving,' then he took the backs off the barbecues which let a rush of air in and we were off. Everyone was seated on the bridge in the fading light, looking out over the lovely gardens tended by Roland, who pointed out Jupiter in the sky, and the Countess joined us for the first barbecue they had ever had at the château.

The passengers were absolutely beside themselves and thrilled with the whole thing. After dinner, talk turned to all sorts of topics – the funniest of which concerned an older, single man who was on the boat. Despite the fact he looked very happy and fulfilled, the others kept asking him why he wasn't married.

'Well,' he drawled (he was from Texas), 'there was this gal chasin' after me once, so I stopped and she went right past.'

'That's very good,' I said. 'Do you mind if I use it?'

'Not at all.' He smiled his boyish freckled smile. 'There was one other gal, though. She banged on my door for three weeks so finally I had to let her out.'

This man was my competition. He took notes endlessly, wrote down all the meals and snapped 36,000 photos. He snapped flowers, lettuce leaves, the side of the boat, the bar, the lock – anything he could find. It was so sweet and he was very pure and delighted in everything, like a child. It turned out he was a wealthy banker.

Roland was convinced that men in the New World were very macho and badly brought up and let the women carry their own suitcases. Jonathan conversed intelligently about why he thought France was the perfect country, asked me questions about the relationship between nuclear testing and the importation of New Zealand lamb into France and got all my jokes. I managed to squawk out a few songs while Huw stood in the shadows with his arms raised to me, just stopping short of howling at the moon, and a passenger who was a classical pianist sat down at the shonky piano and somehow coaxed a bit of Chopin out of it. All in all it was a fine evening, and when they left, Roland kissed the women's hands. They all said they would never wash again. I didn't want to leave. Every time I visit a château I become hooked on the historical drama. For hundreds of years a potent cast of players ruled, murdered, played, haunted and adulterised like mad behind the thick walls of European castles, and walking on the same floors as they had walked on never ceased to grab me. Within minutes of looking at a painting of a previous inhabitant I would 'see' them walking through a room and wonder whom they were going to visit down which secret passage. The Château Longecourt was such an eccentric little castle and the countess and Roland were so approachable, I decided to ask if I could come back and talk to them more about their family history – to which they kindly agreed.

We all floated into the pretty port of Dijon in our love boat (love boat because we actually liked all the passengers that week) and prepared for the slap-up last night dinner. The best tables were dragged out from the dining room onto the deck, covered in white tablecloths, flowers, silver and candelabra. I cooked them *poivrons rouges Piedmont*, another recipe Louise's chef boyfriend had given me, wherein you cut large red peppers in half, core them but leave the stems on. Then they are stuffed with chunks of skinned tomato, lots of garlic, salt, pepper and fresh basil or thyme. You roast them in a hot oven drenched in olive oil for about an hour or until they are melting and browned on top. Baste frequently. He served them on a bed of melted aubergines, and I served them on a bed of salad greens, the juice from the cooking acting as the salad dressing. This utter deliciousness was followed by eye fillet with anchovy sauce, tiny green beans neatly lined up together and sautéd potatoes. There were three birthdays amongst the passengers so I made a huge birthday cake, the girls cut the lights and we sailed out with all the candles lit, singing at full throttle.

They all left in the morning with kisses and hugs and I was picked up and driven to my next barge, moored at Vandenesse-en-Auxois in the beautiful Ouche valley. On the way I read in the newspaper that the Paris transport authority was halving fares on buses and métros for the next two days (22 August) to encourage motorists to use public transport during their regular summer pollution alert. Paris had been plagued for a week by high ozone levels because of car exhaust fumes and the heatwave. The police had lowered speed limits and begged drivers to leave cars at home, which no one did. It was at level two, which means they tell old people and babies not to go out – just one slippery digit away from level three, which means free public transport and no cars. I thanked my lucky stars I was living the heatwave out in the countryside. According to the French Meteorological Service it was the longest heatwave this century, with temperatures over 30 degrees for three weeks solid. In fact the weather in Europe had been nutty all summer – a very early hot spring, cold and rainy July and a furnace in August, with everyone talking about global warming.

Of course in France when you think about weather you automatically think about wine. You have good wines and bad wines but it is always the weather that controls everything. The grape harvest began in Bordeaux a week ago, a month earlier than usual and it has been a century (1893) since there has been such a precocious *vendange*. The Château Haut-Brion premier grand cru classé Graves whipped their white grapes off the vines in the middle of August with the reds following a week later. Winegrowers have to obtain a precarious equilibrium between acid and sugar. The aroma of the grape grows with maturing then reaches a peak before dimming, so one must pick as close as possible to this aromatic summit. It's all terribly dramatic and nerve-racking. This year the vines flowered a month in advance, which is normally the sign of a very good year, and although it was too early yet to tell if it was an exceptional year or not, all the signs pointed to it.

This barge was full so I didn't get a passenger cabin. When I jumped on board at the lock, the pilot tried to put my suitcase downstairs in the chef's hovel but I said, 'Oh no, no. I'm not sleeping down there.'

'Well, where are you sleeping?'

'It's too hot down there. Give me the best of the worst you've got.'

They put me in a crew cabin which was very nice, with all the comforts save for air-conditioning. I immediately nicked the fan from the vegetable storage and from then on, it spent half its life in the kitchen and the other half in my room.

Later on I decided to eat at Pascal's restaurant and épicerie. Anything to get away from the hellhole of a kitchen and staff dining room, situated in the dark, airless, viewless bowels of the barge. They were busy: his wife Monique said they weren't taking any more customers, but Pascal said seeing as how it was me and I was such a *charmante dame*, he'd make an exception – and the wife smiled daggers at me. She sat me down looking over the canal and redeemed herself by offering a kir, and her little girl, all dark flashing eyes, bare feet and tiny frilly skirt, plonked a whole baguette on my table. The hot pink and blue evening illuminated the castle at the top of Châteauneuf, water swished through the lock gates, and the bridge traversing the canal was lined with box flowers. Just over the bridge several barges were moored as well as ours with evocative names like *La Reine Pédoque*, *Lady A*, *Niagara* and *Saroche*. I thought Niagara was a bit much considering the utter passivity of the canals. I was happy to be there in the fresh air, listening to the water in the lock and watching the day fade away. A little boy walked past wearing a big smile, potatoes in all his pockets and down the front of his shorts and arms full of freshly picked beans. My *coq au vin* arrived and the cat whinged loudly at my feet.

There was a buzzer under the floor of the épicerie that went off every time anyone went in or out of the shop, which meant it rang all night – enough to drive anyone up the wall. Now the cat was on the table standing over my food, and with the darkness arrived candles, moonlight and a few stars. All the tables were lined up on the grass verge of the canal and the children were running in and out helping with the service. Across the canal in front of us was the restaurant Lucotte, closed for August unfortunately. The inexpensive bill came. One can only be grateful one is alive.

Next day in 34 degree heat I sat on my bed eating Roquefort on a chunk of baguette and drinking red wine full of ice-cubes, typing and waiting for the passengers to arrive. This boat definitely didn't feel like the other one, either in terms of classiness or in terms of fun and friendly staff. It seemed to be very much the poor cousin of the others in spite of it being very pretty and doing a much more picturesque route. The housekeeper said hello without smiling then basically ignored me. I missed Louise and her friendly, courteous, helpful ways already. There was no uniform for me to wear and no effort made to find some staff shirts. The male staff, although very nice, seemed to reach new heights of the normal boy-laziness and randiness. At the last minute I realised there weren't enough smoked duck breasts to do the salad so decided on avocado with salsa – but there weren't enough avocados. This was a bad start and might even end in tears. I then had to take the goat's cheese from the housekeeper, as there was nothing else, and served it grilled on toast with salad. This was a large group of 20 so there could be no cheating – and there were difficult customers who didn't eat strawberries or fish or shellfish or tomatoes or meat, to make things even more pleasant for me. A bunch of losers in other words. I loathe vegetarians and wonder why anyone would come on a tour like this if they didn't enjoy good food. Patrice said this neuroticism is the fault of American doctors who can't think of any other ways of making money, so invent allergies and food fads for people. There were no compliments or thank yous from the staff for the food I prepared for them. That was my first day.

Patrice, the tour guide, was the bright spark on this boat. The last time I had seen his stocky little person was at a crew wedding I catered in 1988. He never stopped talking and laughing and telling indiscreet stories about who was getting up to what with whom, and he could go back 10 years if need be. We went over the story of how Jean-Marie had been caught in bed with a housekeeper whose husband turned up with a shotgun. Jean-Marie said he wasn't the slightest bit scared, but Patrice said he was white. As he lived nearby, Patrice slept at home so unfortunately we only saw him when he was picking people up or dropping them off. He would throw himself into the kitchen like a fireball, kiss me and say, 'Ça va, *ma poule*?' talking non-stop in his gravelly voice. Just looking at Patrice made me laugh.

French chefs on the barges do quite different food from the English or American ones. They do what the mediocre French chefs have always done with little originality or zinging flair. The food seems tired and unoriginal to me. For example they use powdered veal stock, which of course tastes industrial – something a good chef would never do in a month of Sundays. I know it is not practical to make real jus on a boat, so why use it at all? Why not just make a fresh sauce from roasted tomatoes or a fish sauce from fishbones, cream and wine? This chef had ordered lots of pre-prepared things like terrines to make less work for himself, which I thought was quite a good idea but completely unacceptable on the other barge which expected much higher standards. The crew on this barge were astounded when I told them I was accustomed to cooking a hot meal and even desserts for lunch on the other boat.

I endured a week in the third world they called a kitchen, where I never saw the light of day, there was no ventilation and I got to smell the rotten odour of *écluse* (lock) walls regularly. The staff were boring, unfriendly and ungrateful, save for Matt, the matelot and a sweet French cabin girl called Aline. These two never failed to thank me or help me when they could and Matt took on the task of entertaining me. A tall, nice-looking boy, he had girls coming out his ears and I couldn't quite figure out why. He didn't seem to have the charm or animal sexuality of certain famous barging predecessors, but as the tedious days went by I realised what it was – he was just a very nice, fun person, not macho, no attitude and very generous of spirit. His one fault was he was just a boy who couldn't say no: two-, three- and four-timing girls without telling them. The other cabin girl had the most revolting eating habits and enthusiastically threw everything out every day without consulting me. One day I found this stupid girl smothering industrial mayonnaise all over an eye fillet steak. She lived on biscuits, junk and mayonnaise from what I could see, while surrounded by the best food money could buy – AND was having an affair with the regular chef, whose food she refused to touch. Vegetables and salads made her sick. Also, to my astonishment the pilot regularly threw wine down the gurgler. The housekeeper who I had been told was *spéciale*, was married to the pilot. Spéciale in French is not a compliment – it means unusual or difficult. Two more different people you couldn't hope to meet. He was so relaxed and passive he was almost asleep, and she was the *dominatrix par excellence*. She wasn't without humour and I liked her strong personality but unfortunately it was tempered with neither warmth nor charm.

This very pretty barge, built in 1928, was 38 metres long and five metres wide – the standard Freycinet size. Freycinet was the Minister of Public Works in 1890 and he standardised the size of the locks and draught on the principal canals of France. She was bought by the company in 1978, transformed into a hotel barge and has been plying the Canal de Bourgogne ever since, making her the most well-known and maybe oldest of all the vessels that pass through the waterway system. But nothing worked on this boat. The washing machine was so hopeless the girls couldn't even change the passengers' towels every day, and the laundry floor was constantly flooded. Having opened two new packets of crew shirts for myself as the housekeeper refused to provide me with some, I couldn't get them washed. They were still sitting on the floor two days later, so I had to wash them by hand and hang them up in the bathroom. The generator was borderline suicidal and you could only use one appliance at a time, the air-conditioning worked maybe half the time, and the motor regularly crapped out. The management refused to replace cracked plates (so the staff said) so the chef had to surreptiously buy them from another budget. In spite of all these working conditions, the crew provided great service and the passengers never knew what they had to endure. I had worked on this barge nine years ago and it was exactly the same, but the thing that saved it at that time was the crew, who drank like fish and sang and partied every night. I remember I used to make the pilot a cooked breakfast every day and take it up to him at the wheelhouse. When I did that for Matt one morning, the crew took half a day to close their mouths again. One day it suddenly rained and the temperature went down. In the space of two days the heatwave was completely off and we were wearing jumpers.

Having finished my semainus horribilis at Dijon, I strolled around the fabulous market before meeting my old friend Agnes for lunch at the Bistro des Halles. The food was as good as ever and we caught up on all the news over a red pepper mousse and lamb with scalloped potatoes. In the afternoon I talked Matt into driving me back to the first barge to complete my third and last week. Huw and Louise were there but most of the rest of the crew had changed. That night they made a barbecue on the towpath next to the barge and we sat huddled around it in our jumpers, hardly believing that two days ago we were fainting from the heat. They told me of their traumatic week in my absence – horrendous passengers, bad food, air-conditioning problems and the entire lock system breaking down at one point. That was just the tour. Before it even started two hoons had come on board on Friday night, wanting a drink. When it was explained that it wasn't a public bar they trashed the place, breaking a chair over the chef's back, bashing the matelot in the face with a bottle and generally spreading terror wide and far.

By a stroke of luck my return brought a boatload of wonderful, polite, appreciative passengers. Ruth and Norman, Sharlene and Chuck and their friends read passages from the Bible to each other, didn't drink much and thought everything everyone did for them was just wonderful. Huw of course insisted I show my books to them and I wondered what they would make of the F words and stories of men, horrible American passengers and such when they got to them. Of course they were far too polite to mention it and talked about my interesting recipes! As the week progressed Huw, Louise and I realised we had a very boring crew and missed our previous cabin girls dancing on the tables, wearing too-short shirts and talking in incomprehensible accents. On the 30th of August the matelot called his parents in England on the cellphone, which was working for a change, but when he came back he was white. We all stared at him. Princess Diana had been killed in a car accident in Paris. Most of the crew were English and everyone was in a state of shock and disbelief. The death was all over the French news, radio stations in England didn't play music for a whole day and everyone was baying for the blood of paparazzi everywhere.

Two weeks after my first visit I returned to the Château de Longecourt, bringing with me two white deckchairs we had appropriated from them by mistake after the barbecue. The barge manager drove me over in the bus and refused to talk to me, even when I spoke directly to him. Like all psychopaths, he could be charming and expansive or odious and closed, depending on which way the wind was blowing, and had absolutely no insight into his pathology. A classic bully, his stress and emotional problems manifested themselves in obesity and an inability to communicate with other people in any real sense. Wonderful and brilliant with the passengers, he controlled the atmosphere in the crew quarters with his tantrums and ominous silences. Many staff had left because of him and yet he was still there. Up until now I had been '*la charmante cuisinière*' and could do no wrong. Now, for no obvious reason, I was persona non grata. The crew were very relieved that I had joined the ranks of the nonexistent. That left the two new cabin girls, so I guessed they had about a week to go. His blackness was so obvious that when we arrived at Longecourt Roland asked if we were at war. He was in his uniform of jeans, T-shirt and cigarette – still the sardonic, slightly shy smile from dark eyes and two deep lines on either side of his mouth. This time he had read my book and was quoting from it, which is the point where I always realise, with regret, the disadvantage of having exposed myself.

Roland made me coffee and we sat outside in the main courtyard where he immediately set to interviewing me, wanting all the spaces in the book filled in, with no reticence shown in the intimate question department. His curiosity and comments were naively but sagely direct, in a way Anglo-Saxons never speak, and I didn't know whether it was because he felt he knew me, or whether it was just his nature. Questions like, 'How do you feel about being single?' and 'Where is your husband?' and 'Why don't you have any children?' and 'When you say butter, what kind of butter do you mean?' and 'How did these people in your book feel about what you wrote about them?' He said he had the impression I observed my life without really participating in it – and scanned me in a way no journalist had ever come near.

We were joined by his mother, Madame de Saint-Seine, this serene woman with her black eyes and gentle manner. Although they were entirely charming and open, I had lost the moment. Now that I was there officially with a notebook, pen and camera, everything was different and artificial. They didn't really want to talk about the château and their history anymore, they just wanted to sit and drink coffee and enjoy themselves.

'There are 32,000 châteaux in France,' said Roland. 'Why

do you want to talk about us?'

'Because our little lives would all be poorer without access to France's ancient soap operas through the castles. I happened to meet you so it's you I'm talking to.' He smiled his sardonic smile. I kept trying to turn the conversation back to them but they insisted they weren't interesting, they had done nothing, they had lived in the village all their lives. They didn't want their photos taken and I think they had told their story so many times and been photographed so often, they just wanted to relax. Maybe it was because they had read my book *Fête Accomplie* and were afraid of me. In a way I was happier just to be in their company and took few notes, Roland escorted me around the château and I ended up in their private kitchen, watching the Countess top-and-tail the beans he had just picked, and playing this-little-piggy-went-to-market with the granddaughter. This toddler was the sister of Jonathan, a child with alabaster skin, ringlets and dark slanted eyes like the women in the paintings on the walls of the castle. Surrounded by love, she was delightful and affectionate and scribbled all over my notes, which was only correct.

The Saint-Seine family have owned the château since 1830, for five generations, and recently there was a family reunion of almost 300 people carrying the Saint-Seine name. Madame de Saint-Seine married the count, who was a lot older than her, and had four children, the eldest of whom is the mayor of Longecourt. One entered the château through large iron gates and was faced with a large, ornate building with two slightly uneven towers on either side. On the left side was the original entrance, now covered up, big enough to allow a carriage and horses to enter into the château. I regretted the sealing of this door as I happened to see myself riding through in an ornate carriage drawn by six black horses. The Italianesque stucco facade covering the entire outside of the château like the icing on a cake, had half fallen off to reveal the bricks and mortar of its previous status. This marbling and trompe l'oeil was continued inside on columns and walls. When châteaux were fortified they were little communities unto themselves with their own priests, large kitchens, gardens, animals and coveting of the neighbour's wife. When under siege, the whole village could shelter there indefinitely and want for nothing, save a bit of peace and a few less arrows landing on their heads.

Firstly Roland took me to the ornate little chapel which resembled a mini cathedral, with portraits of ancestors painted in tiles on the floor, coats of arms on the ceiling and a private gallery on a mezzanine. Inside the front door of the château was a long gallery with walls covered in paintings of ancestors and a heavy Dutch cabinet full of the Countess' homemade jams. To the right of the gallery was the huge old kitchen, no longer in use – a room I would have liked to spend at least half my life in. Now cleaned back to its original off-white, it had once been almost black with the cooking of centuries. A large armoire was groaning with shining copper pots, there was a long table in the middle of the room, and if one looked carefully one found naughty sculptures on some of the pillars. A fireplace the length of a wall was lined with beautiful little cupboards and in the central pillar was a tiny holy water font, now Roland's private hidden ashtray. There was an antique skittles table with bronze clowns, and paintings on the walls of how the kitchens were in the old days – dark, unhygienic and smelly.

There were several salons downstairs, beautifully restored and decorated with frescoes and flowers Roland had painted around the ceilings. On this floor and the second floor were the large bedrooms with en suites for paying guests, all embossed wallpaper, 18th-century screens, brass bedsteads with canopies, tapestries, heavy drapes, and named for the guests who had stayed there in the past – Catherine de Medici, Charles IX etc. I always find it amazing that aristocrats can let someone else sleep in the rooms they have spent their most intimate moments in, but I think it's like writing autobiography – you cross a barrier where you are no longer attached to the emotional content of an event or a room. Roland said he was afraid of these rooms when he was a child. He had nightmares and imagined all kinds of ghosts and monsters. I envisioned a sensitive, brooding child wandering around the long corridors, lost in the labyrinth of rooms and inherited memories of past deeds. At the end of a corridor I saw a locked door and asked what was behind it. The Countess said it was the old, unlived-in part of the château and I didn't want to go up there. I assured her I did, so Roland unbolted the door and we all mounted the dusty winding staircase, going from gloomy room to gloomy room. It was like being in an attic. If I had had the time I could have figured out the history of the château just by examining the objects in these rooms with their 12th-century floors – wool mattresses, old cradles and beds, trunks, tools, clothes – treasures to my eyes.

We locked the old door behind us, walked down the hall and, going up the staircase, we entered the *grand salon* on the second floor, nothing short of surreal in its Versailles-like splendour. If this room failed to take your breath away and convince you minimalism was for the birds, I don't know what would. Roland opened the windows and shutters to let the afternoon light fall in stripes and patches on the ornate gold-framed mirrors, paintings, grand clock over the fireplace and voluptuous décor. It was hard to believe this château had been requisitioned by American soldiers during the Second World War and that they had sat at the velvet-covered table, in the antique chairs and on the precious carpets. Roland told me some American guests had sat on the floor in there recently and eaten sardines from a tin with red wine. 'Sardines from a tin!' I gasped. 'Sardines with red wine!' he gasped. '*Oui, des sardines, des sardines*,' sang the little girl. I was invited into their private salon and almost felt like an intruder as I looked at the beautiful photographs of the Countess' children on the walls and the little portrait of her as a young woman, painted by Roland from a photograph. This marvelous room was full of extraordinary things juxtaposed: a huge painting of Marguerite de Bourgogne, a beautiful young creature in an ermine and red satin gown with tall medieval head-dress; a large television set which the child immediately turned on and the grandmother immediately turned off; paintings of kings and royalty, books, mending and antiques. Oh, there are people who say if you've seen one castle you've seen them all, but this is just a philistine sophistication – you have to know where you came from to know who you are.

After our tour tea was made and we sat down again outside to be joined by friends of theirs who had just got back from seeing the Pope in Paris. He had descended from the lofty heights of that cesspool of shady dealings, the Vatican, to a choreographed and designer-clad orgy of clergy and faithful dressed in ice white. Only in France would the clergy be in co-ordinated colours. The friends described it as being a religious experience and like being in the presence of a saint. Roland asked if there were beer stands set up for people. I looked quickly at them and they didn't seem to think it an odd question but I was sure he was being facetious. Reluctantly I took leave of them to return to my kitchen and the serving of the evening meal on the barge. Roland gave me his copy of *Clochemerle* by Gabriel Chevallier, saying I couldn't possibly write about Burgundy without having read such a classic about Burgundian village life. He, the dog and the beautiful child Félicie drove me to find the barge which hadn't quite arrived at the Longecourt lock, where it would be moored for the night. We followed it along the towpath with Félicie hanging out one window screaming '*bateau! bateau!*' and Roland leaning out the other picking me *des baies de sureau* (elderberries) and pretty poisonous flowers. Mimi makes good jam from this bitter little berry. At the bridge we all caught up with each other, Félicie did a tour of the deck, whispered bateau to the passengers who all fell in love with her on the spot and I gave her back to her uncle when the barge rose in the lock, blowing them kisses as they drove back into their privileged world behind the big gates.

I sat on the deck when the passengers were away visiting and set to reading *Clochemerle*. First published in 1934 and still in print, this Rabelaisian chronicle written in a naïve style tells about an era long gone, a style of village life existent only in our memories. But does it? I can tell you, French village life hasn't changed much. Chevallier wrote many other novels plus three follow-ups to *Clochemerle*, which is all about the building of a public urinal in the village. Where to put it and how to deal with such a sensitive issue? Barthelémy Piéchut the mayor of Clochemerle-en-Beaujolais calls it *un urinoir*, Ernest Tafardel the teacher calls it *une pissotière*, Mme la Baronne Alphonsine de Courtebiche calls it *une vespasienne*. There are inaugurations, hallucinations, scandals, craziness and personal dramas lived out in much the same way as they are today. An awful lot of country people in France live the same way their ancestors did, never leaving their village and not letting so-called progress within a kilometre of them. Piéchut is described thus:

> L'un de ces hommes, âgè de plus de cinquante ans, grand, rouge de teint, encore blond, offrait le type pur d'un descendant des Bourgondes qui peuplèrent autrefois le Rhône. Son visage, dont les vents et le soleil avaient craquelé l'epiderme, vivait surtout par deux petits yeux gris clair, entourés de fines rides et perpétuellement clignés qui lui donnaient un air de malice, tantôt cordiale. Mais la bouche, qui aurait pu fournir sur son caractère des indications qu'on ne lisait pas dans son regard, demeurait invisible sous la moustache tombante, dans laquelle s'enfonçait le tuyau d'une courte pipe noire, mâchée plutôt que fumée, qui

sentait à la fois le marc et le tabac. Le personnage paraissait de forte charpente, sec, monté sur des jambes hautes et droites, avec une pointe de ventre qui était négligence musculaire plutôt qu'embonpoint véritable. Bien qu'il fut vêtu sans recherche, à ses souliers confortables et circés, à la qualité du drap de son habit, au faux col porté avec aisance un jour de semaine, on le devinait cossu et respecté. On sentait l'autorité dans sa voix et ses gestes rares.

On the last day, after waving goodbye to our lovely group, I had lunch at the Bistro des Halles with Huw and the pilot. I had forgotten my lipstick and on the way home Huw just couldn't stand it and leapt into the nearest pharmacy to buy me one called Volcano Red by Phas. Later on he presented it to me gift-wrapped with a condom and a flower – *Please think of me when you use these.* At the table behind us in the restaurant I heard a film crew talking about our barge so I asked them who they were and what their business was. They were with the television station France 3 Bourgogne Franche-Comté and had hired the *péniche* for the launch of a new programme called *Les Dimanches Malins*, to air on Saturdays at 5.30 p.m. The idea was to give people ideas as to what to do on a Sunday in terms of cooking, gastronomy and the constant search for authentic regional Burgundian products. There would be lots of advice and practical information given around a central seasonal theme – food writers, famous guests, unknown artists defending the ancient art of living well, lost recipes, secret addresses, market and fair visits, fleamarkets etc. It was to be presented by a well-known personality, Jean Maisonnave – a man of the theatre, gastronomic critic and columnist. Very attached to his home turf of Burgundy, a defender of authentic products, open and curious about everything, Jean is famous for being a big man with a big mouth and bursts of laughter. In France they don't expect a gastronomic presenter to look good

– and there he was in his crumpled shirt that I suppose had been white at some stage, huge belly full of years of good Burgundian beef, and messy hair. His personality seemed to be as big as his physique.

They arrived on the barge later that afternoon with hordes of press to give a preview of the show and stuff champagne and hors d'oeuvres down their throats. I sat at the back in bare feet as the heat was on again, and got talking to a very pretty woman, Marianne, who was the communications person for France 3. She introduced me to the only person in the room who looked interesting, a journalist with shaved head, a silver feather hanging from one ear, black clothes and black suede winklepickers. Thierry was with another journalist, Jacques, and we had an enthusiastic get-together after everyone had left. They described themselves as old rockers. Somehow he persuaded me to give him the only copy of my book and we decided to keep in touch. A week later I received an extraordinary two-page fan letter from him that was both touching and open-hearted.

I was almost sad to leave the barge and my new friends, but knew I would have to lie down very still for at least three weeks to recover. The day after I left I got the news that Louise had resigned her job to work for another company. She could no longer tolerate working with the manager, knew nothing would change and felt the company was always going to protect him. Another unfortunate postscript to my stay on the barges was that the moisture and dampness ruined the screen of my laptop, obliging me to replace it for huge amounts of dosh.

The evening I arrived back in Auxerre chez Frédéric and Kathy, we were invited to Catherine and Emmanuel's place for a North African couscous. We don't know a lot about North African cooking in the New World but because the French colonised a lot of these countries, their dishes are found everywhere in France. It is an ancient cuisine gorged with flavour and the historical influences of both Africa and the Orient. They do very perfumed desserts using cinnamon, orange-flower water, almonds and nutmeg. Couscous is made from rolled *semoule* or semolina, and was traditionally served at the end of the meal but has now become a major dish on its own. I hadn't eaten a good couscous since I'd been in France, and the best place to eat one is in someone's home. In Moroccan cooking they use lots of nutmeg, cinnamon, cumin, coriander, ginger, paprika, parsley, pepper and saffron. In her tiny kitchen, Catherine was cooking the vegetables, lamb, chicken and chickpeas in separate pots varying in size from small to huge. In a real couscous the grain or semoule is hand-rolled and steamed four times, a feat of not inconsiderable love and devotion – and this is what Catherine had done, not leaving out the loud complaints about having a supposedly macho man who didn't help her enough and two male children who did nothing but exhaust her. She had rubbed the grain in butter and steamed it for three minutes in a steamer, then laid it out on a platter to cool. This process was repeated four times, the last time adding olive oil and raisins. In France you can buy *couscoussiers* (covered, two-storeyed couscous cookers): the vegetables and meat cook in the broth in the bottom pot and the grain steams over it in the perforated top pot. Just before serving, courgettes were added to the vegetable pot, the couscous was steamed for the last time and the merguez fried.

All was brought to the table in large platters amid applause, along with a bowl of spicy harissa or Moroccan chilli sauce. Everybody dived on the food, first covering the plates with the light, tender, perfumed semolina then choosing potato, carrot, turnip, tomato, courgette or chickpeas according to taste to put on top. This was then covered with the broth and harissa was mixed in with spoonfuls of broth and poured over the lot. Next the chicken was cut up and passed around with the lamb and merguez. It was a real feast that one could keep adding to indefinitely. You can also make a fish couscous or a vegetable one comprising chickpeas, onions, aubergines, carrots, potatoes, courgettes, green beans and tomatoes. There were mostly men at this dinner, and everyone was making it clear that only the French know how to live and eat. They didn't know anything about the rest of the world and saw no reason why they should, and they gave amusing imitations of what it would be like to be a tourist abroad. Kathy found this particularly hard to put up with from the French, and felt she was constantly being penalised and put down for being a foreigner. It was funny, but in the end, boring and xenophobic.

I also talked to the chef of one of the best restaurants in Auxerre, Barnabé's. Jean-Luc Barnabé takes people on truffle and wine tours between 15 September and 15 December. The Burgundy black truffle is a little-known cousin of the Périgord truffle. With its hazelnut taste, crunchy flesh and very delicate aroma, it apparently offers equally remarkable gastronomic qualities. Jean-Luc gives people all sorts of options, including tramping out to the forest in your wellies to find the truffles, Burgundian wine-tasting, visiting Chablis, a tour of Auxerre, a feast of guess what, and how to cook with guess what. This is what you get if you have his special truffle menu:

> Salmon marinated in Burgundian truffles
> Shrimp and truffle lasagne
> Calf's tongue with truffles and mashed potatoes
> Chèvre and truffle salad
> Crunchy pear tart with truffle ice cream

For Frédéric's birthday dinner Kathy cut up melons with cured ham and made a salad from peeled tomatoes and fresh mint, grilled duck breasts in the fireplace, roasted potato cubes and garlic in its skin (they say *en chemise* – in its shirt – in French) in goose fat and Frédéric dragged out some very good wine. The best was a 1990 Moulin de Bajac Montbazillac that we drank with the chocolate cake. Jean-Luc and his tall, gorgeous English wife Jane were there with their three perfectly behaved children. Francis, a wine merchant friend from barging days, and Frédéric went into a delirious conversation about the wine:

'It smells of flint ...'

'Yes. Like a train that has just come into the station ...'

'Hot metal on cold. Maybe in November ...'

'No, wait. I can smell pineapples in a box. No, just the box ...'

'Honeysuckle. You know– that honeysuckle at the top of the street. Not the one on the porch ...'

I find the French very poetic in the way they do everyday things. Frédo left me a note on the door written in cherry juice from fallen fruit on the ground – a sweet, runny, pink letter. Men kiss each other on both cheeks and put their arms around each other. A woman at the market told me how to tell the difference between male and female melons, going into sensual detail about colour, aureoles and stems. We danced outside on the terrace in the rain, got out all poor Frédéric's best eaux-de-vie and welcomed more visitors who arrived at 1 a.m. after a jazz concert. Guests never leave a dinner party before 1 a.m. – having to get up early for work is not considered an obstacle and the ones who leave at 3 a.m. do the clean-up.

One evening Frédéric cooked a *petit salé*. This is a winter dish which we immediately turned to, hardly had the weather begun to chill. Burgundians love their provincial, family dishes and the petit sale is a classic French everything-in-one-pot dish like *pot-au-feu, cassoulet* and *potée*. There are as many variations as stars in the sky. This is how Frédéric did it. He soaked a lump of salt pork in cold water overnight to get rid of some of the salt then fried diced carrots, leeks and onions in a big pot in duck fat rather than butter, which he considers gives the dish a greater creaminess. When they were golden he threw in half a kilo of green lentils with a bouquet garni, garlic and pepper. He then added the pork, covered the lot with water and simmered it, covered, for an hour. At this point you can add the sausages cut in large chunks and simmer for another hour. Alternatively, prick the *saucisse de Toulouse* and *saucisse de Morteau* (smoked pork sausage) with a fork and simmer separately for half an hour to get rid of some of the fat, then add to the lentils and pork in the last half hour. Some people cook curly cabbage with it also, an addition I find delicious. The final result should be luxuriously smooth, and one eats it with lashings of Dijon mustard and huge glasses of Brouilly wine.

I never got sick of going to the Auxerre market on Friday morning because I always met friends, made jokes with my favourite stallholders and bought the best potatoes in the world. As with all things of value in life, you have to know where to go. The merguez came from a certain Arab butcher on the left side, a handsome man with his apron tied in a big knot at the back; the mixed salad came from old Mme Lorne near the middle who gives you a tiny *ardoise* (slate) to write the prices on, which she adds up at the end; and the goat's cheeses must only be bought from a woman who knows the stage of ripeness of every single cheese on her stall. Mme Lorne also had some big, ugly farm tomatoes which she urged me to buy rather than the perfect, flavourless ones next door. It was to be my last big dinner in Auxerre and the people I had become fond of had been invited – Jean-Luc and Jane, Abdallah, Catherine and Emmanuel and another couple, Jean-Michel and Marilyne. I knew with this mixture of merry souls, the risk of a memorable evening was dangerously high, so I wanted everything to be perfect.

Frédéric and I raced off to the market with our baskets to quickly buy things, in spite of the fact that I was supposed to be in Chablis interviewing someone and he and Kathy were supposed to be in Paris picking someone up from the airport. Emmanuel was at the market so when Frédéric raced off, we stopped at the market café for a quick natter. As soon as he saw the bottle of dark straw-coloured liquid on the bar his eyes lit up. 'Ah. *Le bourru est arrive. Génial.' Bourru* is the first pressing of the new wine with only a few days fermentation and only comes out just after the vendange in September. It's sweet, low in alcohol and really spells autumn. This one came from Bordeaux and the Burgundian ones would be out in a few weeks. Next I drove over to the frozen food place called Piccard to pick out two small but perfectly formed New Zealand legs of lamb to shut the xenophobes up.

A sunny but chilly Saturday morning was spent in the kitchen, making coffees for friends who stopped by and wandering out to buy fresh baguettes to spread foie gras on as we worked. Abdallah flew in in his usual manner – the smile coming first, followed by the long, slim limbs, talking a mile a minute, giving us a spray of his new perfume and loping out again. It's a pity *The Greatest Salesman in the World* has already been written, because he could write it. His powerful energy, spiritual commitment and success in business make him a formidable presence, if slightly spoiled by a lack of sensitivity and a certain macho quality of the meridional man. I made the lemon and almond tart that I never get sick of and will be eating when I'm 80. Kathy was making *chèvres sur toasts* – rubbing thick slices of country bread with garlic then covering them with paper-thin slices of garlic here and there for good measure. Next she crushed red peppercorns in a mortar and pestle with black pepper and coriander seeds and rolled rounds of chèvre in this mixture, placing one on each slice of bread. Each cheese was topped with half a teaspoon of honey and put aside to be grilled.

I threw myself into grilling aubergines, long green peppers, courgettes, carrots and tomatoes all cut lengthways and sprinkled with olive oil, dill, rock salt and pepper. The flat smelled wonderful, wonderful, wonderful. Frédéric trimmed the lamb then made a big bowl of parsley, garlic, breadcrumbs and lemon juice blended to a thick, creamy paste. Placing the legs and all the ratte potatoes in the roasting dish, he spread them with this paste, covered all with tinfoil and left to sit until roasting time. He was so paranoid about getting in my way and starting a fight that he always asked if he was disturbing me.

'No darling, you're not in my way at all. So long as you don't ask in a horrified manner what I think I'm doing, all will be calm and Zen.'

'I have said nothing, Peta, I trust you have noticed.'

'You've been pretty good and I have learned something from you Frédo. I have learned to be patient and tolerant.'

He gasped and looked at me with giant eyes. 'And you think I haven't learned that with you! Did it ever enter your head for one minute that you are a terrible and capricious woman?'

I exploded into laughter. 'Not for one minute – it has never occurred to me.'

It was a good night, although there were varying opinions on that the next day. Dinner parties in France can be a kind of blood sport and detrimental to one's health simply because some of them end in tears and even violence. Personally I like a heated debate unless I'm losing, and think if the room's too hot, leave it, but there are softer, gentler members of a table who always want to compromise and make everyone happy. It's hard to combine people who bring babies, people who bring new techno music, quiet people, loud people, married people, single people. Every individual has an idea of what they consider a good time and it doesn't always add up to the same thing. Abdallah was over the top as usual, endlessly fuelled by Emmanuel: they revert to childhood after one drink. On the other side of me was Jean-Michel, a handsome sporty man, intent on having me feel his rippling muscles, whichever one came to mind first, and across from me the revelation of the evening, his wife Marilyne, a funny, attractive woman who sparkled and laughed all night. Some people fell asleep, some people read a book and some people wept with mirth. One thing was for sure – the food was indisputable. Kathy's goat's cheese toasts, once grilled, were a melting mixture of goaty, musky flavours to swoon over, especially with the Sancerre wine. There was also a premier cru from Domaine Laroche which was disappointing and nothing near the finesse of the Sancerre. The potatoes, having roasted in the lamb juices and garlic/parsley covering, were completely hallucinogenic and *tip-top*, according to Abdallah. Emmanuel thanked me for my vinegar tart. Well, I like a tart tart.

There is so much counterfeit ghastly, so-called Chablis in the world, mostly produced by Australia and the US, that when you taste a real, racy, refined Chablis from Chablis you realise it is inimitable. The difference is so marked, you don't have to be the sharpest quill on the hedgehog to get it. One real one is worth 20 fake ones. I had met a tall, dark-haired beauty called Lorraine Carrigan at a barbecue and it turned out she was the public relations person for Domaine Laroche, a Chablis winemaker. Lorraine is a very determined young Englishwoman from Newcastle who, having finished a degree in geography, decided she wanted to work in France in the wine industry. She started in Champagne then came back to work at Domaine Laroche. On a rainy September day I drove over to the rather ordinary village of Chablis, not far from Auxerre, to have Lorraine show me around. The cellars and offices are in a beautiful, listed building called the Obediencerie or Prayer House, an old monastery, originally Michel Laroche's home. The Chanterie is now reception and the old dining room is a waiting room with huge walk-in fireplace and long polished table. The tower that rises through the house is 10th century with the steps turning anti-clockwise, and the rest of the house has been added onto over the centuries.

In 877 monks from Tours turned up with the relics of St Martin and hid them in the cellar of the monastery they constructed – a little crypt that is still there and intact. Across the courtyard from the surprisingly small cellars is the 13th-century press, which is still used once a year in a special ceremony. On the other side of the road the monks built their church, the église St Martin, which looks like a small cathedral or basilica and was apparently built as a prototype for a cathedral elsewhere. The first level of the church is Roman, the next Gothic with flying buttresses and the bell tower and certain additions were constructed after the revolution. The Roman door is covered in horseshoes as St Martin was the patron saint of horsemen, and above it are the marks of *fleur de lis* chipped off during the Revolution. In 887 the monks took themselves and their relics back to Tours, but some of them stayed in Chablis, chose the best slopes and planted Chardonnay vines, producing wine very similar to today's Chablis.

Most grape-growers in Burgundy were farmers who grew enough grapes to supply themselves with wine and this is how the Laroche family (Jean-Victor) started five generations ago, in 1850, with one hectare in vines. By 1976 Michel's father Henri had six hectares and still ran a farm, his son became an oenologist and now Domaine Laroche comprises more than 100 hectares of prime Chablis vineyard, including some of the best grand cru and premier cru plots, as well as holdings in Chablis and Petit Chablis. Jean-Marie's father sells his grapes and some of his wine to them. The crucial thing that turned the fortunes of Domaine Laroche around was the discovery of a way to stop the terrible periodic spring frosts destroying the crops. One could never rely on a crop every year, which meant great hardship for the growers. They invented two simple but effective ways of controlling the frost – a *chaufrette* or smudge pot and an *aspersion* (sprinkler system) and they worked like a charm.

There are varying opinions on the quality of Laroche wines but Michel Laroche's approach to winemaking is aimed at creating the ultimate expression of what Chablis should be in terms of authenticity, purity and 'typicity'. He says to produce the best Chablis you need to produce the best grapes, and the poor, flinty soil, northerly climate and Chardonnay grapes combine to make the elegant, complex and structured wine so appreciated by those who like his. The 'Kimmeridgian' limestone soil containing millions of fossilised oysters dating back 150 million years, is what is responsible for the classic steely, floral bouquet of Chablis, its delicate, crisp, refined flavour and underlying flintiness.

There are three things which strike one at first, each of them typical aspects of Chablis which will evolve throughout the life of the wine. One of them is the smell of cut grass – not green, but slightly dried. The second is the honey character, which will develop further with age. Finally there are those unique mineral undertones – 'you can smell the soil,' says Michel Laroche. 'My grandfather's wines were always a deep golden green with oxidised, powerful flavours, but today our wines are straw-coloured with hints of green and we are looking for fruit and elegance. On feast days my grandfather would easily finish off 48 snails with a bottle of Chablis ... I would definitely not be capable of that today.'

On a fresh, fair Sunday Frédéric, Kathy and I set off with Mimi to discover a restaurant in the country, recommended to us by Abdallah. Le Moulin at Venoy, half way between Auxerre and Chablis, is a charming old mill complex of hotel and restaurant, and a haven of gentleness and quiet. The owner and chef Jean-Pierre Vaury and his wife Marie-Cécile are also unstressed, serene and softly welcoming and they've imparted this way of being to their waiting staff, who were unusually courteous and attentive. It was a large restaurant full of families, country people and groups, and completely devoid of yuppies, chic bourgeois or vulgar tourists. The décor was unpretentious to a fault – maybe Vivienne Westwood can put pink tablecloths and red walls together, but it didn't work at Le Moulin – and the advantage of the suburban décor was that only nice, unpretentious people would go there. And then there was us. Mimi, who loves colour, was dressed in a vivid, royal blue blouse and red vest, a cloud of pale blue shadowing her beautiful cornflower eyes. Our hostess, in contrast, had half a pot of blue eyeshadow on, with eyebrows drawn almost to her ears (not that this detracted from her sweet nature).

The chef himself, dressed in his kitchen whites, took the apéritif orders – a big tall man in his fifties with very black hair and a warm smile. He was born in the mill, which was owned by his great-grandfather, so he knows the territory and its gastronomy like the back of his hand, specialising in genuine country cooking. We chose the five-course menu, in spite of the fact I was never eating again after Mimi's photos. The food was so light and beautifully cooked in small portions, that it wasn't too much, even at midday. After an *amuse-gueule* of marinated fresh anchovies I tried the calf's foot salad, a gelatinous horror which I immediately pushed over to Mimi. The most generous thing I could say about it is that it is an acquired taste.

The best course in the meal was the pastry-wrapped andouillette with Chablisienne sauce. It was from the house of Soulier, the best andouillette-maker in Chablis – small, perfumed and full of herbs. The fillet steak was perfect and the vegetables overdone as is traditional. Dessert enriched our lives in the form of a light-as-a-feather tarte fine aux pommes. This apple tart, borrowed from nouvelle cuisine, was a small round of flaky pastry topped with very finely sliced apples and glazed. In my opinion it's a vast improvement on the regular heavy apple tart – and desperately easy to make. Cut out rounds of flaky pastry the size of a glass coaster. Cut apples in half, peel and core them. Place face down and slice very finely, then fan out quite densely on top of the pastry. Sprinkle with a pinch of sugar and a little butter. Bake in 200°C oven for 15 minutes. Remove from oven and glaze with heated apricot jam.

The wine list was formidable, but Frédéric managed to choose an Irancy red and we got into a conversation with a vigneron couple at the table next door. They were a M. and Mme Duprés from Courgis next to Chablis, peasant grape-growers all dressed up in their Sunday best. They smilingly told us they went to a different restaurant every Sunday, and gave us a few good tips for other ones. Like most grape-growers in Chablis their vines were inherited from the family, their daughters married into wine-making families and they now sell their juice to the Chablisienne co-operative, no longer making their own wine except a little for their own consumption. They receive a monthly payment for this and consider they make just as good a living, if not better, as they would if they were independent. Their one complaint was that bureaucrats who never set foot in the vineyards make the crucial decision of when the vendange or harvest will start, not the grape-growers. This year Chablis would start picking on 22 September, so they were enjoying the calm before the storm.

The cheese trolley was a feast of milk in a divine state of decay. I chose a runny Époisses washed down with marc, and a Chaource. Époisses is the cheese of Burgundy and is very hard to buy anywhere else because production is so small. It is made by one person called M. Berthaut in one village called Époisses. Napoleon supposedly loved it, and it was very popular at the beginning of the 20th century, but the Second World War killed production until M. Berthaut got his act together in 1956 and started making it again. There are also a few people making artisanal versions which are very good. Époisses is not for the faint-hearted, with its sticky strong-smelling rind, but bite into the melting interior and you will be rewarded with a slightly salty, metalic but sweet milky flavour so adored by the Burgundians. Chaource is another Burgundian soft uncooked cheese that is eaten rather fresh at about one month old and disappears in your mouth like snow. Le Moulin is really the perfect place for Sunday lunch with family and friends, old-fashioned in every way and leaving one with a lingering desire to come back and be cossetted again.

The very cultivated Mimi had reproached me for indulging my interest in gastronomy and neglecting the fabulous history and culture of Auxerre, a town after all officially titled 'City of Art and History' – so the very next day I took myself on a cultural tour. Just as the real wealth of Burgundy is found underground in wine caves, its real history is also found under the ground in crypts, places I find much more interesting and moving than the church above. Crypts are always the oldest part of a church and are usually the only remaining part of the original. Sometimes several churches have been built, destroyed and rebuilt on top. My first stop was the St-Etienne cathedral around the corner from Mimi's house. I knew the interior from concerts, with its elegant sculptures, splendid stained-glass windows and impressive organ, but the crypt, all that was left of the original Roman church, was lovely in its meditational calmness. With its almost completely intact vault, eerie white walls and the magnificent faded mural of 'Christ on Horseback' once so vibrant with colour, these rooms exuded the grandeur of human experience. The plaque on the wall at the entrance quoted the florid prose of the Book of Revelations evoking Christ's triumph – 'And now I saw heaven open and a white horse appear. Its rider was called Faithful and True. His eyes were flames of fire; his cloak was soaked in blood; he is known by the name The Word of God. Behind him dressed in dazzling white linen, rode the armies of heaven on white horses.' No one does that now. Things were so glorious and exciting in those days.

A five-minute walk away is the St-Germain Abbey, an almost intact monastic complex founded more than 1000 years ago and considered a holy place of great significance from the Carolingian Renaissance (the time of Charlemagne). There is a high school attached to it now of which Jean-Michel is the headmaster. The crypt is really quite amazing and one leaves the whole complex feeling as if one has been meditating for an hour. St-Etienne was probably born in Auxerre in 378 into a wealthy family. He went to university in Gaul and Rome, went hunting, had a wife and family and generally led the life of a privileged man. He was involved in politics and did lots of good works, so the people of Auxerre rewarded him with a bishopric, which meant he had to give everything up, including his designer wardrobe and his wife and family. He assumed this honour and became a very holy man, travelled all over the place to spread the word, evangelised Gaul and Great Britain and eventually died while away preaching in Ravenna. This is when the real story starts, because only upon death did he really become famous and influential which is what I assume will happen to me. The place where his body was buried at St-Germain Abbey, became a place of prayers and pilgrimages. The sarcophagus is still there along with other ones – in fact the whole place is a necropolis for the bishops of Auxerre.

There are ninth-century frescoes on the walls, the oldest in France, still barely visible and protected by very dim lighting. Frescoes were different from murals in that the procedure was more complicated. The frescoes were painted on a surface made of sand mixed with slaked lime and clay. The whole work was covered with lime wash to make it even, then on this still wet lime the painter spread the colours thinned out with more lime. The four colours used were white with lime, red ochre, yellow ochre and iron oxide. Three of the frescoes are of St Stephen who was punished by the Jews for making too many converts to Christianity. There is one where he is surrounded by them with a look of pure hallucination or religious ecstasy on his face – and this is ninth-century stuff! Nowadays, of course, he would be considered a schizophrenic, but in those days it was *de rigueur* for religious aesthetes. The construction of the crypt is in three barrel-vaulted naves resting on two oak architraves, supported by four Gallo-Roman columns with four Carolingian capitals (foundations). In this very precious place it was impossible not to be affected by history and I felt privileged to be there. The complex is in continuing restoration and there are archaeologists in permanence working in the crypt to loosen its secrets.

Leaving Burgundy was like leaving any other place when you've been there for a while. Everyone knows well in advance you're leaving and yet when the time comes they are completely astonished that leaving actually involves leaving. I had stayed longer than planned in order to catch Gael's birthday party at Le Moulineau on Saturday night, and intended to catch the 11.30 a.m. train on Sunday morning. There's nothing to beat a country party: obviously that train and I didn't connect, there were mumblings about how it would be nice if I had a last lunch with Mimi etc. etc. and the next train was at 1.15 p.m. after all. I could see I was looking for excuses to stay forever. Kathy, Frédéric and I stood at the kitchen bench preparing our last meal together – ratte potato salad with mayonnaise and shallots. It's always a good idea to cut onions for a farewell lunch, that way it's easy to blame your tears on them. We sliced up jambon de Parme on their little slicer, opened a pot of *rillettes* (shredded pork

Rillettes
Shredded Pork Pâté

1kg pork belly. (Have the butcher bone the pork and remove the rind.)
sea salt
freshly ground black pepper
500g pork back fat
2 cloves of garlic
1 bouquet garni

1. Rub the pork belly well with salt and leave overnight in the fridge.

2. Cut pork into little strips about the size of match sticks and twice as thick. Cut the fat up in the same way. Crush the garlic cloves. Preheat oven to 120°C.

3. Place pork, fat, garlic and bouquet garni in an earthenware or ovenproof dish, season with pepper and pour over a cup of water. Cover the dish and cook in oven for four hours. The pork will now be melting and swimming in fat.

4. Turn the pork out into a wire sieve standing over a large bowl to catch the fat. When drained and cooled a little, gently pull the meat apart with two forks until it is in fine shreds. Taste for seasoning. Place lightly in an earthenware or china bowl and pour the fat over the rillettes. Cover and refrigerate.

paté, see recipe above) made a bean, chèvre and tomato salad with our favourite ficelles and packed one of their ghastly frozen ice cream pies. This was the one gastronomic slip-up in their repertoire. The take-away Lebanese was great, the packaged dinners were quite good but the frozen desserts were baffling for such a household. I bought them a huge bunch of flowers and a bottle of cognac, which they mumbled was unnecessary. How could cognac be unnecessary? Aside from potatoes and friends it's probably the most necessary thing I can think of. We put everything in baskets and carried the last-supper down the road to Mimi's, where we dined on the terrace in the sunshine. She showed me the first crayon drawing she had done from the photos. It was a simple, beautiful pastel of a woman in a long black dress and large hat holding a basket of fruit. She was sitting in the garden surrounded by trees and flowers and looked exactly like my youngest sister Desirée.

Encore

Paris

WHEN I ARRIVED back in Paris in September for my last five days in France, it was still sunny and warm and the city was in a good mood. This time I stayed at Renate and Nillo's place in the 20th arrondissement. Their house is extraordinary in that, to get to it, one walks through a less than glamorous neighbourhood from the Port des Lilas métro, past seedy bars and ugly apartment buildings and down a long passage. Then suddenly at the end one opens a gate and walks into a lovely little garden with deckchairs, up the steps and into a world of light, beauty and orderliness. The three-bedroomed house had white walls covered in bright, contemporary art, white and black furniture, white tiled floors and halogen lighting hanging everywhere like fairy sculptures. Leading off the kitchen was a terrace with garden and table and chairs. Here Renate lives with Nillo, her two little daughters, her mother-in-law and the dog.

I struggled up the passage with my suitcases to find her playing in the garden with the beautiful daughters. We all fell on each other and the girls sat on top of us as we caught up on the news over Riesling and marinated olives. Six-year-old Camille had given me her little bed to sleep in for my stay and three-year-old Liza was my guardian, getting into bed with me every morning and saying in my face, '*Tu dors Peta?*'

While Mamie (Nana) occupied herself with childcare and mumbling that her work in the house was never done,

I sat at the kitchen table watching Nillo cook. He'd spent all afternoon sanding, stripping and oiling antique kitchen implements which he collects. There was an old wooden mandolin for slicing vegetables, ancient weights in a wooden box and a very ornate German spatzle maker. Nillo and Mamie always ate early with the children and a separate later dinner was made for Renate and me, either by Nillo or Mamie, who also did the dishes afterwards. Renate called her mother-in-law Maman and so did I. Maman considered I couldn't make a bed, wash a sock or iron a dress to save myself so she insisted on doing all this for me. If I left a stocking on the floor by mistake, when I came home it was washed and folded. Nillo is of Spanish parents brought up in France and Renate is German, so the cooking reflected their origins – sometimes there was a sort of potato tortilla with lots of olives on the side and sometimes red cabbage cooked for hours with sliced apples, duck fat and a little sugar. That night Nillo cooked us sautéd potatoes on top of which was fanned slices of duck breast and a cream and grainy mustard sauce.

Renate produces television films and series for a German/ French company and gets dressed up to the nines every day to go into the office and make those big bucks. In spite of the fact that she and Nillo have a 24-year-old son, they turned around and made two little girls almost 20 years later. She's a workaholic, eats creamy sauces, is as slim as a pin, and looks about 30 with her short blonde hair, cupid lips and dazzling blue eyes. Her wardrobe is Parisian chic, designer and runs to racks in two rooms. Her bathroom is a hermitage, a refuge, a sanctuary of perfumes, makeup, magic potions, lotions, soaps, scented tissues, body scrubbers, huge mirrors and every species of beauty cream known to mankind. Either she was born and will remain beautiful in spite of gravity or all this stuff really works. I'm still struggling with it.

I hit the town for my various rendezvous and snatched

lunch at a madly busy brasserie at St-Honoré. The little *tickets de caisse* piled up in front of me – the meal, the wine, the coffee, all had separate compartments and all were added up at the end in a great flourish of the till. It was sunny, everyone was sitting good-naturedly on top of each other, the patronne was happily humming in the controlled chaos they called service and everyone knew how to play this fast game of eating at lunch time. I realised that Paris will always be like this. Parisians are born stressed, they thrive on it and for them, it is life. No matter how tough things get, they always find a way (how? why? are they genetically programmed?) to make it all wonderful, give it humanity, lift it with humour. In France, when I talk about the other side of the world that I come from, people always get a look on their faces that says 'Yes, for a holiday but what do you do there, where does your money came from, what do you drink?' It bothers them that there's hardly any people there and they might lose the sense of themselves in all that free space. I say, 'That's fine, that's how we like it, we think it's stressful when the sheep prices go down.'

I decided to blow a day's budget on a coffee at Les Deux Magots on Boulevard St-Germain, always a good place to think uncharitable thoughts. Two well dressed women behind me were complaining about their children in the most vulgar terms. I caught a look at them in my little mirror as I applied lipstick and realised that this was a device I should use more often. They were old, rich, paper thin and sharp as snakes. Americans come to this café a lot to pretend they're doing movie deals, the women (and sometimes men) being easily recognisable by their strange, surgically altered faces. Frighteningly sunbed-tanned people walked past looking like radiation victims and the waiters were straight out of Central Casting with their black vests, floor length starchy white aprons and handle bar moustaches. There were couples who had nothing to say to each other, resorting instead to avidly studying the bill or peering longingly at the décor. If I am studying the décor of a café, I am in big trouble with my dining partner – normally it's a question of getting the person to shut up so I can say what is surely more urgent, more important, funnier and more incisive than anything that has gone before.

Les Deux Magots is a landmark in Paris, first opening in 1885 on the place where there was a shop of the same name. An important cultural landmark in Paris, it was a literary café where the likes of Verlaine, Rimbaud and Mallarmé met to exchange an idea or two. Later on André Gide, Picasso, Fernand Léger, Prévert, Hemingway, Sartre and Simone de Beauvoir hung out and existentialised; in fact, Simone de Beauvoir wrote there all day to keep warm. In 1933 le Prix des Deux Magots for literature was created, but now it's not so much writers as the fashion and political world who grace the velvet banquettes.

I spent one evening at Renate's watching unfathomable German soap operas she was assessing for her company. They were full of fat-paunched men with receding chins saying things like *klatzenhausenschmauzenianein* all the time to their blonde, peach-skinned, blowzy wives. The comedy was set in a camping ground by the beach and you could almost see the boom and lights on what was quite obviously a studio beach with perfectly coiffed and heavily made-up actresses. This was most unlike the camping grounds I spent disagreeable portions of my *jeunesse* in, where there was sweat and heat and swimsuits going up your backside and concrete showers and no body cosmetics around at all. The camping setup was like a stage set with everything you would have in your home but never take on holiday – coloured lights, white chairs, false turf, artificial flowers in pots, plastic lace tablecloths (Okay, I don't have plastic tablecloths in my home), full table settings and a slimy, grey supper of pickled herrings. After lunch they all leapt up and danced to Abba and there was shrieking coming from locked caravans at three in the afternoon. That bit reminded me of a certain neighbour's beach house but aside from that I was agog. Beside me Renate was doubled over with laughter.

In the interests of studying every aspect of French food, I accepted an invitation from Renate to lunch with her and her colleagues at her work canteen. Before we walked in she looked at me with very wide eyes, dug her Gucci nails into my arm and said through her teeth, 'You have the right to say nothing, Peta, you understand? No comment.' Yes I understand and I'm grateful I have been invited and I won't embarrass you in front of your boss. Of course the food was revolting. Canteen food is canteen food. We drank lots of rosé to drown it, the boss came to our table to be introduced to a famous food critic (she always made my credentials up, depending on whom she was talking to, a business trait I admire) and I got the old-fashioned look from Renate. The best part of lunch was the Illy automatic coffee machine. At the counter when you pay for your inch-square bit of industrial camembert and trough of grey stew, you may also buy a compact little disc of coffee which you insert into a machine and press a button to obtain hot, fresh express.

On my last day I decided to try Alain Ducasse's old style bistrot, Aux Lyonnais at 32 rue St Marc in the 2nd. Fortunately I had made a reservation, because the place was packed to the gills in the traditional French style – i.e. 3cm between each table, with well-heeled, conservative *gens du quartier*. Here there were no chic peacocks, no women watching their thighs. Everyone was happy and the service was unusually polite. As is customary for a foreign woman dining alone, I was given the most dishonourable table right next to the kitchen. One kir later and I had forgotten about that. A bowl of *cervelle de Canut* (marinated goat's cheese) with toast fingers was immediately placed in front of me. It was deliciously sour and salty and gave me strength to peruse the 28€ menu of the day. I decided to order the herrings with warm potatoes, a decision ridiculed by the charming, witty Maitre d'. '*Hors de question Madame*,' said he. 'Why would you come to a Lyonnaise joint, only to turn your nose up at our fabulous *charcuterie*?' You are quite correct, *Monsieur*,' I said, 'please accept my apologies. I would now like to order the charcuterie platter.' I was rewarded for this choice by being presented with a wooden board on which was a little pot of *canut*, warm potato, warm *saucisse de Lyon*, tiny croûtons and sauce *gribiche* mixed together; two different pork terrines, various paper thin slices of *saucisson* and *gratons* (fried pork rind). Accompanying this was a little container of larded sea salt, a pot of *cornichons* (little pickles) and a linen bag of sliced sourdough and baguette. The perfection of produce and attention to detail was heart-stopping.

Obviously I was full after the charcuterie and feeling at peace with the world with the help of a *première cru Gevry-Chambertin*, but the Maitre d' who revealed himself to be Eric Mercier, was having none of it. In due course my *boudin noir de l'Auberge Iparla* arrived – a big, fat slice of tender, fragrant congealed blood swimming in a little pool of *jus* with carrots, peas and lardons. The provenance of the meat at Aux Lyonnais is so important to Ducasse, there is a note at the bottom of the menu which states that in accordance with decree No 2002–1467, the restaurant and its suppliers guarantee the pedigree of all the meat served. This heavenly dish was followed by my dessert of rice pudding with red berry jelly. When I couldn't get more than a few mouthfuls in before giving up, Eric threw his hands in the air and said, 'I give up with you ... I am saying nothing'. 'But I can't,' I pleaded. 'Take it slowly, Madame, just like life'.

This old bistrot has always been called Aux Lyonnais and has served Lyonnais cooking since 1890 – Ducasse bought it in 2002. The decor is typical over-the-top, turn-of-the-century art deco with tiled floors, huge ornate mirrors, zinc bar, art deco lamps and lovely pink and green flowered tiles around the walls. The tablecloths resemble over-sized white tea-towels with red check stripe down the side. An air of safety, respect and tradition prevails. Upstairs is a lounge and enchantingly beautiful bathrooms. To the food writers who are addicted to pontificating about the demise of French cuisine and how only foreign muck are to be seen eating in the so-called temples of gastronomy, I have this to say: Get a life, and get it at Aux Lyonnais. This old fashioned, high quality, honest food is what the rest of the world is now craving. The price for the menu, kir, glass of wine, water and café was 54€ – not for the faint-hearted but worth it.

Renate and I both had planes to catch – she to the festival at Cannes and I to London, so we shared a taxi. We looked as though we came from two different planets. I had my comfortable look on – flares and a jumper and a slash of lipstick. She had her comfortable look on – power suit, Chanel shawl over the shoulder, dripping in gold, designer sunglasses and full makeup. Upon arrival at Charles de Gaulle we immediately lost each other and I didn't see her again. I turned and all that was left was a waft of Givenchy.

Epilogue – Culinary Adventures

SINCE THIS BOOK WAS first published in 1998 I have returned to France every year to visit friends and family. I have continued to make television food shows and write gastronomic travel books. When you pass through a place like Uzès, you can never just pass through. Passing through intimates you have been unmoved, you breathed but didn't inhale, you looked but didn't touch. This is impossible in Uzès and it only hits you when you return, why you had to come back.

As I write, it is 30 degrees and I am gorging myself on Bouzigues oysters and *tellines* (tiny oval shellfish) sautéed in Pastis and olive oil. I decided my culinary adventures would be a week long and include accommodation, cooking lessons, visits to vineyards, truffle hunting, artisan guest chefs, olive oil makers, etc., picnics, restaurants, market shopping and general immersion in the sunny, intoxicating Languedoc/Provence lifestyle. In my first three weeks I bought a traditional lavender-picker's hat – the straw ones with the huge brim and small crown, pink and brown striped espadrilles and a cheap diesel Fiat to buzz around in. Armed with these three things, I got just about anything I wanted as I spent my days driving through sleepy villages and ancient stone vineyards.

The maps of the Languedoc-Roussillon are so covered in vineyard signs, you can hardly read them – it is the largest wine producing area in France. The Languedoc (originally called Occitania), so named because the people used to speak the language of Oc (now called Provençal and closely related to Catalan) rather than French, and some of them still do, has always attracted me more than the more glamorous, fertile Provence to the east. It is dry, old, staunch, influenced by its closeness to Spain and so far not completely inundated by tourism. There are bull fights, *abrivados* (bull running in the streets), siestas and the people are friendly, reflective and a little sober rather than ribald and charming like their close neighbours. Here the colours are not the cornflower blues and searing yellows of Provence but more muted – washed out sage, dove grey, biscuit and pale blue.

The region of Languedoc-Roussillon was formed in the 1960s by merging two historic provinces. It stretches in an arc along the coast from Provence to the Pyrénées with its northern flanks bordering the Massif Central. Because the Languedoc's borders have changed so often, and this particular part of it is so close to Provence (actually called Provence by some people), it doesn't respect culinary limits. This food is made to be seen, felt and even listened to before you eat it. It embraces all the produce and richness of the whole south. It is a modest, robust cuisine and all the great ingredients are here – *sanglier* (wild boar), *ratatouille*, *pissaladière*, lemon thyme, anchovies, rosemary, tapenade, red Camargue rice, saffron, olive oil, seafood, fish from the coast, and of course the entire region is dominated by wine. They eat meat grilled in the fireplace over *ceps de vignes* – old gnarled grapevines that have been pulled up for new ones, every kind of goat cheese imaginable and olives with every glass of rosé. In

France there are registered 'Remarkable Sites of Taste' and Bouzigues and its oysters is one of them.

One of the best markets in the area is held on Wednesdays and Saturdays in the beautiful Place aux Herbes in Uzès. Here you might fill your basket with live prawns and trout, foie gras, smoked duck breast, fennel bulbs, fresh figs, *Gaussian*, preserved lemons, olives, fresh cèpes and grilled mushrooms, fresh almonds, olive oils and of course the specialty of the region – their fabulous Pélardon goat cheeses at every stage of maturity. Or you can buy nothing and just stand in the middle of it all in the sunshine, revelling in the strong Languedocien accents. Uzès is one of France's 500 *villes d'art* where *Cyrano de Bergerac* starring Gérard Depardieu was filmed. It is a sparkling gem of a medieval town with old houses, lofty towers and narrow streets full of interior decorating shops and art galleries. It is famous for the long-standing House of Uzès, home of France's highest-ranking ducal family, who still live in Le Duché (castle) dominating the town.

Languedoc-Roussillon is one of southern France's great old provinces; you have to let go of time there; people will not be hurried. They will say to you, 'you can call as often as you like – it won't make me come any faster'. If you invite a new friend to dinner too quickly, they will find excuses not to come. Months later they will say, 'you have invited everyone to your house for dinner except me'. The shop opening times are pasted on the windows. They might say 'open from 10 until 12 and 3 until 7' but they don't really mean it – the hours are just a philosophical idea which never gets in the way of life. They mean they will turn up when they feel like it. Meanwhile, you, who have an appointment with them, wait in the heat like a marinated sardine, and when they arrive smiling and fragrant, without exception they will say, '*Oh Madame, je suis desolé. Je ne suis jamais en retard – aujourd'hui est exceptionel.* (Oh Madam, I'm sorry. I'm never late – today is an exception.)'

Before the First World War Provence and Languedoc were equally popular backwaters, of interest mostly to winemakers, peasants, rabbits and olive growers. Then Provence pulled ahead and everyone going south for a holiday drove straight to the sea and turned left. Provence became glamorous, expensive and fashionable but the Languedoc remained a backwater, relatively unknown and inaccessible. Foreigners and French people bought up large in endlessly sunny, hot Provence then two things happened: (1) it got too expensive (the Riviera is ruined); and (2) low-cost airlines became a huge catalyst in opening up cheaper, more authentic Languedoc. You can now fly every day from Stanstead in England to Carcassonne, Montpellier, Nîmes and Perpignan. Provence was cool and stylish but what did the Languedoc have to offer? Well, the landscape is sublime, there is lots of sea, there is no hype, fewer people, dramatic history and artists and writers who live there consider it 'the thinking man's Provence'.

It's a lovely life there and I can see why every second person who comes, wants to open their very own B&B and be part of that life. The natives, on the other hand, do nothing but complain, chase foreign women and wish they could go and live somewhere else, n'est-ce pas? Quaintly, folk still bring their canines with them to restaurants. Where I come from you would go straight to prison for this but in France it is still perfectly acceptable for dogs to sit quietly at their master's feet in posh restaurants. This and bullfighting are two of the things which make the south of France exciting and slightly naughty – you always get the feeling you are breaking the rules and getting away with it. Nevertheless, the Languedoc-Roussillon province is soaked in blood from its violent past. Protestants were massacred in their thousands by the Catholics. I was told about an old house that was bought recently. When they started renovating, the new owners pulled down a wall and behind it were eight skeletons lying on top of each other.

I drove down to Marseilles to visit Michèle where I found her and her friend Jamil touching in their support of my cooking school project. In her filthy (intellectuals don't clean) but madly eccentric house, Michèle had made a stew and overcooked pasta. During this boring, pedagogic dinner on the terrace, the subject of the school was broached. Jamil passionately congratulated me on my rip-off scheme but counselled me not to go so far as calling a tourist, superficial, bullshit experience a 'school'. He proposed rather to call it culinary tourism or at a push a cooking course. He, who had been in the food business all his life, knew much better than I the ins and outs of the business. He who had cooked a fish stew for three million – a feat I could only dream of achieving. I didn't know the meaning of work (I have to say owning two restaurants, writing eight books and presenting television shows for 12 years had seemed like work at the time). All this coming from people, with respect, a lot less successful than I – a failed psychologist and a failed restaurateur ... but to be fair, we did have that in common. I also am a failed restaurateur – my restaurant in Paris almost killed me. Maybe therein lies the rub – jealousy, defensiveness, disrespect. There's nothing worse than a foreigner working hard and becoming proficient in French cooking. It's enough to make you sick ... and it almost did.

Back in Uzès, the attitude was the opposite. Everyone thought it was high time a culinary course was set up as there were hardly any in the Languedoc. In terms of setting it up, to my astonishment, things went exactly how I had planned. I imagined someone would say, 'I've got a big kitchen in a fabulous house and you can use it for your school'. I imagined I would quickly find a cheap, good car to buy. I imagined someone would say, 'I have a big house with lots of room and you can stay with me for a reasonable price and use my kitchen as much as you like'. All this happened in the space of two weeks. I moved into the sixteenth century mansion of Gina and Michael, right in the centre of Uzès, across the road from the famous Les Trois Salons restaurant owned by my friends Paul and Charmaine, who invited me to a party where I met David, who would become my partner in the business. The culinary adventures had gone very well. I have now added Marrakesh and will soon add Rajasthan.

There are some very chi-chi butchers in Uzès with self-opening doors, suspiciously pink meat and all sorts of seductive extras such as designer pasta, terrines and ready-made salads the French so adore – anaemic *céleri rémoulade*, tired *poireaux en vinaigrette*, flaccid grated carrots. There's a lot of money in this town and Parisians love spending their loot on extravagant feasts while on holiday. Everyone in the south makes jokes about pretentious, flint-hearted, extravagant Parisians but the Parisians don't care – like all superior races, they are thrilled with themselves and tolerate the languid, slow southerners with humour. They secretly want to be like them but can't let go of their ambitions, philosophical problems and designer clothes. There are no philosophical crises in southern France – you just work, drink, eat, make love, laugh and then start all over again.

And then there's Djouti Butcher just off the Place aux Herbes. The Djouti brothers, of Moroccan origin, have the best meat in Uzès, recommended to me by good chefs in Uzès. In Djouti there is beautiful, properly hung, normal coloured meat from the Cevennes mountains, and only meat – no ghastly marinades. They also grace the Saturday market with a big stand which is where I had my conversation with one of the brothers about his *mechoui*. This is the spit-roasted lamb done before your very eyes with Moroccan spices. They come to your place and set up in the back yard. On other visits the other brother back at the shop is re-educating me on the correct cuts of meat for the dishes I wish to cook. I asked for lamb shoulder for a tagine. 'No no,' said he, 'not shoulder. You need neck chops – much better.' I asked for rumpsteak for my *brouffade*. 'No no,' said he, 'too dry. You need *paleron* or shoulder,' and he cut it in the traditional thick slices. He was right both times – more unctuous and sweet at the end. My greatest moment came when he shyly said I was as beautiful as his leg of lamb. Coming from a butcher, I chose to take this as a compliment.

When they do a *Fête Votive* in Uzès they pull out all the stops and it lasts for five days. This summer voting festival was started up long ago by mayors to garner favour amongst the voters and involves free breakfast for the whole town on the first day, *bals* (dances), feasting, bridge competitions, *abrivados* (bull running), street music, sheep, donkeys, lamas, cows and farmers on tractors parading down the main boulevard. They also have a strange game called *taureaux piscines* (or swimming pool bulls) where local boys provoke young bulls into chasing them towards a pool and at the very last minute, when the bull is almost upon them, leap into the pool to safety. Supposedly bulls won't go into water but sometimes the animal is so enraged he jumps in anyway. I always applaud wildly when that happens. Every village and town has their Fête Votive and in Uzès, all sorts of other glitter has crept in like a little fairground with rides, American hillbilly bands, Brazilian drummers and dancers and disco. This is the opportunity for the *flics* (cops) to go into a frenzy of officiousness regarding traffic, barriers and general meridional anarchy. They go to huge amounts of trouble to protect the public from the vicious (taped) horns of the bulls by erecting barriers erratically along the streets. (Apparently the bulls don't escape and run amuck where there are no barriers!) Nevertheless prudent persons such as myself stand casually behind trees.

The wines of the Uzège (area around Uzès) are slowly

starting to make themselves known worldwide. Vineyards have decorated the hills of the Uzège since the 6th century BC but, as with the rest of the Languedoc, it's only fairly recent that the concept of very good wine has become important. Fifty years ago it was all about quantity, not quality, but in the 1970s growers understood they had to step up their act, pulled up a lot of their vines, replanted and invested in technology. In a lot of cases the vineyards are owned by the same *paysan* families but they have a completely different attitude. They're still wily peasants but the difference between the wine their grandfathers made and what they're now making is enormous. Incidentally, the word peasant doesn't have the derogatory connotation in French that it has in English – a paysan is a person of the land.

In the New World, wines are labelled by *cépage* or grape but in France the label is strongly based on the notion of *terroir* – sun, climate and soil because it is these characteristics, rather than the grape, that give a wine its unique attributes. This is why AOC (*appellation contrôlée*) was introduced in the 1930s. This classification system specifies a wine's geographic origin and a standard of growing and production conditions, including the yield per hectare and alcohol content. You are obliged to make the wine from a certain blend of grapes but the grapes used are not specified. All this information on the label is very useful to the buyer. However in the Uzège, because they sell so much of their wine to the new world, they accept its interest in cépage and are now marking what grapes were used in the wine. But it isn't that simple. *Vin de pays* or table wine has no classification and is supposed to be a simpler, cheaper wine but in this area they are often better than the AOC ones. *Vin de Pays d'Oc, Vin de pays du Gard* and *Vin de Pays Duché d'Uzès* are all local wines granted the right to use these names under an agreement made by their department, region or town. The Duché d'Uzès is in the process of applying for AOC status and at the wine fair in August on the esplanade in Uzès you would honestly be hard put to find some bad wine.

My favourite winemakers in the Uzège are the Chabrier Brothers, Patrick and Christian, whose mother cries every year when the first drops of wine are tasted. They don't look like winemakers at all; they look like farmers – sturdy with thick accents and a mad sense of humour. They are generous, unaffected, hard working and every few months they email me photos of activities in the vineyard – vendange and pressing at the end of summer, bleak naked winter vines at Christmas and there always seems to be a photo of them drinking. They have been known to turn up at fancy dress parties in the most outrageous, cross-dressing outfits, frozen for posterity by Amanda who then shows the photos all over town. Interestingly, their winemaker Karine studied viticulture in New Zealand and speaks fluent English.

An inevitable part of travelling is airports. Either your passage through these mausoleums all goes right or it all goes wrong. Actually I don't think I've ever had a good time in an airport. I've either been vomiting, fighting unconsciousness or dementia, weeping, angry, bored or verging on medically unfit due to leg swelling due to standing in a bloody queue for an hour. The most useful thing you could ever use in an airport would be a urethral catheter because you can't fit your baggage through a toilet door, the toilets are always occupied and international airports have deliberately set it up so that if you do say 'fuck it' and leave your baggage unattended for more than 30 seconds, they will detonate it. Keep in mind that because I am a gastro-nomad, I am always moving around with 80 kilos of luggage, a computer and a big red bag JUST IN CASE. As with all connecting flights, timing is of the essence so they deliberately made us wait 20 minutes to alight from the plane in London because they had (this is true) misplaced the stairs. I then waited for half an hour for a 'frequent' shuttle between terminals. The people standing next to me were speaking a guttural, Swedish sort of language that I listened to intently, trying to identify. Eventually, to my utter astonishment, I realised the language was English, from some dark, primeval hole of a place in the far south of Somerset or somewhere.

The people next to the aliens were snivelling. Whenever I see couples tearfully osmosing with each other at airports I always want to laugh. Heathrow in particular reminds me of one memorable goodbye from my then boyfriend. We were sitting on the floor next to the point of no return where they have garrotting wires to separate people. The last, last, last call came and he threw himself on my legs weeping, wrapped around them, begging me not to go. Ever since, I've always felt that other men have been particularly undemonstrative in this area. If they're not going to kill themselves when you leave, maybe you shouldn't have been there in the first place.

As a result of the 'frequent' shuttle I was now late for my flight to Los Angeles. I was told to carry my suitcases directly to the plane myself (still true) – through passport control and security where, as is only correct, the security werewolves decided to search EVERYTHING in my possession. 'Please hurry, I'm late and it's not my fault, and why are you doing this to me?' Panicky eyes, breathless demeanour. Their slow dark eyes registered – we must under no circumstances bow to this person, we must not speed up, no one must be given preference. 'Excuse me I'm late, please do my bags ahead of these people who have all the time in the world.' Slow dark expressionless faces.

'Oh no, we can't do things out of order (because that might mean we're human but even worse it might mean you're human).'

'And will you buy me another ticket when I miss my

plane?' I shrieked. Silence. Searching. I grabbed the bags and ran through 36,000 waiting lounges.

'Are you running late, love?'

'No, I'm doing my fast walk and I use luggage for weights.'

I don't understand why more people are not alcoholics; and prescription drugs don't seem adequate somehow. Now I was on the plane, that torture chamber of bad pressure, bad food and bad company. I'm always amazed at how few psychopaths and chainsaw massacrers there are on planes. By the time you get to your seat you have been deliberately driven to the point of dementia, then you're asked to sit still and enjoy your venous system blocking up, and everyone quietly does it. Personally I think the man who hit the headlines for defecating on his meal was making a reasonable statement. We who do nothing are the ones suffering from 'battered travellers' syndrome. We need help. We need to be taught – there is a choice, we are lovable and we can just say no. It's all about self-esteem and triumphing over passivity. I was seated next to a man and his young son so the purser thought it would be hilarious if he pretended we were a family. We assured him I was a tragic widow and he a happily married man but no, if we weren't husband and wife, we should be, we looked made for each other. Son with panic-stricken look on his face as the purser asked nearby people if they would be bridesmaids and best men. Ha ha. Dinner was dog food with rats' breasts in it and dessert was almond essence held together with flour and eggs.

At 6.15 a.m. we touched down into a clear, crisp dawn in this beautiful land I call my home. This land that I truly love. After Paris and Los Angeles the air seemed sweet, pristine and almost alpine. The air is not this clean even in the south of France. I walked into a pretty, ordered, light-filled house, the front and back doors were open to let in the early air onto the polished floors. My room was full of fresh flowers and champagne and pressed linen graced the bed. On my table was a fax from a French friend: 'We miss you already and the only thing I have to look forward to is your return in the springtime with the swallows.' I ask you.

List of Recipes

Index